QUESTAR PUBLISHERS, INC.

A
TALE OF
THREE VIRTUES

Cures for Colorless
Christianity

Steven R. Mosley

QUESTAR PUBLISHERS, INC.
Sisters, Oregon

A TALE OF THREE VIRTUES
© 1989 by Steven R. Mosley
Published by Questar Publishers, Inc.

Printed in the United States of America

ISBN 0-945564-15-5

Cover Design by Jerry Werner

to Bill Shelly

whose grace lives on after him

CONTENTS

CONTENTS

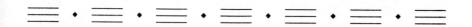

A
Tale of
Three Virtues

INTRODUCTION

I WAS SLOUCHED in a back pew following a worship service—wondering, as usual, why church had to be so boring. The few elderly saints spread out thinly in the wide sanctuary had dispersed slowly around me, and the wobbly organ music had trickled away altogether. I felt empty. Why did the religious life seem to attract mainly the old—those able to slip into sanctity by default? I had to admit there was very little that really attracted me about these conventional religious rites. And yet here I remained, in body at least, among the faithful.

I had noticed a blind man sitting alone near the front of the church. He lingered too. There, I imagined, was another isolation that echoed mine. Nothing seemed to have touched him, either.

In the rows in back of him, several grandmother-types were seated singly by the aisle, one after another. They also waited in the silence, with their heads bowed.

Very slowly the blind man, a stocky gentleman, rose from the pew, fumbled for a huge book thick with Braille lettering, and slipped it under his arm. He then turned uncertainly to make his way toward the rear of the sanctuary. Immediately one of the ladies reached out and clasped his hands tightly. They exchanged a few animated words. He stepped forward, and the next lady reached for his hands in greeting, then the next. Each woman beamed as she spoke his name and expressed her delight in seeing him.

In this way the grandmothers formed an unobtrusive escort, guiding the man's steps to the foyer. He wasn't just led like some lost child; he was carried along exuberantly.

As he came closer, his face transfixed me. Around sunken, glazed eyes, his features radiated an intense joy. Even I could see that the feeble, wrinkled hands of the old women had pierced deeply through his solitude.

SOME TIME AFTER being jolted awake from my sullen reverie I decided to take a long look at virtue and what it can reveal. So many acts of religious goodness seem to fall mute and flat in the world. Yet others speak with eloquence. What makes the difference? So many of my peers have burned out on being good, or simply been bored out of the pursuit of righteousness. Is there a particular kind of holiness that can inspire our contemporaries, instead of putting them to sleep?

This book is an attempt to get a handle on the expressive virtues, qualities that can become much more than just pale abstractions for us to aim at. I've concluded that they can best be experienced as a great tale, an epic that sweeps through Scripture and through heroes of faith down through history—heroes who, in both quiet and spectacular ways, modeled a winsome artistry of the spirit. In these pages I try to show how we can become part of the story, how we become inspired participants in a divine drama. By means of a dynamic art that the Word reveals, we can move beyond a routine religion of dull duties, and into artful goodness—a challenge worthy of our greatest energies.

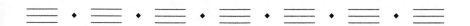

ARTFUL
GOODNESS

1

A Moral No Man's Land

STEPHEN DEDALUS, growing up religious in Ireland, had a pressing problem: His adolescent lust just wouldn't leave him alone. He found himself reimagining every demure and innocent girl he met as some wench with a leering face, "eyes bright with brutish joy." The youth's single-minded pursuits left him with a "keen and humiliating sense of transgression."

Stephen, the sensitive poet-protagonist in James Joyce's autobiographical novel *Portrait of the Artist as a Young Man*, saw with mounting despair a verse in the book of James coming true in his own life —the verse about how he who offends a single commandment is guilty of all of them. He found that lust bred "pride in himself and contempt for others, covetousness in using money for the purchase of unlawful pleasures, envy of those whose vices he could not reach to and calumnious murmuring against the pious, gluttonous enjoyment of food, the dull glowering of anger amid which he brooded upon his longing, the swamp of spiritual and bodily sloth in which his whole being had sunk."

Drawn and quartered by the seven deadly sins, Stephen felt a "loveless awe of God" and grew ever more fearful of His wrath, which seemed aimed squarely at him in the sermons he had to listen to at school. Hell with all its torments, also elaborately described from the pulpit, seemed to open its mouth for him. After struggling for some time with a sense that "his offence was too grievous to be atoned for," Stephen finally caught a glimpse of God's mercifulness one day in church and wept his way to repentance. Asking for forgiveness in a corner of the dark nave, "his prayers ascended to heaven from his purified heart like perfume streaming upward."

Walking home, Stephen saw the whole world differently. The muddy streets seemed jovial, and an invisible grace pervaded him and made his limbs light. The boy had not known how beautiful and peaceful life could be with a soul pardoned and made holy by God.

His sense of grace persisted; now instead of fantasizing about seduction he imagined himself "as a priest wielding calmly and humbly the awful power of which angels and saints stood in reverence!" For a while the mysteries of the church and its ceremonies attracted him; its sanctity beckoned.

One day a priest encouraged him to consider taking up holy orders. Stephen was at first excited about such an honor, but then, looking up into the man's face, he was struck by "a mirthless mask reflecting a sunken day," and stopped cold. He began wondering— What would a future confined to the holy life really be like? Suddenly it seemed "grave and ordered and passionless." He remembered a stifling odor from the long corridors of the parochial school he attended and the smell of moist air above the stagnant, turf-colored water at its baths. These sensations spoke urgently to him. His pulse quickened, and he gasped for air as if smothering.

Some deep instinct within the boy awakened at the approach of the holy life and "armed him against acquiescence." He was repelled by the chill lifelessness of such an existence. The words "Reverend Stephen Dedalus" conjured up a fearful countenance: "eyeless and sour-favoured and devout, shot with pink tinges of suffocated anger."

Stephen realized that the call to the holy life simply "did not touch him to the quick." He wondered "at the frail hold which so many years of order and obedience had on him." The prospect of pursuing such an artificial perfection seemed unbearable: "Not to fall was too hard, too hard…"

So the young man left parochial school and headed for the university. There he found a calling that *did* touch him to the quick: the spirit expressing itself "in unfettered freedom." Art was his answer. The passionate pursuit of beauty called to him as piercingly as the cry of an eagle flying high. It was definitely not "the dull gross voice of the world of duties and despair, not the inhuman voice that had called him to the pale service of the altar."

Art would fulfill his deepest longings where religion had not. He now saw sanctity as a net flung over the soul to hold it back from flight. He vowed to become "a priest of the eternal imagination, transmuting the daily bread of experience into the radiant body of everliving life."

THE DEDALUS COMPLAINT

Stephen Dedalus instinctively felt a cleavage between being a complete human being and living out the type of holiness he had seen. It wasn't just the reticence of the carnal nature confronted with moral demands; this youth had cherished the state of grace after his conversion and had responded to the call to be holy. But that calling didn't hold up; it withered into the "pale service of the altar" and dissolved in the featureless faces of the pious. The goodness Stephen saw was not compelling; it wasn't worth dedicating your whole life to.

His aversion to religious goodness resonates widely in our age. His experience is an archetype of the road away from religion that today has become a congested freeway. His complaint looms over all who would like to take their faith seriously.

When aroused to try winning over unbelievers, most Christians focus on making it easier to believe. Our contemporaries in this secular age seem to have a hard time grasping accounts of angels and demons, miraculous birth, resurrection, and second coming. So we struggle to make these truths tangible in a world that does not regularly bump into them.

But there's another problem, one that involves perhaps deeper instincts: the problem of who's got the good life. For the great majority, goodness—quality of life—is what first draws attention; experience speaks louder than doctrine. Most people are moved to believe because they are attracted by and drawn into a way of life that happens to include certain beliefs. Very few turning points are based on abstractions. Not many of us (unfortunately) go around seeking truth, but all of us are after the good life. And our perceptions of what the good life includes generally determine what beliefs we cling to.

Stephen Dedalus, and one assumes James Joyce as well, had his doubts, but he wanted to believe. The mysteries of the faith attracted him precisely because they were glorious mysteries. But something else tripped him up: the failure of religious goodness to compel.

Too often believers have trivialized goodness by concentrating on their various denominational brands of legalism, becoming a "peculiar people" set at odd angles to the world rather than being an attractive light illuminating it. As a result, our morality calls out rather feebly. It whines from the corner of a sanctuary; it awkwardly interrupts pleasures; it mumbles excuses at parties; it shuffles along out of step and slightly behind the times. Such virtue doesn't play well on prime-time TV or in top-forty tunes. It's often regarded by our secular contemporaries as a narrow, even trivial, pursuit. Compared to, say, efforts to achieve world peace and end world hunger, preoccupations with jewelry, foul language, and whether women should preach in church don't seem very earth-shaking.

FENDING OFF THE ANGELS

There are some things about Stephen Dedalus's coming of age that I deeply identify with. I spent four high school years at Christian boarding schools, surrounded by order and duty, ambivalent about the pull of religion. The great moral issues of my world were boys' hair sneaking below the collar, girls' skirts edging above the knees, and anybody listening to rock radio stations. Our Bible teacher happened to be a quite likable guy, but when he sensed that the school might be on the edge of revival, the first action he proposed was "dress reform," lining the boys up in a long row and urging each of us not to wear our pants too tight.

Still, even within those boundaries, I had no aversion to believing; God and His Word and His acts beckoned nobly to me. I did struggle with doubts, but it was a struggle I wanted to win.

Religious *goodness* was the tricky thing. It did not confront me as a challenge to take on but as a fear in the back of my mind. I was afraid of what kind of person I might turn into if I became completely religious. The few who had fallen altogether into that state projected a forbidding image: virtue wrapped around them tightly like packing wire, faces pinched into benevolence, bodies aligned on the straight and narrow like boxcars laden with holy freight.

In my particular subculture they always wore white, starchy shirts and dark slacks, carried large leather-bound Bibles, and spoke in King James English. They had memorized great quantities of doctrinal information, such as the details of the symbolic beasts in Revelation, and they wielded ever-ready proof texts proclaiming that our church was the true one.

Most of my peers at school likewise saw religious goodness as a threat. The holy life seemed to plead for the privilege of shriveling them. To ward it off, my roommate Joe faithfully carried a miniature pack of poker cards in his inside coat pocket during church services. If a sermon got too pressing, he could always reach in and finger the ace of spades or queen of hearts. The cards were his security, preventing angels from getting too close.

It wasn't just fanaticism that threatened us. It was simply a common goodness that seemed drained of life, colorless. I'm sure our sinful natures were a big factor in all this aversion. But there was something more. We saw no signs of the good life, or the great life; nothing compelled us. Indifference and boredom were just too easy, too much a fitting response to our religious environment.

A Pale Slice of Life

Like most everything else in today's world, conventional religious goodness is able to position itself in people's minds with only one label, projecting one basic image; it's seen primarily as *something which avoids evil*. It means avoidance; the absence of.

This defensive image lies at the root of the inability of most religious goodness to inspire. The pious confront a world full of threats —anarchic rock lyrics blaring out everywhere, suggestive TV shows on every station, riotous parties in every neighborhood, decadent materialism all over the mall—and have to turn away. The world is portrayed as morally toxic—like tobacco smoke continually blown in one's face. The easiest sermon to preach is one on why the world is going to hell. The quickest religious bestseller is one that red-letters a new hidden danger out there threatening the faith.

When the center of morality is avoidance—when virtue is a matter of continually whittling life down to proper size—it's all going to appear quite pale and stifling. If our primary focus is on remaining unspotted by the world, we'll invariably narrow our way down to pettiness in preserving our peculiar slice of religious turf undefiled. Evil seems all-encompassing, so our turning away becomes frantic flight. We must build ever higher, ever stricter barriers against the encroachment of the world. Morally safe activities steadily decrease; the "true way" of holiness steadily constricts.

Again and again, the watching world sees the pursuit of holiness derailed into eccentricity when avoidance is carried to its logical end. (A certain Madame de Genlis concentrated on "purity of manners" to the point of once reprimanding the man arranging her library for putting books by male and female authors on the same shelf.) When it becomes life's focal point, "goodness" seems to lead away from humanity into some sanctimonious perversion of it—a pale slice of life lived out with a vengeance. If pursued with too much regularity, sanctity seems perilous. Surely then, many people conclude, a little goodness goes a long way.

Tragically, conventional religious goodness manages to be both intimidating and unchallenging at the same time. The thought of spending one's life always vigilant, ever defensive, guarding against the evils of the world, fills people with dismay. It's just too hard not to fall. And yet, though extremely difficult, the prospect doesn't arise as a great challenge, either; it doesn't seem worthy of life's best energies.

Normal Sin

Confronted by the apparent perils of the virtuous life, most of us have settled on a different picture of ourselves, a different ideal. Part of the humanist legacy is the belief that to err is human. This is not an unhealthy perspective at first. People need to know they're not perfect; they commit sins. But slowly this fact has been turned on its head. We now are reassured about our normalcy by our sins; we've come to identify our humanity with our flaws. The belief that moral failure is an essential part of healthy humanity is our ace of spades we can finger when the call of holiness brushes by too close.

"I'm only human" commonly means "I make mistakes." Fine. But is holiness, or its pursuit, then *less* human? That subtle message has been sinking in for generations.

We tend to link the capacity to sin seriously with maturity and adulthood. Vice is an adult phenomenon; G ratings are for kids. Thomas Szasz writes in *The Second Sin*, "A child becomes an adult when he realizes he has a right not only to be right but also to be wrong." A *New York Post* columnist echoes: "The greatest right in the world is the right to be wrong." These are the slogans of a secular age that no longer buys holiness as a credible pursuit.

Consistent virtue seems more mechanical than human, as Isaac Asimov implies: "Part of the inhumanity of the computer is that, once it is competently programmed and working smoothly, it is completely honest." Even with tongue in cheek we reveal our ironclad assumption: To err is human.

Of course we all struggle with moral problems. It would be terribly unwise to hide from that and become paralyzed by failure. The tragedy comes, however, when people give up the struggle. What's at issue, and what has changed, is our goal as human beings, our identity, what we perceive as the good life.

Whereas we used to revere them, we are now embarrassed by idealists and saints. We make excuses for them—they come from a troubled background or have an uncanny gift. Those who have engaged in heroic deeds of righteousness are "larger than life." They don't really fit into the human scale of things.

Contemporary moral slogans tend to move in only one direction: lowering our horizons. The moral world has been steadily shrinking. Our most telling specialty is turning human frailty into something heroic.

When Stephen Dedalus turned away from the chill of moral orderliness he conjured up a new ideal:

> To live, to err, to fall, to triumph, to recreate life out of life! A wild angel had appeared to him, the angel of mortal youth and beauty, an envoy from the fair courts of life, to throw open before him in an instant of ecstasy the gates of all the ways of error and glory.

Stephen, the whole human being, boldly asserted:

> I am not afraid to make a mistake, even a great mistake, a life-long mistake, and perhaps as long as eternity too.

The courage of the modern man is tied to his capacity for great mistakes.

Contemporary biographies celebrate this fallibility. The slogans we come up with to summarize a life are revealing. Take Dashiell Hammett, the real-life ace Pinkerton agent who wrote *The Maltese Falcon* and other classic detective novels. Summing up Hammett's "deep and steadfast" code of honor, his biographer says: "He played no one's game but his own." That's it? It has a ring to it, but it seems morally neutered. Cool self-centeredness is recast as singular virtue. The subtitle to Hammett's biography, *A Life on the Edge,* echoes the conviction that real life lies on the borders of morality, not at its center.

F. Scott Fitzgerald, a writer who partied his way into creative limbo, draws another telling biographical summary: "If Fitzgerald created his own hell, he also survived it heroically." Lowered expectations.

D. H. Lawrence, gifted writer of *Lady Chatterley's Lover* fame, could be kind and sensitive and also inexplicably cruel—as on the day at dinner when he told his young daughter her mother didn't love her or anybody else, then threw a glass of wine in the mother's face. A biographer tells us that to be Lawrence's friend was always interesting: He might behave with intimates like an angel one day and the devil the next. But whatever else, it was always a "full-blooded relationship." Again we get the feeling that decency by itself would not be full-blooded; the virtuous are only half-human.

A corollary to this is the widely held myth that genius almost requires distorted moral character. We hear anecdotes of the great excusing their petty cruelty by referring to their artistic gift, and few question it. A similar myth asserts that mental instability, or even a touch of insanity, is a prerequisite to artistic achievement. Vincent van Gogh is the classic example here. What most people don't realize, however, is that he could not paint at all during his mental seizures, but only during days of lucidity. What makes him heroic is his desperate struggle against the affliction that he knew was destroying his ability to create.

Just as people create in spite of mental handicaps, so they also create in spite of moral handicaps—not because of them. Moments of moral insensitivity are not the key to greatness of any kind. It is the struggle against our ethical failures that makes us grow.

But in a world where our expectations have been lowered, we must reinvent ideals and imagine new heroes. The womanizing star who dies an alcoholic is lauded: "Some measure out their lives with coffee spoons," but he "poured his out by the bucketful..." We have come to a pathetic kind of abundance: men grow heroic by their incontinence. Those who don't drink themselves to death are merely measuring out life by the spoonful.

The merely virtuous are typically urged, "Why don't you live a little?" That generally means, "Why don't you sin a little?" Transgressions seem the obvious alternative for someone trying to grow out of a repressed life. That's where you go for the gusto. Mere goodness, in contrast, is all the color taken out. The often-quoted line "Happy families are all alike; every unhappy family is unhappy in its own way" hints at the banality of conventional virtue. One-dimensional do-gooders are not taken seriously; they're admired, perhaps, but only in the way a nicely cut french fry is admired.

ALLERGIC TO ABSOLUTES

We have to admit there is a kind of frailty that helps make us "more human." Uncle Freddy's forgetfulness becomes a cherished family joke; Grandad's dozing off in mid-conversation makes him all the more endearing; Mom's jumpiness makes her a delight to tease. But these traits that bind to a personality and help define it are very different from moral errors.

Sin is cruelty. It's hurting other people or yourself. Take a good look: Every time you fail morally, somebody suffers. And it's usually the weaker and more dependent who must suffer for the "humanity" of the stronger. Children are a great destroyer of our comforting myths about the charm of moral lapses. When we live alone we can usually get away from those we hurt. But children reflect back our every nasty habit and we view it in all its ugliness; we don't see endearing faults but personalities deformed because of our anger, impatience, insensitivity, unfairness.

Sin is cruelty. It sounds a bit different for us to blandly pass off the aphorism: "To be cruel is human. I'm only human, I've got to be cruel." In this light our revolution of lowered moral expectations doesn't look quite so benign.

A world-class American actor once met a lovely, fun-loving woman named Susan. He fell in love with the girl. But, as a biographer put it, "He was a very married man who took his obligations seriously. His middle-class, Midwestern background made no allowances for secondary romances. If he was stern with his children, he was sterner with himself."

So how did he respond, this paragon of virtue? He didn't sleep with Susan right away. His "Boy Scout" morality restricted the romance to only a few kisses. At length he walked into his wife's bedroom and told her he'd met someone and wanted a divorce. She accepted this rather quietly and even wished him good luck. "She was absolutely wonderful," the actor recalled. Her complete nervous breakdown wouldn't come until a little later.

This man closed the door on his wife and went out to start a new life, greatly relieved that he'd done the right thing: "I had been honest with Frances, fair to my children, virtuous toward Susan, and, finally, honorable with myself."

Astounding bit of insight. It's like complimenting someone on a nicely healing lobotomy, oblivious to all that has been destroyed. This is the kind of "virtue" we end up with after desensitizing ourselves to the call of holiness. It's human to err. As long as we're polite in our cruelty and don't make a scene, we can walk away with our heads held high.

Sometimes we go beyond lowering moral expectations and attempt to rule them out altogether. In a greatly constricted world it's not hard to become allergic to ideals and absolutes.

Fictional characters sometimes best echo our picture of ourselves. Here's a reviewer summing up author Bernard Malamud's work:

> He admires the sheer cussedness of his characters, their backs to the wall, squabbling in the maw of annihilation. He relishes the cranks and eccentrics who, destined to suffer and die, still insist on making noise in a vast, indifferent universe.

There is something admirable in many of Malamud's characters, but there's no question that the world has shrunk. Meaningful virtue is impossible, making defiant noise against the meaninglessness the only heroism.

Novelist David Grossman spent seven weeks in Israel investigating the daily lives of Palestinians and Jews. His impressions of many West Bank Jewish settlers as intransigent and arrogant led him to write:

> I fear life among people who have an obligation to an absolute order. Absolute orders require, in the end, absolute deeds; and I...am a partial, relative, imperfect man who prefers to make correctable mistakes rather than attain supernatural achievements.

Grossman's modesty is commendable, but to get there he feels obliged to deny absolute values. The problem with Arabs and Jews throwing rocks at each other, he implies, is that they're pursuing "supernatural achievements." If we just weren't so obsessed with absolutes, he says, our mistakes would be more correctable; we'd have less heroic violence breeding its own kind.

But the central problem behind Arab-Israeli fighting, and most other chronic conflicts, is really the kind of absolutes that have been chosen. God and truth and right are reduced to property claims, the insistence on defending my turf no matter what the cost. Yet, instead of attacking these imposter absolutes we take refuge in a lower aim; we vow to scale down our moral achievements, as if there were a surplus of them in the world.

Can absolutes make people arrogant? Yes. Food can make people fat. A kitchen knife can be used as a weapon. But they aren't the problem.

In the absence of compelling moral values, other things rush in to take their place. Slogans reach for transcendence: "Buick, Something to Believe In." Or this bumper sticker with wit and bite: "Tennis is not a matter of life and death. It's more important than that." The question we face is not whether we're going to have absolutes or not, but which values we're going to stand on.

Something will arouse our deepest passions. A former mental patient living near Los Angeles decapitated his roommate after they'd argued over possession of a girlie centerfold. The defendant in a murder trial in Nottingham, England, explained why he'd killed his girlfriend: She'd deliberately turned off the TV during the replay of a soccer game. But it wasn't just any soccer game, it was the National Soccer Championship.

Yes, we have passions, and we choose our absolutes. The big issue is, which ones?

The movie *Terms of Endearment* struck me as an example of striving for excellence in a shrunken world. It was a fine accomplishment in simply laying out life as it is. In accepting the Oscar for Best Actress for her role in the film, Shirley MacLaine spoke of the writer-director's intense commitment to honesty, and his working hard to make something "truthful." The story *was* truthful in giving us a realistic picture of certain obviously flawed individuals, their marriages, friendships and adulteries. And we can learn valuable lessons from looking at "real" characters in "real" situations.

Listening to MacLaine talk about the struggle to produce the film after several Hollywood studios rejected it, one got the sense of a holy quest, people involved in a noble cause. For the secular, perhaps that's the only kind of ideal there is, the only absolute. We hear spoken accurately an intimate part of life, and we feel it together. It can be a moving experience.

But a small detail at the end of the film tripped me up. A young widower abandons his children, saying, as if this explained everything, "I never thought I'd be the kind of father that would do this." Other relationships had already dominated the film: a mother and daughter painfully coming to terms of endearment; the mother reaffirming herself through a refreshing free-spirit/obnoxious boozer; a young married couple falling apart. The movie brought in a bit of heroism by having the young wife die of cancer.

Then, almost as an afterthought in the plot, comes her husband's decision to drop his two motherless young sons. His mother-in-law will take care of them. This incalculable disaster in the lives of two boys slips through as one more honestly reported event. But I wanted to yell. To me it made everything else in the film secondary. In that light, who cares what happens to the Shirley MacLaine character? Adults can cavort and betray each other, but when two kids are permanently handicapped by the unspoken fact "This man is our father and he doesn't want to take care of us" —somebody should scream bloody murder.

The film, however, did not stray from its restrained true-to-life calling. It excelled at that. But I had the sense of another nicely healing lobotomy. Everything was so well done, but what about the destruction, the cruelty? No one ached at the absence of goodness.

WE'RE ALL CAUGHT in a double tragedy. Religious goodness fails to compel, and the world has lowered its moral expectations accordingly. Most of us turn to a more comfortable world of moral limits. But something important of our humanity has been lost.

When we can't cry out against the cruelty we're less human. When we give up the struggle, a crucial part of us is gone. We've closed the door on great deeds; the call to holiness collapses; the heroic disappears. The sky has closed in on all of us, secular and religious. The secular don't want to hear about moral heroes, and the religious don't want to hear about saints.

We stand awkwardly in this moral no man's land as in a badly framed photograph that cuts off the subject above the eyes. Faced with intimidating goodness we lower our aim, slink back into the comfort of mere human error...and cope.

2

INTO ACTS
OF ART

THE MORAL NO MAN'S LAND held me fast for some time back at my Christian boarding school. I remained fearful of a virtue that seemed to shrivel its host. Yet something—I suppose my parents, my upbringing, even the church—had left me unable to give up on radical rightness. I could not shake off the absolutes stirring in my bones.

My fears didn't really dissipate until I discovered a goodness that rang a bell. One day a kid named Bill Shelly entered our world of miniature rights and wrongs. He came to our Midwestern school from the West Coast. The first thing that struck us about Bill was that he worked rather cheerfully. Some of us students were employed at a furniture factory as part of a summer work program. Bill was stuck in the paint room at the end of an assembly line, a noxious place that left you sick at the end of the day. But Bill painted dressers and cabinets smiling as if he weren't all there. He was alert all right, but somehow he wasn't confined to that gloomy factory.

He'd been places, and not just geographical ones. His life was going somewhere. How could anybody have goals surrounded by miles of nothing but corn?

Bill was sincere, never pretentious, and never corny. We noticed him say grace at meals, but he never wore a white shirt. That was a new trick.

Something somehow made him terribly content. We couldn't figure it out. Once in a while he even talked about things he'd read in the Bible, but he didn't speak King James English. Bill was the first peer I'd known who made goodness seem both attractive and accessible.

One evening I was walking back to the dorm from supper and caught traces of purple, orange, and magenta in the sky. Quite a sunset. I hadn't noticed too many sunsets before. Toward the west the sun was flaring out and its golden rays were reflected in scattered clouds all the way across the heavens. I had never seen so much color; our usual flat gray ceiling of a sky was now alive with it.

Then I noticed Bill, sitting alone out on the football field bleachers. He was there with his Bible, looking at the sunset too.

That was the moment it hit me: Goodness could be a welcome part of your life. At least Bill was comfortable with it. Everything he did suggested he actually enjoyed it. Nobody had told him what to do. There were no rules requiring Bible-reading on the bleachers. Bill was making something happen. He wasn't just putting in time.

I looked out over the expanse of rolling hills turning purple in the haze. Maybe there was a goodness that took in the whole, something as expansive as this flaming sunset, something as inspiring. It was just a hint out there, but the mere possibility of virtue solidly in the flesh struck me to the bone.

The sun, digging deeper into the horizon, cut a majestic path far ahead through the clouds. After staring a long, long time, I made my way slowly toward the bleachers.

IF WE'RE TO FIND A WAY OUT of the Dedalus Complaint and also escape the counterpoint tragedy of lowered moral expectations, we have to reimagine virtue and rediscover its original passion. We must radically alter the way we think of being good. A new energy is desperately needed in an environment increasingly numb to the spirit. We must have a deeply rooted momentum going for us in order to push out the boundaries of our shrunken world. It won't do to just buckle down and try harder, pushing our pettiness to the limit.

If we go back to the New Testament call to holiness we find something very different from the pale, chill order of conventional goodness. There is an intense vision in the epistles that's remarkably close to the passionate ambition of an artist. We see Paul, as an up-and-coming Pharisee, throw away society's approval in favor of pressing toward a high calling that had laid hold of him. Definitely compelled, he urges us to make righteousness a consuming pursuit. He never wants to stand still; he always wants to grow in grace, being transformed from glory to glory. He proclaims that conventions like circumcision mean nothing and that the only thing that counts is new creation. Resolutely following Christ's manifesto, Paul knows we must create new wineskins to express the new wine fermenting in our spirits.

After much reflection, I believe we can best reimagine virtue through the paradigm of making art. From the petty and pedantic we must recover goodness as what God originally intended it to be: an art form, a highest calling, something with eternal resonance.

As we try to rediscover virtue, there is much we can learn from the way art is created and the way it works on people, the way it drives artists to devote their lives to creative effort. Great works of art and spiritual accomplishments have more in common than is apparent on the surface. We can begin to see some important connections by looking at a fundamental biblical principle: the dynamic relationship of law and spirit.

THE STRUCTURE THAT FREES

Law is used in various senses in the Bible. It can refer to the Old Testament system of sacrifices and ceremonies or to a method of achieving salvation. Here we will use it in its primary sense as the expression of God's moral character.

Law is a black and white photograph of what God is like, or God in outline form. Scripture does not present God's law as some arbitrary code plopped down on the world, but as something inevitable, ingrained in the universe.

God's law is unchanging; it doesn't need to be revised, amended, or updated. "All his precepts are trustworthy," writes the psalmist; "they are steadfast for ever and ever, done in faithfulness and uprightness." And in another psalm: "All your righteous laws are eternal." God's laws express His eternally consistent character.

In the New Testament, James calls God's moral demands "the law of liberty." The law points the way not toward restriction or mere avoidance, but toward liberation. Looking at that perfect law and following it is like mastering the basics on the piano or the basics of draftsmanship. Knowing these principles is what enables an artist to express himself musically or visually. He is free to perform. In James's view, liberty is not a vacuum, the absence of slavery; it's the ability to *do*. Freedom is the power to fulfill our destiny, and the law is the prerequisite for that freedom.

Elsewhere in Scripture the law is defined as good, spiritual, and holy. God described His creation as "good" repeatedly in Genesis 1. The fabric of creation—harmony, color, emotion, rhythm—is good. Artists who master these principles move and enlighten us. The moral form of that creation is good, too. God's moral law is every bit as basic, every bit as inherent in creation.

The law creates a space for growth. Those who "walk in the law of the Lord" are considered blessed. There's room to walk in the law; it's a healthy direction. I don't know of anyone who is threatened by the laws of composition or color harmony. Artists like Bach and Mozart were not intimidated by chord structure and scale, but eager to excel through them.

The common Old Testament refrain "Your law is my delight" likewise suggests that the law is something unthreatening which one can admire, like beautiful coloring and ingenious harmonies. The Hebrews' ideal was to "follow all the words of this law." They carried those words in tiny boxes strapped to their wrists and foreheads, symbolizing the value they placed on living in that precious space the law creates. Symbols, having a borrowed life, can of course dry up and die. Admiration can wither into legalism; basic principles can shrink into petty regulations. But there is still much to learn from the essential Hebrew contribution: an appreciation for the creative potential of law.

The pinnacle of Hebrew admiration is Psalm 119. Rhapsodizing on the priceless heritage of God's precepts, the psalmist makes the law musical. He longs to meditate on those statutes; he treasures every word in his heart. He gets up early to seek God's words and then through the day waits eagerly for sunset so he can meditate on them again in the night watches. One is reminded of someone poring over a masterful orchestral score.

In the law he finds something "sweeter than honey" and more precious "than thousands of pieces of silver and gold." Four times he declares with feeling, ""How I love your law!" It is a lamp for his feet, a good counselor, and a great inheritance. Through it God sustains and revives him. Reminding us of James, the psalmist writes: "I will walk about in freedom, for I have sought out your precepts." To him, God's commandment "is exceedingly broad."

Today it is hard for us to relate to Psalm 119. Our concepts of law and legality are very different. The law, for us, is an impersonal entity imposed by impersonal institutions. Our encounters with it generally involve offended traffic cops, clogged courts, convoluted tax codes, zoning ordinances, or a maze of propositions on the ballot. Typically, we bump into the law as a barrier. So this biblical poet's enthusiasm is puzzling. How could moral demands be so stimulating?

To understand the psalmist's admiration we have to see the moral law as he did: as an expression of God's character. The law revealed God to him; it was very personal. In the Old Testament, "the word of God" and "the law of God" were often used interchangeably. So the law celebrated in Psalm 119 includes God's word in general, His revelation of Himself in Scripture. Those precepts and statutes over which the psalmist waxed eloquent were not isolated entries in a thick code book. They were brush strokes that helped fill in the face of the Almighty, one more series of notes in the great score that expressed God's character. The law helped the psalmist know God and admire him, so naturally he was eager to learn all he could.

That's the secret. He was admiring God, and he enjoyed discovering more about Him: "Open my eyes that I may see wonderful things in your law." Of course he also appreciated the law as an invaluable guide in his life, but it was a *personal* guide, a personal word from the God who loved him.

In the history of Israel, it was the rediscovery of the law after years of neglect which led to revival and reformation. The law beckoned the Hebrews back to God, their great heritage, and away from idolatry.

In 500 B.C., Ezra the scribe took a few Jewish stragglers, most of them virtually paganized, from Babylon back into Judah, now a Jehovah-forsaken wasteland. He proposed to create a new cultural order with all the richness of the old. What did this scribe have? Only one thing: the law. And Ezra succeeded.

The law, the structure of goodness, gives us a rock-solid foundation for spiritual achievement. Goodness is not some subjective oozing; it's expression within a structure.

NOT ENOUGH

Many artists echo the writer of Psalm 119 in their appreciation of essential truths, of fundamental forms in the world. Even a romantic painter like Delacroix, reacting against a rigid classical style, valued "the hidden symmetry...the equilibrium at once wise and inspired, which governs the meeting or separation of lines and spaces, the echoes of color, etc."

American sculptor Horatio Greenough perceived the artist as someone "tasting sensuously the effect of a rhythm and harmony in God's world..."

Gino Severini, a twentieth-century futurist, declared:

> An art which does not obey fixed and inviolable laws is to true art what a noise is to a musical sound. To paint without being acquainted with these fixed and very severe laws is tantamount to composing a symphony without knowing harmonic relations and the rules of counterpoint.

Most artists would not be so dogmatic, but almost all would confess a longing to uncover eternal laws in the world they reflect upon. The law is the foundation, an essential prerequisite to the expansive, creative virtue which I call *artful* goodness.*

---

* In this book I'm using "artful" in its simple and primary sense of "exhibiting art or skill," and I hope we can avoid its other connotations of "tricky, cunning," and "artificial."

But the law is not enough. Another element is needed. By itself the law can point us toward imitation, but not art. In fact, when isolated from the Creator God, the law can become stifling. People drift toward external details and focus numbly on the letter of the law. Delacroix's criticism of boring art applies to pedantic goodness: "Cold exactitude is not art....The so-called conscientiousness of the majority of painters is only perfection applied to the art of boring." People merely trying to render duty, merely trying to copy, invariably come up with less than the law. As Delacroix elaborated, "Continual caution in showing only what is shown in nature will always make the painter colder than the nature which he thinks he is imitating."

The law, good in itself, essential for art, capable of showing us the way to liberation, continually runs into the barrier of our carnal nature—our tragic twist away from expansive goodness and toward petty selfishness. Sinfulness includes a bent toward the trivial*We don't naturally ascend; we flop around. We guard turf, take offense, strike back, put down, complain—all effortlessly. We grasp spiritual values only by taking pains.

The carnal nature recognizes only the most obvious pleasures and quickest rewards—or punishments. Listening to an enthusiastic testimony about someone's "new life in Christ," it hears only that he doesn't do this and that anymore. The part about a "personal relationship with Christ" floats through the mind untouched. The carnal nature is reductionist. Presented with some church's doctrinal portfolio, it retains only the impression that "they don't drink or dance."

Externals can be efficiently passed down from generation to generation. The turbaned Sikhs have preserved their tradition of uncut hair for centuries, the Amish their horse-and-buggy lifestyle. A certain form of liturgy is repeated faithfully through the decades, father to son to father to son. Not eating pork, wearing veils, not painting fingernails—these things snap right into a culture. People without a shred of interest in spirituality can zealously preserve these "standards" through the centuries. But when it comes to passing on love, patience, or peace—that falls apart within a few years. It's incredibly fragile.

This is one of the tragedies of our fallen nature; we don't naturally retain what matters most. We're sieves, letting priceless qualities flow through and keeping back all the dirt clods. We go for the tangible trinkets every time.

This doesn't mean externals are bad. It simply means that's all the carnal nature can handle. It's incapable of truly creating; it can only imitate an outward form. It's a laborer fulfilling a quota. Artful goodness is utterly beyond it.

In trying to raise us above the pedantic, God had to deal with this problem of our sinful nature. On a legal level He absorbed its worst consequences by sacrificing Himself on the cross. He took on Himself the deadness of the carnal nature. And He laid down His own perfect life as a substitute for our chronic failure. The result: acquittal, justification.

THE MISSING ELEMENT

On an experiential level God unleashed His Spirit to transform those who accept His sacrifice. He attacked the hopeless dullness of the carnal nature by pouring His own creative energy into us. As Scripture repeatedly tells us, it is the Spirit who gives life; we're made alive by the Spirit; through Him we escape the deadness of the flesh; He resuscitates mortal bodies.

Paul in Romans 8 introduces the new factor of the Spirit: "Through Christ Jesus the law of the Spirit of life set me free from the law of sin and death." People are spoken of as born of the Spirit, renewed by the Spirit. This is the missing element. For artful goodness to occur, law must be combined with God's Spirit. The Spirit is the resource who turns the form of the law into art.

The creative energy of the Spirit bears abundant fruit: love, joy, peace, patience, kindness, goodness, faithfulness gentleness, self-control. God's Spirit within us is presented as a potent brew, the muse's magic: "We were all given the one Spirit to drink." To the Ephesians, Paul presents being filled with the Spirit as an alternative to getting drunk. That strong spirit produces expression: Believers "speak to one another in psalms, hymns and spiritual songs." Conversation is lifted to art. The Spirit-filled make melody with their hearts to the Lord, getting beyond the dull chant of the carnal laborer, giving voice to inner qualities.

Having the Spirit means that God Himself is at work in us. Just as an artist is possessed with his idea and must express it, so the Spirit-filled are God-possessed and must express Him.

So how do we get it? Or, perhaps more accurately, how does He get us? Paul suggests a simple answer in his rhetorical question to the Galatians: "Did you receive the Spirit by observing the law, or by believing what you heard?" The rest of the epistle suggests, or shouts, that they received Him when they heard the gospel and believed in it. They heard the Word; they placed faith in it; they received the Spirit.

One way we express faith is by asking, praying. Jesus tells us explicitly (Luke 11:13) to ask for the Spirit. The Spirit comes to us as we look at the Word and converse with God about it.

This is true not only of our initial reception of God's Spirit when we begin the Christian life but also of how we grow in the Spirit thereafter. We still need to hear the Word, believe in it, and be filled with the Spirit.

The Word is the source of our inspiration; the story of God and His saving acts inspires. We need to place faith in it on a continual basis. How?

We could define faith functionally as a kind of attention, a way of looking. The artist, especially the painter, develops a disciplined way of looking at the world. He looks carefully; he finds new ways of seeing the ordinary; he puts things together or tears them apart. The artist looks with intensity, involving his intellect and emotions. Then, when some insight develops, he tries to give it expression on canvas.

The Word is our world, the source of our art. We need to look at it carefully, using the same intense involvement with which the painter looks at life. We must find new ways of seeing the familiar, and involve our intellect and emotions. Then, when insights develop, we give them expression. On a practical level, this is how we place faith in the Word, how we "let the word of Christ dwell in you richly."

The Spirit is really not so mysterious or complicated, though His work is supernatural. God must be present to produce inspiration, but our part is direct and simple: We have to look at the Word and respond to it in prayer. Perhaps it's too obvious for a lot of people. Believers tend to try all kinds of techniques and activities except the essential discipline of looking at God in His Word.

LIGHT TO PAINT WITH

Artists frequently wither when they begin simply copying another artist whose work they admire, instead of gaining inspiration directly from nature and coming up with fresh ideas. Delacroix complained, "All those young men of the school of Ingres have something pedantic about them." They had imposed a "mass of fixed opinions" on themselves, imitating a human master instead of creating.

Law and Spirit represent a dynamic process, not a mechanical two-step. We receive the Spirit through the Word, but the Spirit also helps us see more deeply into the Word. The two are mutually reinforcing. "The Spirit searches all things, even the deep things of God," Paul tells the Corinthians, and then explains that this very Spirit is ours. He enables us to understand God in a profound way and to gain insights that are completely beyond the reach of carnal thought patterns.

The Spirit recognizes *God* in the Word, not just data. That's the essential difference between the psalmist leaping for joy over God's law, and those who turn it into dry, external requirements. The Spirit comes into our hearts crying, "Abba! Father!" when we look with faith, when we practice a disciplined seeing and respond to God in prayer. We look at the Word, and finding a personal revelation there, we shout "Daddy!"

The Spirit is our essential means of turning from imitative acts toward inspired expression. We are urged to live by the Spirit, walk by the Spirit, sow to the Spirit, grow in the Spirit. God's purpose is that "the righteous requirements of the law might be fully met in us, who do not live according to the sinful nature but according to the Spirit."

This is how we arrive at the new covenant in which the law is written in our hearts and minds. That eternal moral form is internalized and enlivened. This is how we get to those mysterious phrases: "the law of liberty," "the law that gives freedom," "the law is spiritual." They sound almost like a contradiction in terms. But the Spirit changes everything. He turns law into artful goodness—creative expression. The law becomes light, not a rule book, and we can paint with light. The Spirit fleshes out the black-and-white photograph of the law into full-color expression.

The law must be fulfilled is a statement repeated over and over in the Bible. The law calls for expression just as the principles of musical harmony and composition do. It demands fulfillment, and only the Spirit can answer the call. The Spirit compels us to turn the forms into art.

Art is always something compelled. The angel which Michelangelo saw in that block of stone must be uncovered, that last symphony Beethoven heard through his deafness must be given exact shape for an orchestra, those wheat fields in southern France that van Gogh saw vibrating vividly with color must be captured on canvas.

You feel the same compulsion in John's first epistle. After his opening lines of testimony he declares, "These things we write, so that our joy may be made complete." His experience with grace just had to find expression.

Possessed by the Spirit, human beings become God's workmanship, created in Christ Jesus for good works. "Offering up spiritual sacrifices acceptable to God," we are "living stones" built up on the living Cornerstone, Christ. Goodness is more than just putting round pegs in round holes and square pegs in square holes; it is offering up sacrifices to God, works of art that rise like incense above the world and echo God's qualities, making Him feel there are people down here who resonate with His instincts.

Spirit and law are the basic dynamic behind artful goodness. Admiring God in the Word (faith) produces creative energy—inspiration (from the Spirit)—which uses biblical teaching (law) to produce good works (artful goodness).

LIKE A NEWBORN CHILD

Back in high school Bill Shelly hinted to me that such a thing as artful goodness could exist simply by relaxing with his Bible on the bleachers under an expansive, brilliantly colored sky. Others have made the quality quite explicit.

Late one evening three men conversed in a small flat in Budapest: a Lutheran pastor named Richard Wurmbrand, his landlord, and Borila, a huge soldier on leave from the front where Rumania was fighting as a German ally during World War II. Borila dominated the conversation, boasting of his adventures in battle and especially of how he helped exterminate Jews in Transmistria. He had killed hundreds of them, he said, with his own hands.

Wurmbrand was not a man to remain silent about cruelty, so he protested—quietly and with bite: "It is a frightening story," he told Borila, "but I do not fear for the Jews—God will compensate them for what they have suffered. I ask myself with anguish what will happen to the murderers when they stand before God's judgment."

The soldier quickly took offense and the landlord had to prevent an ugly scene, saying both men were guests in his house and steering the conversation to more pleasant things.

Eventually it came out that the Jew-killer was also a lover of music. While serving in the Ukraine he'd been captivated by the songs there and now wished he could hear them again.

Wurmbrand thought to himself, *The fish has entered my net!* He told Borila: "If you'd like to hear some of them, come to my flat. I'm no pianist, but I can play a few Ukrainian melodies."

This Borila, his huge bulk horrible as the smell of death, was a prime example of the evil that conventional religion must turn away from. He was a moral pollution to avoid at all costs, a subject not just cut off somewhere above the eyes, but all but morally decapitated. The last thing a man on guard against the evil world would do is invite him into his home, exposing his family to such a spectacle.

But Wurmbrand brought Borila downstairs into his flat and began playing Ukrainian folk-songs—softly so as not to awaken his wife and baby son. After a bit the pastor could see the soldier had been deeply moved by the melodies. He stopped playing and said, "If you look through that curtain you can see someone asleep in the next room. It's my wife, Sabina. Her parents, her sisters, and her twelve-year-old brother have been killed with the rest of the family. You told me that you had killed hundreds of Jews near Golta, and that is where they were taken. You yourself don't know who you have shot, so we can assume that you are the murderer of her family."

Borila leaped from his chair, his eyes ablaze, looking as if he could strangle the pastor. But Wurmbrand calmed him by proposing an experiment: "I shall wake my wife and tell her who you are and what you have done. I can tell you what will happen. My wife will not speak one word of reproach! She'll embrace you as if you were her brother. She'll bring you supper, the best things she has in the house."

The pastor then came to the punch line: "If Sabina, who is a sinner like us all, can forgive and love like this, imagine how Jesus, who is perfect Love, can forgive and love you!" He urged Borila to return to God and seek forgiveness.

The man melted. Rocking back and forth he sobbed out his confession: "I'm a murderer; I'm soaked in blood..." Wurmbrand guided him to his knees and began praying. Borila, having had no such experience, simply begged for forgiveness over and over.

Then the pastor walked into the bedroom and gently awakened his wife. "There is a man here whom you must meet," he whispered. "We believe he has murdered your family, but he has repented, and now he is our brother." Sabina came out in her dressing gown and extended her hands to the huge, tear-stained soldier. He collapsed in her arms, and both wept greatly. Amid the overwhelming emotions of grief, guilt, and grace, they kissed each other fervently.

Finally Sabina went into the kitchen to prepare some food. Wurmbrand thought his guest could use a further reinforcement of grace since he was laboring out from under such horrible crimes. So he stepped into the next room and returned with his two-year-old son, Mihai, fast asleep in his arms. Borila was dismayed. It had been only hours since he boasted of killing Jewish children in their parents' arms, and this sight seemed an unbearable reproach. He expected a withering rebuke. Instead the pastor leaned forward and said, "Do you see how quietly he sleeps? You are like a newborn child who can rest in the Father's arms. The blood that Jesus shed has cleansed you." Looking down at Mihai, Borila felt—for the first time in ages—a surge of pure happiness.

Later, after rejoining his regiment in Russia, Borila laid aside his weapons and volunteered to rescue the wounded under fire.

REDISCOVERED PASSION

For Richard Wurmbrand, goodness was not something that evil constantly threatens to overcome. *It was something that can overcome evil.*

I admire the ingenuity with which this pastor wielded the weapon of goodness. He deftly brought a brute into a confrontation with the beauty of grace. He was not heavy-handed, but skillful. And his acts were such a revelation. Sabina's embrace embodied volumes of theology. The child sleeping in his father's arms propelled truth to the marrow.

This is an artist at work. Even Stephen Dedalus, longing to transform "the daily bread of experience into the radiant body of everliving life," would have found him inspiring.

Artful goodness means going beyond our chronic defensive fight against evil. In our conventional efforts to be good, it's usually sin that dictates the rules and the battleground. Too often sin becomes the focus of our attention. We're alarmed over it and warned about it; we're defining it, reacting to it, avoiding it, overcoming it, careening around it. It's about time something else took center stage. There's something great we can express with our lives; there are qualities luminous enough to turn into art. The driving force of the good life, the best life, is positive expression, not defensive reaction.

Van Gogh carried on his fierce struggle against madness because he had something to express:

> In a picture I want to say something comforting as music is comforting. I want to paint men and women with that something of the eternal which the halo used to symbolize, and which we seek to give by the actual radiance and vibration of our colorings.... Ah! portraiture, portraiture with the thought, the soul of the model in it, that is what I think must come.

The artistic drive compels people to put up with all kinds of hardship in order to capture something eternal, something that matters. George Bellows suggested art as "the finest, deepest, most significant expression of a rare personality." The German expressionist Max Beckmann explained, "What I want to show in my work is the idea which hides itself behind so-called reality. I am seeking for the bridge which leads from the visible to the invisible." Charles Sheeler spoke of perceiving and expressing a "universal order."

If virtue is ever to rise above that pale and monotonous service at the altar in a greatly shrunken world, it must capture this same drive to express, to become a bridge between the visible and the invisible. There have been men and women through history who've gone beyond conventional religious goodness and demonstrated a robust, colorful virtue that constrained their contemporaries. Like Richard Wurmbrand, they knew artful goodness. We'll meet some of these artists of the Spirit and study their works as one might peruse a great painting, deciphering the beauty and uncovering the meaning.

To see just how goodness can become positive expression, a compelling picture on the canvas, we'll look at three qualities that can serve as primary colors. These essential virtues make possible many others, opening up a whole spectrum of spiritual hues.

The First Virtue

LIGHT
HUMILITY

3

THE INVISIBLE
VIRTUE

AT THE FURNITURE FACTORY where I first met Bill Shelly, I used to drive a forklift. My job was to retrieve flats of deacon benches, hope chests, and six-drawer dressers and delivering them to a man of indeterminate age named Arthur who loaded the boxed pine into neat stacks in a railroad car. Arthur seemed physically incapable of hurrying, his movements as deliberate as a minute hand. But he wasn't at all lazy. In fact, you almost never found him at rest. Boxcar after boxcar, trailer after trailer—he filled them with a peculiar intensity.

Arthur was so different from me. I was seventeen and erratically active, racing around on my forklift, clambering over forty-foot stacks in the warehouse for a stray deacon bench, dodging the staples of the piece-work guys gunning for me. I often dropped things —entire stacks of dressers tumbled down on the roof of my forklift, much to the boss's dismay. Arthur never dropped things. He just kept plodding along, arms thick and solid with labor, skin darkened by labor, clothes confined to labor. He seemed to expect nothing more in this life than sweat.

Once in a while I tried to get into Arthur, but I could never really penetrate his benign and slightly nervous exterior. He seemed to be always avoiding himself, gently turning aside personal questions as if someone had made an indecent remark. During break time he remained in the corner, out of the way, never really in a conversation, always commenting from the edge. I had the impression Arthur was a faithfully religious man, reverent from a long distance, a distance he seemed to feel inevitable. Among his profane co-workers Arthur would go out of his way to avoid the appearance of evil, but he never preached at anyone.

This man seemed the embodiment of humility to me, invariably self-effacing. At the same time I was distressed by my inability to put a finger on a self there somewhere within the striped overalls. In my idealistic youth I felt a keen desire for Arthur to be somebody, but he remained deliberately overshadowed, consciously avoiding any "me" coming to the surface. I couldn't escape glimpsing in his weathered features a measure of self-hatred.

Arthur remains a character I can still only imagine drawn to scale. I don't know how or why he was ticking. But he remains in my mind the haunting image of a humility black as a nightmare.

UNSEASONABLE VANITY

Humility has become a virtue known chiefly by its aberrations; only a multiplicity of frauds hint at the real thing. Charles Dickens's oily character Uriah Heep whines his way into advantageous position by making a spectacle of his meekness. There's nothing like an overly humble character in fiction to arouse our suspicions. *Why is he being so nice? There must be something wrong.* Pious lowliness in mystery plots is a sure sign of murderous intent.

Most real-life attempts to be meek sound terribly awkward. Leonardo da Vinci once enumerated his manifold abilities to a potential patron, the duke of Milan, and ended the letter with the words, "Your Excellency, to whom I commend myself with all possible humility." Evidently, humility wasn't too possible in the light of all his accomplishments. The Roman consul Cato, observing that monuments were being erected in his honor, declared, "I would rather people asked why there is *not* a statue to Cato, than why there is." The ego polishing up its humility.

Thomas Mann was once introduced to a successful American author who groveled before him, saying that he was nothing but a hack who could hardly call himself a writer in the presence of so great an artist. Mann later remarked, "That man has no right to make himself so small. He is not that big." False humility often leads us to such nonsense as this anonymous Irishman's declaration: "In this country one man is as good as another…very often a great deal better."

Whether on the stage, before the camera, or simply in conversation, humility has often seemed more a symptom of malady than shining virtue. Today it appears more foreign than ever. There's no room for it in our slogans. We can't say: "Let's look out for number one and be lowly about it"; "Seek self-fulfillment with utmost humility"; "Meekly go for the gusto."

Humility—the real thing—is all but extinct in the age of self-promotion. And, like some dodo bird of the soul, it appears charming only after becoming irretrievably lost. We gaze fondly at heroic lowliness as a museum artifact, after it's mummified in the stylized costume of a medieval saint. In the present environment we can hardly put a healthy finger on it, and sometimes—on days when the blustery, loud-mouthed present tense gets to be too much—we actually ache in humility's absence.

The trouble is that humility isn't something you can really pursue as an isolated virtue. It's awkward to try to make yourself more humble. The more you cast a disparaging eye on that ubiquitous self, the more it dominates your perspective. You get wrapped up in the folds of the garment you're trying to discard.

One ends up with all kinds of self-conscious imitations. Most of us have known people with a habit of putting themselves down. I once worked with another teacher who sometimes would go on at length about how terrible he was doing in his classes. His self-evaluation was so bad that basic human decency required the rest of the faculty to tell him he was a fine teacher doing a good job. After a while, however, it became clear that by dumping on himself he was really fishing for our compliments—which we dutifully gave him, without enthusiasm.

This is *sleight-of-hand humility*. The hand pointing inwardly with such decimating accusations suddenly switches into a palm panhandling for flattery. We all want to feel good about ourselves, of course. But genuine humility is a result of that, not a means to that end.

Sleight-of-hand humility is something people usually engage in subconsciously. *Jockeying for position* is a bit more premeditated. This attempt at humility requires that we become very conscious of how we're perceived.

William Congreve produced plays of such sophisticated wit and brilliant dialogue that he became the leading dramatist of the English Restoration. He owed his fame and fortune to the comedy of manners. But Congreve, preoccupied with status, entertained a low idea of his profession and regarded his works as mere trifles beneath his class. He eventually gave up writing to be a retired gentleman, passing time with the boys at the Kit-Cat Club.

When Voltaire, who admired the man's plays, came for a visit, Congreve responded that he would see him "upon no other foot than that of a gentleman who led a life of plainness and simplicity." Voltaire, as one might expect, saw through the pretension. As the Frenchman recalled, "I answered that had he been so unfortunate as to be a mere gentleman, I should never have come to see him; and I was very much disgusted at so unseasonable a piece of vanity."

The point is, Why make a big deal about how you're regarded?

Even attempts to be placed in what appears to be a humble bracket betray a vain preoccupation with place. Who cares? Be happy with who you are and what you do.

Jockeying for position in the guise of humility leaves a bad taste in our mouths. And yet, in trying to make ourselves humble, it's hard to avoid. We aim at placing ourselves in a posture that can be labeled humble, but the attempt only makes us ever more conscious of levels and brackets, of how we're seen.

Then there is the type of humility that is not so much manufactured as inherited. It's not a trick; it comes naturally. But it's naturalistic, an environmental humility. People who've never learned to lean into the wind, who have abdicated their will to the prevailing forces, stake a claim to it—and thus the spineless are mistaken for the meek.

These are the wimpy personalities who would like others to provide for them and control their lives. People who say, "Oh I could never do that; I'm just not good enough," are sometimes simply lazy. They enjoy basking in the soft light of "humility." Putting themselves down becomes an excuse for inaction.

Most weak people deserve sympathy. Few of them decided to be gutless. Their home and companions, as well as their genes, shaped them to a great extent. They have extenuating circumstances—but they do not have humility.

For a lethargic person looking for respectability, this *warm-blanket humility* is all but irresistible. It's a cover-up for nap time, a kind of failure that asks for pity. But pity is the last thing the truly humble desire. They don't want a chorus of sympathetic eyes drooping their way, throwing a spotlight on their unfortunate selves. They don't want that cocoon around them.

STEWING IN OUR OWN JUICE

Conventional humility seems to distort people, and it leaves most of us with a bad taste in our mouths. Yet its absence leaves a hole. The alternative—the self-centered life of the proud—has drawbacks that are even more serious. When we lower our moral expectations and settle on familiar old selfishness as guiding star, our humanity constricts. If we follow it far we run into a dead end. There's nothing quite as dull as a person wrapped up in himself; nothing quite as frightening as an individual whose reference points are all internal.

When everything gets sucked up into self the result is a kind of implosion. Jake was such a case. I met him one day hustling for bus fare at church, greasy hair hanging limp, face an unearthly off-white, shirt and pants emoting some vague, unresolved argument. Even from a distance he couldn't hide that tentative shuffle of the emotionally disturbed. He could speak only in barely audible bursts, sentences spurting out as if on a quick prison furlough. His eyes never rested on any one object and his self-conscious hands constantly fumbled for a natural gesture that never came.

He had a lot to be self-conscious about. And he obsessively queried me about what people were thinking of him—right now, that boy over there, that woman glancing. It seemed like a perfectly rational concern at the time. He was a spectacle, displaying the abused look of those always ready to dodge a blow to the psyche.

Jake won my sympathies and I tried to help, jumping confidently into chaos. This adolescent in his mid-twenties persisted in asking, knocking, seeking (like a good Christian), and on occasion I responded. Jake always needed to go somewhere, and I took him around. I came up with dimes for phone calls and bus fare (so he could wander off from home to meet reluctant friends). But his desires were always so pitifully focused on this very minute, getting away, getting the ride, getting his way, avoiding other considerations at all costs, that I couldn't get any meaning out of him.

I turned behaviorist and tried to force just one healthy conversation into his jittery thoughts. We went over simple statements that people make to each other: How have you been? Did you have a good day? Jake wasn't retarded, but his feverish concentration on the thing he wanted right now consumed all normal interaction. I thought, *If I could get him just once to show a flicker of interest in another life...* But each time we managed a few spurts of dialogue, the conversation quickly collapsed into the bottomless abyss of his self.

Jake turned out to be a heart-breaking, maddening tragedy. He manipulated total strangers for all they were worth without even the briefest introduction. He was forever running away from the horror of himself, forever caught more deeply in it.

Counseling was recommended for him, but he was deathly afraid of it, terrified that those smooth talkers only wanted a reason to lock him up. We begged and assured and bribed and set up meetings and threatened, to no avail. He promised and lied (the two seemed indistinguishable to him) his way from one moment's demand to the next.

Jake demonstrated self-awareness with a vengeance, his thoughts always spinning in that vortex. No impulse could drift out to take root in human or divine nourishment. He was the most self-centered person I have ever known, and the most profoundly disturbed. I don't think that's a coincidence.

In Ibsen's *Peer Gynt*, the mad director of an asylum declares:

We're ourselves and nothing but ourselves.
We speed full sail ahead as ourselves,
We shut ourselves up in a keg of self.
We stew in our own juice...
And get seasoned in a well of self....
There are no thoughts or sorrows outside our own.

The self is not quite that divine source of light, truth, and guidance that pop religion has made it out to be. Selfishness can lead to its own nightmares.

So this is our dilemma. We badly need to escape the self-centered life of the proud; we don't want everything to implode into the self. But a healthy kind of humility seems as elusive as shadows at midnight. The more we try to focus on our "low" position, the more darkly self-centered we become.

How do we escape the two tragedies of Arthur and Jake? Gazing around at our present environment, there seems to be no way to get there from here. Meekness isn't—and can't be—advertised. So who has the real thing?

THE PIG, THE SNOB, THE PIONEER

In an old, scratchy photograph one can see him at the age of six, dressed in hunting costume and holding a toy gun, staring out at the world sulky and truculent. That faded image proved to be prophetic. Through the rest of his childhood, Charles de Foucauld established a record as a violent-tempered and domineering boy. Later, as a fat, slothful adolescent, Charles was sent to a Jesuit boarding school in Paris, where he became (as he later recalled) "wholly an egotist, wholly vain, totally impious." He was expelled, though politely, since he came from a good family.

At twenty-one, having made a clean break with religion, de Foucauld became a sublieutenant with the Hussars. Military duties were light and he had lots of money with which to entertain friends in a richly furnished apartment. He showed off a succession of expensive mistresses at lavish parties.

After he established his unique style of dashing obesity, Charles's good-time companions admiringly nicknamed him St. Cyr the Pig. He was a pig and also a snob. When a friend suggested he install his mistress at his personal hotel suite, Charles objected indignantly: "A fox is a foul beast, but even he doesn't sully his earth, nor does a de Foucauld his family."

Years later Charles would remember, "I felt a painful void, an anguish and a sorrow... each evening as soon as I found myself alone in my apartment; it was this that held me dumb, depressed, during what people call entertainments." Still, the sublieutenant managed to keep the swirl going around him for some time.

When fighting broke out in Morocco, Charles galloped in with the Hussars to establish order. While stationed there he continued to indulge his appetites, but he also became interested in the Koran and its manly religion of Islam—total surrender to the will of God. In that harsh desert land he was fascinated for a while by something that contrasted so completely with his life of soft pleasures.

Back in Paris on leave, the cavalryman rediscovered his family. They were more than just French aristocrats; they possessed an intelligent, cultured piety that attracted him. Charles especially noticed his cousin Marie. What a beautiful person she was, so different from himself! Marie always seemed to make the Christian life a delight and an adventure. One day he told her wistfully, "How lucky you are in your faith."

But that luck was making its way inexorably toward him. Charles began dropping into churches to check on the faith he'd abandoned. He was moved to repeat one brief request: "My God, if You exist, make me know You."

Distinguished guests often attended the de Foucauld family's social affairs, and one evening a popular priest named Abbe Huvelin came by. Huvelin's combination of sanctity and intelligence had a magnetic influence; whenever he preached, the church was packed. Charles was introduced to Huvelin and liked him immediately. While they were conversing, a pretty lady came up to the priest and gushed, "Oh, you always look so happy! I wish you would let us into your secret." Huvelin, who was crippled with rheumatism, replied gently, "I've found that the way to happiness is indeed very simple."

"What is it?" she asked eagerly.

"It is to deprive oneself of joys, madame," the priest said with a smile. He went on to explain that religion isn't just something to give comfort. Christ in Gethsemane was not just comforted; He was fortified to endure the trial. For Charles, listening intently, these words seemed the perfect moral challenge, something as nobly pure as the North African desert he'd come to love.

Soon after, Charles confessed his sins and received communion. With the help of Huvelin, he clambered over the remaining intellectual obstacles to faith and then fell under the spell of the divine perspective: "As soon as I believed there was a God, I knew I could not do otherwise than to live only for Him. God is so great! There is such a difference between God and all that is not God!"

Finally Charles had found something big enough to consume his vanity and overpower his voracious ego. His indulgent self found an exit from itself, from its pettiness and anguish. Eventually Charles expressed this radical and quickening escape by serving as a Trappist monk in the Sahara and adopting a minimalist lifestyle.

In the middle of the desert, near a lonely French army post, he built a rustic chapel of palm beams. "Very poor," Charles admitted, "but harmonious and pretty." Four palm trunks held up the roof; a paraffin lamp threw light on the altar. He drew the fourteen stations of the cross on packing case boards, and on white calico he painted a large figure of Christ "stretching out His arms to embrace, to clasp, to call all men, and give Himself for all." Later Charles added to the chapel a few cells for guests and an infirmary.

There he cloistered himself, marking out his island of devotion with a circle of pebbles. He rose in the dark early hours to pray and meditate, then received visitors, greeting them at the door dressed in a white *gandourah* (the flowing robe of the desert people) on which he'd sewn a red cross, wearing a *kepi* hat with a white cloth hung down his neck to protect it from the scorching sun. Coming to see this unusual pioneer were numerous Arab tribesmen (he quickly picked up their language) and French soldiers, as well as many poor, to whom he gave barley and dates.

Charles had something in mind beyond meditation. His was a missionary outpost, an evangelistic strategy, not just some heroic display of introversion. He had become aware that in Morocco, a country of ten million inhabitants in an area as big as France, not a single priest could be found in the interior. And in all the vast Sahara there were only a dozen missionaries. No people seemed more spiritually abandoned to him than the Saharan nomads. Charles determined to offer the divine banquet "not to relatives and to the rich, but to the lame, the blind, and the poor." He set about to love the nomads "with that all-powerful love that can make itself loved," and to "pray for them with a heart warm enough to bring down upon them from God a superabundance of graces." That, he was assured, would result in their conversion.

NOT DUTY, BUT DEVOTION

On excursions to desert settlements Charles encountered proud, veiled Touareg warriors, as well as hungry nomads afflicted with ulcerated eyes, malaria, typhus, and gangrenous cuts. Slowly the Trappist earned their trust. They came to delight in this wiry, holy man who spoke their language and required neither flattery nor gifts, but happily bestowed medicines, soap, flour, sugar, tea, and needles.

One woman, whose child Charles had saved from death,

declared, "How terrible it is to think of a man so good, so charitable, going to hell because he is not a Muslim!"

Among those who came to the chapel to chat were black slaves who exhibited raw ankles, chained wrists, cheeks branded like a camel's, and backs scarred from lashes. Charles could not be silent. This penniless priest began begging and cajoling his superiors for money so he could purchase slaves and set them free. More importantly, perhaps, he wrote influential friends in France, urging them to start a campaign pressuring the government to have the slaves declared paid servants. "It is the greatest sore of this country," he wrote. "They are subjected to daily beatings and gross overwork, and if they attempt to escape they are shot in both legs. And when their work is done, they are expected to roam around and pick up what food they can find. There is no remedy but enfranchisement; slavery must be abolished…No economic or political reasons countenance such immorality, such hideous injustice."

It's remarkable how far out of his fat, indulgent, vain little self this man had traveled. He who had grown up amid aristocratic ease endured the harsh desert and his even harsher discipline with an easy cheerfulness. Charles explained that in prayer he saw his Lord infinitely happy and lacking nothing—"Then I, too, am happy, and I lack nothing; Your happiness suffices me." He came to possess an unshakable sense of the self consumed in Christ, which enabled him to greatly expand his identity. Charles could live among the North African Arabs as one of them, like any Touareg clinging precariously to an oasis. He retained no official position, subsisted on dates and barley bread, and occupied his tiny sanctuary simply as a neighbor always there to help when called upon.

Eventually he would translate more than six thousand verses of Touareg poetry, working laboriously to render the meter and idiom of these love songs in flawless, clear French, creating one of the world's great anthologies of primitive verse. In the end he gave the Touareg language a grammar, a dictionary, and a literature, both prose and verse.

Charles's radical humility did not erase his will, or snuff out the fire in the belly that had driven him on his adventures as a charming rake of the Hussars. His will was just more sharply aimed now; the fire burned white hot. Charles was compelled to express something eternal in that wasteland of sand. He longed, above all else, to imitate "the hidden life of the poor and humble Workman of Nazareth." His extraordinary life did not arise from a sense of overbearing duty but from intense, even passionate, devotion. "I love our Lord," Charles once wrote, trying to explain why he became a Trappist.

"And since I love Him, I cannot bear to live a different life from His, an easy and honoured life, when His was the hardest and most despised that has ever been." Another priest noticed him on several occasions spending an entire night kneeling in the church, "conversing with his beloved Jesus...his face shining with a gentle joy."

This intimacy with his Lord gave Charles a profound security in his calling. Through his ascetic lifestyle he was making his own statement as an artist of the spirit; he never insisted that others copy him. When he sent a young Touareg to France for a visit, he carefully arranged that everything be pleasant and comfortable for him there. While traveling with a certain Brother Michael, Charles would cover him with his own cloak during the night (he himself was hardened to the desert cold, he explained), and would provide the brother with coffee and barley cake in the morning though he never had breakfast himself.

Charles submitted to a demanding religious rule, but by centering all on God he made it seem effortless. "He holds up equally my soul and my body," he said, assuring his friends. "I have nothing to carry; He carries it all."

On rare occasions, when Charles found someone who could understand something of his feelings, he tried to share "the immense happiness one enjoys at the thought that God is God and that He whom we love with our whole being is infinitely and eternally blessed." This is the theme one finds over and over in his letters. Charles was intensely happy that God is God. He felt "drowned in God." Here was someone rejoicing not just in God's blessings but in God Himself. He was devoted not to a sublime feeling in the soul, but to a separate greatness.

TO APPRECIATE Charles de Foucauld one must see him as an artist expressing a theme through his austere and tightly focused life in the Sahara. It was a theme that consumed him: the sacrificial life of Christ. His religious duties centered on the adoration of Christ's sacrifice, represented by the sacrament of bread and wine. He felt this to be at the core of human life. This act was meaningful enough, full enough, to occupy a lifetime. And this, to him, was his most significant accomplishment in the Sahara: simply worshiping Christ crucified. In contemplating the Eucharist he wanted to become "like the divine Food Itself, usefully devoured."

He was always seeking to do it in the most desolate places, where Christ had not been lifted up before. Charles's adoration is etched against the mile-high massifs of the Ahaggar, the rolling sands, the dry rounded stones of ancient river beds. His worship was a fiery gold sunset played against beige and gray rock.

It is hard to measure such a work of art, hard to critique its color and form. But his contemporaries had glimpses which proved to be revelations. A member of the White Fathers traveling with Charles from France to Ghardaia recalled that he had never met anyone with such a supernatural radiance. "It was as though inside the frail priest someone was always singing for joy, so that, if you were quiet enough, recollected enough when you were with Charles, you, too, could hear Him."

At one point Charles asked the White Sisters at El Golea to show him how to make communion bread. But each time he tried to bake the dough he would burn it, having fallen into ecstatic contemplation of "the Host." He had to beg the sisters' pardon amid the smoke of blackened wafers.

After Charles's death at the hands of rogue tribesmen, his life could be summed up in the few possessions discovered at his chapel: a breviary, a cross, a chalice, linen, and candlesticks. That is all. An eloquent still life, each object essential in the composition, laid out with passionate conviction.

4

ADMIRING THE ONE
WHO CHERISHES

IN THE CANVAS of Charles de Foucauld's life I find a compelling picture of humility. It strikes me as a direct expression of his awareness of a great God. Charles the piggish egotist met the Almighty head-on and was re-created as an unassuming giver of life in the desert.

I may admire de Foucauld only from a distance—but it's okay to admire an artist from a distance, to see the whole body of his work and applaud respectfully. He doesn't demand that I either imitate him or get out. We don't all have to subsist on barley and dates and adore the Host from 2 to 5 A.M. But all of us *can* worship God from the heart. It's our heritage, too.

At times I have a peek at what drove Charles de Foucauld in his worshipful desert quest. During moments of devotion when I sense how marvelous and many-faceted God's character must be, I am struck by the thought, *Yes! Just to bow before Him right now, that's meaningful enough for a lifetime. To have done this equals all that a human being can accomplish.*

I must admit the feeling doesn't last very long. There is much in me and around me to distract devotion. I drive on L.A. freeways and want to shout back at the guy gesturing obscenely who wants to go 66 m.p.h. to my 64. I have a "position" to maintain at a media center. Entertainments of every sort bulge out from my TV, ready at my beck and call. I'm a long way from Charles's chapel in the desert.

But the one thing I cannot do after knowing de Foucauld is to shrug off pride and self-centeredness with an "I'm only human" banality. Those traits are an aberration. Charles defines for me an essential aspect of being human. He helps us put a finger on that elusive, invisible virtue called humility, suggesting this functional definition: *The humble find their identity in relation to someone greater.* Their opposite number, the proud, find their identity in relation to someone they think of as lesser.

I'm aware that the word *pride* can be used in the positive sense of self-esteem, but in this book I'll use it in the sense of insecure egotism. The people called "white trash" were a classic example. Many of the poorest white Southerners propped up a sense of self-worth by identifying themselves as non-niggers, insisting they were better than blacks. Better than Jews, too. The proud are constantly on the lookout for an inferior they can peg with a knowing smirk or cutting remark. With this food they nourish their identities.

The humble, however, nourish their identities on an esteemed friend, a hero, God. The key word here is *admiration.* The humble have the capacity to look up, to admire and respect loftier qualities. They enjoy others' successes rather than feel threatened by them. This heroic humility beckons us out of our selfish ruts. We long to express the greatness of God, somehow, even in comfortable suburbs. Such humility is the natural result of seeking God.

That's one reason an unbelieving age finds meekness such an oddity. Even if we want it in theory, we can never quite find a place for humility in contemporary secular life—and not just because egotism, by default, is the major alternative to religion. Humility simply can't be had as an isolated commodity.

In 1937, Lin Yutang published a best-seller called *The Importance of Living.* In a section entitled "Why I Am a Pagan," Yutang gave his objections to the "presumptuous arrogance" of Christian theology. He became a symbol of the sophisticated, cosmopolitan Asian scholar, and wrote several books on Chinese and Indian culture and philosophy. But then he ran into a very basic problem:

> Below the surface of my life a disquiet, born of both reflection and experience, began to set in. I saw that the fruit of the humanistic age of enlightenment was an age of materialism. Man's increasing belief in himself as God did not seem to be making him more godlike. He was becoming more clever. But he had less and less of the sober, uplifting humility of one who has stood in the presence of God. Much of contemporary history seemed to me to indicate how dangerously near the savage state that man, lacking that humility, may be, even while he is most advanced materially and technologically.

Yutang's disaffection led him to a study of the "awe-inspiring simplicity and beauty of the teachings of Jesus." He learned to admire Him and discovered at last the "uplifting humility" he believed so necessary to healthy human life.

Humility is the reflection, the mirror image, of admiring God. It is not something we *do* to ourselves; it's something we absorb in worshiping and giving thanks to God—in particular, the sovereign, personal God of the Bible. We rarely become humble by admiring an ideology, though we may regard it as greater than ourselves and give it our ultimate allegiance. Ideologies don't call us into a love relationship. It's easy for the self to absorb any abstract doctrine as My Opinion. It can become a prop in our chronic staging of the I Am Right scene. But the God who appears to us in Scripture is not so easily manipulated.

Charles de Foucauld's humility became an act of art because it reflected a great God; he was expressing something profound, not just fulfilling an external obligation. He traveled out from himself, constantly awed that a man could embrace the Almighty. He simply admired too much to ever be caught self-consciously posing as the humble holy man.

ADMIRING HIM MORE

Larry's employer had just told him how much he valued his work, how glad he was to have him on board, and that he was going to give him a raise. When Larry received his first newly adjusted paycheck, he felt a bit of a rush; it was nice to be appreciated so concretely. He was leaning back in his chair at the office, feeling expansive, enjoying the scenery out his window (which seemed particularly lovely that day), when suddenly he thought, *Wait a minute. Maybe I shouldn't feel good just because of this. I should be content being a servant, looking for no pat on the back.*

Larry, as a good Christian, wanted to resist something called self-exaltation—one of those nebulous dangers that are hard to put your humility on. He was afraid to enjoy praise via a pay raise. Like a lot of sincere believers he was in the habit of deflecting compliments and yanking the self out of the spotlight before it got warmed up. All this to protect that slippery virtue, humility, which can seep out when you least expect it.

Larry's sincere attempts to avoid pride arose from the wrong starting point. Those who flee from compliments are saying, in effect, "If I admire something about myself (or enjoy it when others do), I won't be able to admire God as much. My identity with Him will be diluted."

It's true that big egos can belittle God, and that flattering attentions can turn our heads away from a sense of His majesty. That's a problem. But the answer is not to avoid compliments like the plague and try to lie to yourself about your abilities. The answer is simply to admire God—that's the right starting point. If you feel a danger of becoming big-headed, don't concentrate on hammering in that head with disparaging remarks. Concentrate on magnifying the greatness of God. His character is vast enough; there will always be more of Him to admire.

When you're complimented, thank people sincerely. Enjoy it, appreciate it, and toss it up to God in celebration because you see your talents and abilities as gifts. Every spotlight thrown on us is a chance to beam up praise to God. That doesn't mean we should always shuffle nervously in the light. It's okay to feel the warmth, which can make our thankfulness all the more heartfelt. When you're feeling good, enjoy it. To be humble, don't do anything to yourself; do something toward God.

It's when people stop thanking and worshiping God that egos start inflating. That's the danger. When praise stops here at my feet and the natural flow is plugged up, humility gets shoved out.

LOVING, SEPARATE, HOLY

Obviously the kind of God we worship has a lot to do with the kind of humility we experience. The principle fact here is that we bow before a God whose love for us is infinitely intense. He is the ultimate "significant other." That's security.

Pride rears its bloated head precisely when we feel aching holes in our self-worth. It is a patchwork of posturing and pretension that we nervously lay over our bevy of insecurities. We value ourselves in direct proportion to how the people we value regard us. Being accepted by drinking buddies is nice, but it generally produces no great sense of self-worth. The love of a father, on the other hand, whom a child regards as his universe, is of tremendous importance. So when a holy God cherishes us, and we can hold on to that cherishing as steadily as de Foucauld did, the result is a wealth of security, a self-worth rich enough to give away, an identity that can blossom in the desert.

This profound security produces a buoyant, enlightened quality that we can call "light humility." It is very different from the dark, burdensome humility of those trying to put themselves down in all kinds of self-conscious ways. Light humility can be expressed only by those secure in their admiration for a loving God.

Things get a bit paradoxical here. You would think that those with low self-esteem could slip right into humility with no problem, and that those with healthy self-esteem would find pride a natural garment. But the opposite is true. The defeated do sometimes grope around in dark humility, but they rarely find the real thing. And the secure do have self-respect, but they don't seek to get an identity from something lesser than themselves. Instead they are free to express their admiration of the divine in many, sometimes radical, ways. Their hand is loosed over the canvas.

Light humility expresses a God who loves us; it also expresses a God who is separate from us. That's essential, too. He is a significant *other* who gives us an identity. It won't do to conjure up some divine essence inherent in our souls. Saying that we're all God and God is all of us may sound encouraging at first, but it falls apart in the end. If God is all things, in everything equally, then we've just labeled the world differently. We've put a higher sticker price on the same old sedan. Proclaiming that God is everything is ultimately not much different from saying God is nothing.

The biblical distinction between Creator and creature is important here. God is intimately related to us, but He is not us. He is a separate individual seeking genuine relationships with other separate individuals. Light humility does not result from the self claiming squatters' rights on divinity. It arises from the self relating to someone greater.

Another of God's essential qualities is His holiness. God's passion for justice must be included with His compassion for imperfect individuals. The accepting God who gives people self-worth is not a moral pushover. The Bible presents Him as a consuming fire of righteousness, upright in all His ways, faithful to generation after generation. Again, what matters is *Who* accepts us, not just that we're accepted.

A high school student named Ben got into the habit of contemplating the meaning of life during his senior year, and as a result he grew somewhat suicidal. The usual idealism of youth was grinding against the usual disasters in the world. Amid society's dim welter of compromises, pursuing an education or a career or even a life hardly seemed worth it to Ben. In school he had been exposed to the prevailing psychological theme of acceptance-without-value-judgments, but he couldn't bring himself to accept it. It was a lie to accept evil, a lie to say things were okay. He wanted to kick in that smiling facade. He began toying with the idea of ending it all.

Then, amid his gloomy philosophical rumblings, one thought lit up: *If there was just one man who lived a good life, a completely good life, it would be worth it all.* Ben had seen plenty of evidence that even the best of humanity hid pockets of cruelty. But what if there were an exception? That would make a difference.

Ben carried that thought around for a while as his last argument against suicide. Then he spent a holiday at his aunt's house. Without saying anything, this Christian woman reminded him of his days in Sunday school. All those stories about Jesus came back to him. Themes long dormant awakened, and suddenly he realized that here was his answer: Jesus was the completely good man who made life worthwhile.

Ben didn't kill himself, and I was able to meet him years later in college and enjoy the pleasure of his company as a fellow believer. He'd found a relationship with this Good Man.

It is a holy God who extends to us His gracious regard; that makes an enormous difference. He imbues human beings with a sense of freedom and dignity by the way He relates to them. It won't do to have some benign blob in the sky who hands out greeting cards to the indifferent masses. Unfortunately, a lot of people have reduced God to the fast-food essentials: He loves everybody, so slide in and out whenever convenient on greasy, value-free acceptance; I'll take mine without that high-fiber part about holiness, please.

Indulgence doesn't produce secure humility; it simply gives the self-centered an ever-constricting circle to play in. Big egos thrive in part by forming private alliances with some malleable deity on high. Their whims are projected up as the divine will.

The humble, however, sense their responsibility before a God of law. They don't just look up at a frozen smile; they bow before a righteous Lord. They sincerely admire the holy God who has chosen them.

Healthy security must have this combination: righteous expectations and loving acceptance. The God of the Bible expresses both consistently and intensely. He has created each of us for the good life. We aren't institutionalized, abandoned to some ghetto for the morally handicapped, and told that it's okay, we're only human. No, God believes in us and has high hopes for us. But He also catches us when we fall. He accepts our frailty and forgives our moral stumblings. He is able to love us when we're at our worst—and to still believe and hope.

God's ardent expressions of justice and mercy produce a profound sense of security in those who bow before Him. They experience light humility. And this humility, in turn, opens them up to more mercy and justice.

In a way, I've slipped into this subject backwards, finding a certain God in order to define the right kind of humility. But of course the God of Scripture precedes all our needs. Before we begin aching to escape our proud, self-centered existence, He's the way He is. And happily, His qualities fit our deepest needs precisely. We are the work of His hands, and we discover signs pointing toward Him in our innermost being.

MORTAL COMBAT

Besides giving us a separate, loving, holy God to admire, the Bible also fleshes out the humility of those who admire Him. One of the great themes of Scripture is humility in mortal combat with pride. It is a panoramic epic flowing through generations and peoples and empires. Here is the Word we must see as intently as the artist sees nature. We begin to draw the real thing only after knowing this original revelation.

In the book of Genesis, the Creation and the Flood informed men in no uncertain terms that there is a God who is sovereign over the world. In response, human pride constructed its first presumptuous monument: the Tower of Babel, a ziggurat built to compete with Jehovah's promise of protection as embodied by the rainbow. Rather than look up to God, those industrious folks on the plain of Shinar insisted on competing with Him. *If this god is ruler in the heavens,* they reasoned, *we just have to build a taller ziggurat to deal with him.*

The story continues with roughly cut patriarchs running up against this oversized God, who must distinguish Himself from local deities battling over turf. Abraham stared up at numberless stars stretching out over the black heavens and believed a deity big enough to promise the impossible. Jacob ran away from home and his own sin, and found a ladder stretching up into heaven. Later he wrestled with his Lord and was defeated, but gained the coveted blessing. These are elemental encounters, earthy nomads learning to bow.

It is significant that the book of Job—that long, agonized, intellectual wrestling match with the problem of evil—climaxes with the protagonist humbling himself before a sovereign Creator, as if that were the answer. At the end of the book we are not rewarded with a neat formula that unties all the moral and theological knots Job and friends have produced for almost forty chapters. None of the debaters wins. There is only the vivid picture of an infinitely wise God to admire. The only thing human to triumph at the end is humility.

Men humbled before the God of heaven produced their first great protagonist in Moses. He was perfect for the part: raised as royalty but without any desire to be king, fiery for justice, tempered by shepherding. Later generations would look back on his accomplishments and call him the meekest man on earth.

Moses came up against Pharaoh, also perfect for his part. It was an epic conflict: man speaking for a God bigger than himself, versus man speaking for an enormous ego. Moses presented Jehovah's signs; Pharaoh ushered in his magicians. Moses warned of Jehovah's judgments; Pharaoh said he'd never heard of Him. The more this ruler's autonomous sovereignty was challenged, the more obstinate he became.

Pharaoh was plagued by frogs, gnats, locusts. His cattle died, hail destroyed Egypt's crops, but the man hung tough, unbowed. Here the self-centered man was exposed as pathological. He would rather destroy everything than submit to someone bigger than himself. His identity was glued so fast to his own sovereignty that he feared he would lose himself if he bowed.

After the Exodus, during the wilderness wanderings, Moses climbed to extraordinary heights of humility, bearing patiently with the chronic grumbling and moral stumbling of the children of Israel. His career created the great alternative to the Oriental despots who dominated the ancient world: the leader as servant of the people. There in the wastelands of Edom, Sinai, and Meribah, Moses fetched water and bread and quail for the multitudes.

He fell into none of the traps that often swallow up those in power. Moses took advice. When his father-in-law, Jethro, dropped into camp for a visit and saw the overwhelmed Moses trying to settle petty legal disputes, he suggested that honest men be chosen as judges for the people. Moses listened and began delegating responsibility.

Moses was secure. When someone came running up to him with news that two unauthorized laymen were prophesying, right-hand-man Joshua urged his leader to have them restrained. Moses replied, "Are you jealous for my sake? I wish all the Lord's people were prophets."

When Miriam and Aaron began criticizing Moses, jealous of his authority and blinded to his burdensome responsibilities, Moses didn't react defensively but allowed the Lord to settle the matter. And when ambitious Miriam was struck with leprosy, Moses pleaded with God to heal her.

Jehovah himself threw a spotlight on Moses' selflessness by making an offer no ruler in his right mind could refuse. At a moment when most of the Israelites had turned their backs on their leader and their God, Jehovah proposed: "Now leave me alone so that my anger may burn against them and that I may destroy them. Then I will make you into a great nation." Moses' ego didn't rise to the occasion. Instead of seizing the offer of a dynasty he seized the offer of mercy hidden in God's proposal, and interceded for his people.

Moses exhibited selflessness, but he was not a weak leader. He bowed before a holy God, but he couldn't bend before evil. When apostasy reared its defiant head Moses struck telling blows, as when he made worshipers of the golden calf drink their god, melted and watered down. When God reacted against flagrant sin, Moses thundered with Him.

Moses knew exactly who he was and what he stood for. Intensely devoted to the God he met regularly in the Tent of the Presence, Moses could afford to be a servant-ruler; he was the definitive answer to haughty Pharaoh, furiously driving his chariot, leading Egypt's finest to their doom under the Red Sea.

After Moses we enter the wild and woolly period of the Judges, when freelance heroes helped Israel climb into nationhood. They were champions of a peculiar sort. Gideon's army, drastically reduced, threw a vast Philistine force into confusion with trumpets and torches. Muscle-bound Samson accomplished his greatest feat only after being shorn of physical strength, blinded, and led about by a rope. Calling out, "O Sovereign Lord, remember me," he pulled down the temple of his haughty oppressors.

Only humbled heroes can be successful—a theme on which, centuries later, the apostle Paul would put a title: "God has chosen the weak things of the world to shame the strong."

BOWING MONARCHS

The age of kings arrived for Israel in the person of a Benjamite named Saul, son of Kish. His life is a psychological study in how a man moves from healthy humility to neurotic pride and finally falls apart under his obsessions. Chosen for leadership, Saul submitted to the guidance of Samuel, thinking it wonderful that a guy from an insignificant family in one of Israel's smallest tribes could be honored by the prophet's attentions. He had a hold on God; shortly after his anointing as king, "the Spirit of God came upon him in power," and he began to prophesy.

Saul was secure. After he led a dramatic rescue operation to free the town of Jabesh from the siege of an Amorite army, his enthusiastic followers remembered some malcontents who mocked the idea of this unsophisticated donkey driver as king. They began shouting, "Bring these men to us and we will put them to death." Flushed with victory, enjoying popular support, Saul had the perfect opportunity to rid himself of potential opposition. But he quickly squelched the idea. "No one shall be put to death today," he said, "for this day the Lord has rescued Israel." His focus was on the God who had brought victory.

But somehow the focus changed. Saul veered off on his own course. He stepped into the role of Samuel by making ceremonial burnt offerings in the prophet's place. He disobeyed divine commands against keeping any of the booty won in battles with idolatrous neighbors. Saul became autocratic and arbitrary; he was barely kept from having his own son Jonathan executed for going against a foolish order. Then he grew jealous of the exploits of a promising young warrior named David. By now, pride was firmly in place and continually threatening. Saul spent the rest of his life pursuing his rival, alienating his son, groping in the dark for that lost connection with divine power. Saul would look anywhere—even to the mutterings of a spiritualist medium—except up. He would not bow. For Saul, God could be anything except bigger than himself.

David, who became Israel's greatest king, created one of his greatest legacies in a moment of despair: David the powerful showed us how to repent. Summarily exposed by Nathan as an adulterer and murderer, he did not eliminate the prophetic irritant, as most monarchs would do, but humbled himself before his Lord. He sought mercy with heartfelt eloquence in Psalm 51, clutching the hope that "a broken and contrite heart, O God, you will not despise."

Later, in Psalm 131, David seemed to have discovered the profound security of the humble:

> My heart is not proud, O Lord,
>   my eyes are not haughty;
> I do not concern myself with great matters
>   or things too wonderful for me.
> But I have stilled and quieted my soul;
>   like a weaned child with its mother,
>   like a weaned child is my soul within me.

The Psalms in general seem to equate the good with the humble.

> For the Lord takes delight in his people;
>   he crowns the humble with salvation.

The wicked are contrasted with the meek; the humble are said to be guided by God and taught His ways. Jehovah on high looks down with favor on the lowly but regards the proud from afar.

David's son Solomon echoed these sentiments in his proverbs. Humility, he declared, is the prerequisite to wisdom; it comes before honor; it is more valuable than riches: "Better to be lowly in spirit and among the oppressed than to share plunder with the proud."

The monarchies of Israel and Judah provided a stage on which was played out this essential connection of pride to evil and disaster, and humility to goodness and blessing. The bright spots in the history came when kings humbled themselves to seek the Lord; the dark streaks came when kings arrogantly lifted up their hearts against Him.

For King Rehoboam, Judah's first oppressive tyrant, the light broke through when Shishak and his Egyptian army besieged Jerusalem:

"The leaders of Israel and the king humbled themselves and said, 'The Lord is just.' " So God granted them "some measure of deliverance. "

After several military successes, King Uzziah of Judah decided to expand his job description. He entered the sacred temple and began burning incense at the altar. Priests objected; he raged at them—then turned white with leprosy. The chronicler sums up Uzziah with words that apply to so many others: "After Uzziah became powerful, his pride led to his downfall."

Pride brings disaster, but humility can bring great triumphs. Youthful King Josiah initiated a revival and reformation in Judah that for a time turned the tide against idolatry. Jehovah congratulated him: "Because your heart was responsive and you humbled yourself before the Lord...you tore your robes and wept in my presence."

Humility can rescue even the worst of tyrants. Manasseh did about as much as any man could to destroy morality and decency among his people. But then, while a prisoner of the Assyrians, he "humbled himself greatly before the God of his fathers." Manasseh went on to become a just, reform-minded ruler.

Israel's northern tribes finally slinked off into moral and physical captivity, then Judah did as well. The epitaph on this period is recorded in the last chapter of 2 Chronicles. Jeremiah had pleaded with Zedekiah, the last pathetic king to strut onto Judah's throne. But Zedekiah "did not humble himself before Jeremiah the prophet, who spoke the word of the Lord."

In contrast to this disaster we have the story of Nebuchadnezzar. He is King Saul in reverse—moving from world-class egotism to the health and wholeness of the humble. First God interrupted the monarch's pampered reverie with a glimpse of the king's place in the divine plan. Nebuchadnezzar was impressed by God as a "revealer of mysteries." Next Jehovah delivered three steadfast Hebrew youths from Nebuchadnezzar's fiery furnace. Nebuchadnezzar bowed before the heavenly Rescuer, but still his pride lingered—Nebuchadnezzar savored that great temple of Marduk, the seven-storied ziggurat, the hanging gardens. Babylon, which he had built, loomed large, Jehovah shrunk, and Nebuchadnezzar's ego burst out again—and snapped. The ego collapsed in on itself. Nebuchadnezzar became so deranged he crawled around on all fours and ate grass. Finally he fought his way through pride and looked up: "I...raised my eyes toward heaven, and my sanity was restored." This monarch finally had found someone bigger to admire: "I, Nebuchadnezzar, praise and exalt and glorify the King of heaven, because everything he does is right and all his ways are just. And those who walk in pride he is able to humble."

The proud are humbled. The humble are lifted up. In the book of Esther, proud Haman was forced to parade through the streets of Babylon shouting the praises of Mordecai, the quietly loyal man he tried to destroy.

HUMILITY'S DEFINITIVE ACT

Israel's kings were always in danger of falling off the edge of pride, but her prophets still proclaimed the essential values. Isaiah became one of humility's greatest spokesmen, warning that the mighty man would be abased and the eyes of the lofty humbled. He assured his listeners that the meek would rejoice in the Lord and that the One who lives in a high and holy place also dwells "with him who is contrite and lowly in spirit."

Isaiah's greatest statement, however, came from a contrast between two larger-than-life figures. Early in his book, as he prophesies against the king of Babylon in chapter fourteen, he presents us with the picture of Lucifer, "Morning Star," a glorious being who yearns to raise his throne above the stars of God, receive adoration from a heavenly assembly, and arrive at a position equal to that of the Most High. This pompous overachiever was cast down to the earth.

Isaiah's book reaches its peak in chapter fifty-three, where a Suffering Servant appears on the scene, described as a "root out of dry ground," someone without beauty or majesty to make Him attractive. There was nothing outwardly desirable about Him; He was despised and rejected by men. Here the coming of Christ, the glorious Messiah, is pictured as the antithesis of all kingly splendor. Instead of seizing power He pours out His life unto death, meek as a lamb led dumb before its shearers. Yet it is He who triumphs; in the end He is raised up, highly exalted.

This prophecy sets the stage for the great conflict between Christ and Satan, a three-year duel to be played out in Galilee and Judea, and reveals one of its important themes: pride versus humility. The two protagonists embody those two qualities to the ultimate degree. Here is the old conflict of Moses and Pharaoh brought to cosmic size. Satan's ego was so grotesquely big it burst out even in the wide, beatific spaces of heaven. Christ compressed His divinity into what men would regard as a zero.

All the conflicts of the Old Testament lead us to this point. The long struggle of humility to shine in a dark, proud land drives us to Bethlehem, and also points us to the man who stands between the two testaments—John the Baptist. He had to prepare the Hebrews for the new age, and he did so by making a spectacle of himself in the desert, dressed in camel skins, chewing on locusts and wild honey. His passionate harangues attracted huge crowds, and John could easily have built a cult around himself. Instead he pointed elsewhere, to the Lamb of God. And he kept pointing. When his followers warned that Jesus was drawing away all the crowds, John replied, "A man can receive only what is given him from heaven." He had found the contentment of the humble, and he uttered their well-known battle cry: "He must become greater; I must become less." This statement can sound like resignation, the bittersweet words of a man facing retirement. But John was talking about his joy, the joy of the bridegroom's friend at the wedding. Jesus was now joined to the people, His chosen bride. "That joy is mine," John said, "and it is now complete."

The humble can transcend themselves and enjoy the successes of others. A proud man would have been wilting. But John's mission remained bigger than himself.

Now we come to the climax of the Bible and of the story of humility: the God who emptied Himself. The Almighty decided to come into the world as its Savior; the Lord of the Universe would condense His majesty into human form. Of all the grand entrances one could imagine for Him, the least likely scenario would be a feeding trough in a barn surrounded by livestock, shepherds, and two peasants. Here the divine identity is so secure as to become almost weightless; the godhood of the manchild is all but invisible. God didn't need an imposing palace, a groveling retinue, or silk garments to assure Himself that He is royalty. "I am who I am." He can be ignored and still proceed surely toward His destiny. Light humility.

The apostle Paul saw the way in which the Almighty took on human flesh as the definitive act of humility. He told the Philippians that the One who was "in very nature God...made himself nothing, taking the very nature of a servant, being made in human likeness. And being found in appearance as a man, he humbled himself and became obedient to death—even death on a cross!"

JESUS TRAVELED LIGHT throughout His ministry, a rabbi without credentials or institutional support who ushered in the kingdom of heaven on foot and face to face. There were never any trumpets blaring.

When He introduced the nature of His kingdom to a crowd gathered on a hillside by Lake Galilee, His first words blessed the poor in spirit, those who mourn, and the meek.

When adults primed for a mid-life crisis asked Jesus who would be considered the greatest in the kingdom of heaven, He replied, "Whoever humbles himself like this child."

To help us find our true selves, He said, "Everyone who exalts himself will be humbled, and he who humbles himself will be exalted."

The clash of pride and humility came into sharp focus in Jesus' long-running skirmish with the religious elite of His time. The Pharisees' expertise in the Law became possession of the Law; they looked down on this unlettered Galilean who presumed to teach. They guarded their turf, fiercely proud of their well-defined island of religious goodness. Jesus, meanwhile, expanded the Law to its essentials as he spoke with anyone who would listen, on goat trail, sheep meadow and lake shore.

The Sadducees in rich robes and influential positions were also offended by this plain Man on unfriendly terms with privileged Mammon. He didn't flatter those who could help Him. Instead He associated with those whose status had dropped through the bottom of society. The Sadducees couldn't fathom how poverty could be a blessing.

The Pharisees and Sadducees would not stoop to acknowledge a greater spiritual power. Jesus wouldn't abandon his utter lack of position. Irreconcilable differences hardened into active enmity. Pride plotted to rid the neighborhood of this unsightly humility that was a constant rebuke.

And in the end, the lowly Galilean triumphed by laying Himself out on the killing ground of Golgotha. Pride tried hard to mock, but soon choked amid that awful echo of an empty tomb.

5

WATER SPLASHED IN A BASIN

HAVING BEEN SWEPT ALONG through Scripture by the epic of humility, we end up pointed squarely at the teaching of the New Testament where that quality is given explicit authority. Peter advised: "Humble yourselves, therefore, under God's mighty hand, that he may lift you up in due time." He saw the trait as an essential garment of the believer: "Clothe yourselves with humility," a phrase Paul used as well.

New Testament teaching also shows us what light humility *does* —it gives that quality a functional shape. And we begin to see that this primary color embodies many different hues.

First of all, we see it as the great purger, cleansing us from a great deal of common clutter so that good art can emerge.

LIKE AN OCEAN

One evening during Passover season, Jesus' inner circle generated what they presumed to be an intense theological debate on the nature of Christ's kingdom. It was surely a significant issue worthy of their examination, especially since their Leader's rather plain statements on the subject invited elaboration. The question: Just how would the kingdom be organized? Or more specifically, just how would they, its designated heirs, organize it?

No one wanted to compete with Jesus as head of state, of course, but what about those nice little vice-presidential slots? One didn't want to be pushy—but, after all, somebody had to occupy them. Hints were dropped that a seat at the right or left hand of the Master in the kingdom would be greatly appreciated.

They talked this over among themselves probably most of the way through the streets of Jerusalem to the Upper Room, where millennia of Passover remembrances were soon to be given a new substance. That night would create a historic crossroads where two covenants met, intertwined for a few moments, then exchanged the sacred burden of meaning forever. But the disciples couldn't see this coming; they were hammering out specifics about their relative status.

Who would be greatest in the coming kingdom? Andrew and John could stake claim to being the first to make the transition from following John the Baptist to sitting at the feet of the One he called the "Lamb of God." Peter, the discussion's inevitable leader, might interject that he was first to "really" follow Christ, leaving behind his fishing business once and for all there by the Sea of Galilee. Others could quickly point out that they were called that very same day, and likewise made the irrevocable decision to become fishers of men. Judas, clearing his throat, might mention that one who already carried financial responsibilities for the group merited serious consideration.

Several disciples (if not all) were drawn into the competition, and as they put forth their qualifications more and more heatedly, the fabric of their discipleship unraveled. Suddenly all the grotesque posturing of the self stood bare. Its assortment of jealousies, disloyalties, and spite tumbled out and consumed their fellowship. The twelve were no longer followers of the One whose life had mesmerized them. For this hour or two, self-promotion obscured Him.

By the time they climbed the stairs to their rented room, reclined on pillows by the table, kicked off their sandals, and realized no servant was there to perform the customary chore of washing everyone's feet, not a soul felt moved to fetch water. They eyed one another accusingly, wanting to blame someone for the bad feelings each felt guilty about, but still clinging to their personal theology of the kingdom.

Nearby lay the pitcher, basin, and towel, accenting the silence. No one moved to touch them.

Jesus had been deep in thought, contemplating the cataclysmic events to come. But He knew what was on everyone's mind, and felt keenly their alienation. Without a word He rose from His place at the head of the table where wine and bread would shortly embody His divinity, and removed His cloak. The Master slowly wrapped a towel around His waist and poured water from pitcher to basin. He moved with deliberation, but not reluctance.

Every eye in the room followed His movements. Every ear heard the water splashing, filling the basin. It sounded to them like an ocean.

Then Jesus knelt down and washed the streets of Jerusalem from His disciples' feet. He bathed the toes of John, first to come to Him, yes. He cleansed the soles and ankles of Peter, dynamic leader who had sacrificed everything. He washed the feet of Judas, renowned financier, and of Nathanael, great intellectual, and of Philip, who had told Nathanael about Jesus in the first place, and of James, whose mother had first put in a bid for the right-hand position. Jesus washed the feet of all these great luminaries—and the ocean swept over them. They saw who it was, draped in a soiled towel and kneeling before them. Decades later John would remember with a pang: "Jesus knew that the Father had put all things under his power, and that he had come from God and was returning to God; so he got up…and began to wash his disciples' feet…"

The twelve finally got out of themselves, using the leverage that Christ's masterful humility provided them, and their pretensions were flooded away.

This preface to the Last Supper lightened everyone's burden of pride. It was not a groaning humiliation, but articulate, light humility. Jesus made a statement, expressing Himself eloquently. He showed what it means to be human, unencumbered by self-centeredness, and what it means to be God, encumbered with a passion for serving.

TRAVELING LIGHT

Light humility clears away the clutter. It solves a lot of problems that consistently plague us—selfishness in its many forms. We're so easily offended; little slights at the office and careless remarks at home can emotionally incapacitate us for days. We spend countless hours navigating the treacherous maze toward the "in" group, whispering about who's out, negotiating a knowing smile or compliment for the proper effect. Our pretensions multiply, and we become mean toward that end, hurting whoever is handy.

Before we know it, our lives—huge chunks of them anyway—have been sacrificed to pettiness. Defending number one can become a colossal human waste. It grinds up our lives, and we so rarely get our heads above it, always caught in the emotional undertow of the latest threat to our egos.

New Testament teaching asks instead to make a better sacrifice, to humble ourselves to the point of the cross. "Crucify the flesh with its passions and desires." We must take up our own cross; the "old self" must be put to death. This sounds harsh, but we need badly to make a clean break with the encumbered past.

With light humility we don't have to try to untangle the labyrinth of the self; we just move out of it—vacate. Admiring God, centering on Him, gives us that kind of leverage. We can crucify the old because we have something immeasurably better to hold onto.

There's nothing like gaining a little perspective from outside the confines of your ego. Its ponderous baggage lightens up. Humility is a singularly effective lever that upends and scatters all the clutter in our lives—all that gets in the way of good art.

This purging requires a killing of the old self, a casting out of the old baggage, but the New Testament also gives us the flip side: finding a new, more secure identity in Christ. Those humbled before the cross, seeking their identity in someone greater, find it in abundance. The bowed down are lifted up as the chosen, dearly loved children of God, accepted in the Beloved, without blemish, blessed with every spiritual blessing, a royal priesthood, the salt of the earth, instruments for noble purposes, temples of the living God, trophies led in triumphal procession, having a citizenship in heaven. The fierceness of the call to be crucified is more than matched by the fervor with which God names the believer. He gives us an identity that nothing can dilute. No misfortune or slander or failure can erase the fact that we are precious in His sight. Having this, the humble are content.

Part of the identity promised to the humble is "that always having all sufficiency in everything, you may have an abundance for every good deed." The humble realize that "we brought nothing into the world, and we can take nothing out of it." And so, "if we have food and clothing, we will be content with that." They don't make unconditional demands on life; they travel light. Those still entwined in selfish expectations are always bumping into a world of difficulties; they never quite catch up with all there is to gripe about. But the people busily admiring the God who cherishes them find fewer and fewer reasons to complain about life's unpleasant episodes.

Saul the promising Pharisee once lived on the cutting edge of a fierce expectation. He thought the world would bow before his orthodoxy, and he was willing to cut with a sword those sects stubborn enough to work against it.

On his way to make holy war against a group of Christians in Damascus, Saul heard God say that he was actually persecuting the Lord whom he sought so zealously to serve. Saul was struck down to his knees. He sought out the Damascus believers as a seeker instead of a grand inquisitor, and became a follower of Christ.

Saul had occupied the highest stratum of Jewish society; every possible buttress for the self had been built around him. But when he came to know God up close, these all become superfluous:

> A Hebrew of Hebrews; in regard to the law, a Pharisee; as for zeal, persecuting the church; as for legalistic righteousness, faultless. But whatever was to my profit I now consider loss for the sake of Christ. What is more, I consider everything a loss compared to the surpassing greatness of knowing Christ Jesus

> my Lord, for whose sake I have lost all things. I consider them
> rubbish, that I may gain Christ and be found in him.

Paul's intense admiration of God-in-the-flesh made his radical commitment not just possible, but inevitable.

This man traveled light. Completely identified with someone greater than himself, he became buoyant. He lost his place among society's elite; the Jewish culture that had nurtured this brilliant young man now found him to be a scandal. But He had found a bigger place in a more important relationship.

Looking at Paul later, we see the dynamics required to balance this supremely confident man. He could have become as bigoted in his new faith as he had been in his old. His basic instinct of doing battle for truth did not disappear with his conversion. But in his new, very personal admiration, he found the leverage to unseat a large ego: "I have been crucified with Christ." "Christ is all, and in all."

Paul once gave a classic retort to the sentiment that deifies charismatic religious leaders. Because of doctrinal disputes in the Corinthian church, some believers had begun to classify themselves as followers of Peter, some as followers of a leader named Apollos, some as followers of Paul. To all of them Paul said, "Is Christ divided? Was Paul crucified for you? Were you baptized into the name of Paul?"

Here Paul remained lightweight, not sucked into a golden opportunity to advance his status by mining a mother lode of religious devotion. The self didn't get stuck. His identification with the Greater One was quick and sure, as he strove to cut off secondary allegiances by lifting up his Lord in incomparable light.

Thinking of his past as a persecutor moved him to say, "I...do not even deserve to be called an apostle." Yet he also expressed a confidence most of us would find frightening: "I urge you to imitate me." Paul didn't try to pretend some of his actions were unworthy; he could calmly acknowledge successes. He may have considered himself "the least of the apostles" but he could add, "By the grace of God I am what I am."

When forced to compete with other leaders because of their heresies, he came up with a mind twister: "If I must boast, I will boast of the things that show my weakness." When people became arrogant he laid out pretensions with one simple question: "What do you have that you did not receive?"

Retaining a secure identity in the One who had chosen him, Paul could afford a balanced perspective. Was he lauded as a successful evangelist? Well, he planted the "seed" and someone else watered it, but it is God who causes people to grow. Thus he enthusiastically discounted his own eloquence in favor of the raw power of the cross. Saul the self-righteous bigot had acquired the grace of light humility.

In Philippi, Paul and Silas were angrily accused of un-Roman activities by the owners of a fortune-telling slave girl whom they had just exorcised of her abilities. A crowd gathered and threatened these "agitators." Magistrates arrived and, to prevent the mob from beating the two to death, had the missionaries stripped and beaten.

Paul and Silas landed in a dungeon, feet fastened in stocks, backs torn and bloody, ears ringing with the chanted threats of pious pagans jealous for the honor of their gods, hands still twitching from the blows. They lay on the stone and straw until midnight, when they began singing hymns to God. The groaning and yelling in other cells subsided. Prisoners usually make noises in the night to drive away the boredom and despair of its darkest hours, but these sounds were unheard of in these dungeon halls. Thieves, rapists, and subversives listened intently to sweet praise ascending through the damp stone and cold bars.

God, too was moved. He responded with an earthquake that knocked everyone's stocks off.

Stuck in prison, that hotbed of complaint, Paul and Silas made their statement in song: There's something bigger than us here, bigger than our bleeding backs, bigger than our raw ankles. It overshadows our discomfort, and we are content to lie here in its glory, though surrounded by dungeon and the threat of further violence.

OPEN-EYED COMMITMENT

Constantly on the road, Paul was also constantly on the run from his outraged fellow Jews, from outraged pagans, from thieves, and from "false brethren." He spoke for his life before kings and consuls and angry mobs of all persuasions. Often hungry and cold, he frequently had no sure place to lay his head at night, and no assurance it would be attached in the morning.

But ringing through all his letters, in and out of jail, is a contagious joy. His exalted run-on sentences are brimming with glorious truths. He is filled up, satisfied: "I know what it is to be in need, and I know what it is to have plenty. I have learned the secret of being content in any and every situation, whether well fed or hungry, whether living in plenty or in want. I can do everything through him who gives me strength."

That's another prize of light humility: profound contentment. This is not because the humble have no self and so fatalistically accept whatever comes. Rather, they are so filled up, so strongly identified with a great God, that they can absorb a wide range of experiences to good effect. Much less threatens them, and much more challenges them.

Contentment may seem a passive quality—the cow grazing in the lush grass—but as an outgrowth of light humility it becomes fertile ground, the difference between a paralyzed life walled in by difficulties and a productive life in which each moment is lived for all its worth.

An artist can't close his eyes against the world; he has to be open, reactive, feeling, sensing the range of experience. And he talks back. Usually the depth of his expression is determined largely by the breadth of his capacity to experience and understand. Paul was not content with his eyes closed, grinning and bearing it. He was content because his eyes were wide open to see what blessing His God might twist out of adversity, what adventure might spring from apparent doom.

Paul created an artful goodness. And he saw a glimpse of the canvas, the meaning behind the lives he and his "fellow-workers" led: "through glory and dishonor, bad report and good report; genuine, yet regarded as impostors; known, yet regarded as unknown; dying, and yet we live on; beaten, and yet not killed; sorrowful, yet always rejoicing; poor, yet making many rich; having nothing, and yet possessing everything."

Getting off dead center—the stodgy rock of self with its tyrannical expectations and demanding habits—one can move about more in life, extend the boundaries. The humble are flexible, not rigid, when called to self-denial. Charles de Foucauld, for example, could be frighteningly austere, yet on suitable occasions he could also indulge with French officers in their rich table. During visits to France he was usually merry and *bon appétit*.

REMAINING TEACHABLE

Light humility brings contentment; it also produces enlightenment. Those who find their identity in a holy God are continually learning from Him. They are Mary, sitting at Jesus' feet and choosing the one "necessary" thing. They are the ones who exclaim: "In thy light we see light."

Casually glancing at God from a distance, people can assume a knowledge that puffs them up. The proud latch on to a few facts as the whole, and rest in their possession. But those who admire God close up can't wrap Him up so easily; they see far more than they can grasp. An Albert Einstein spending a lifetime pondering the structure of the universe could speak about the little we know compared to all there is to discover. Those with a more casual acquaintance of physics and astronomy are usually quicker to take pride in their absolute opinions.

It's hard to be honest with ourselves without light humility; the self-important inevitably bend toward self-deception. We must be humble to see well. The humble are teachable, enlightened. Secure in the acceptance of an infinite God, they find ever more room in which to grow.

Successful evangelists, those who make a career of dispensing truth in no uncertain terms, don't often seem models of teachableness. Egos are easily inflated in the heated atmosphere of multitudes moved by powerful oratory. Perpetual proclaimers appear least likely to listen well. Yet Dwight L. Moody, one of the most prolific evangelists of modern times, retained a remarkably good ear. This man who could shoot straight about sin and salvation to receptive crowds on both sides of the Atlantic could also respond humbly when God shot straight at him.

During one long preaching tour Moody was traveling by train with a singer named Towner. A drunk with a badly bruised eye recognized the famous evangelist and started bawling out hymns. The weary Moody didn't want to deal with the man and suggested, "Let's get out of here." Towner told him all the other cars were full.

When a conductor came down the aisle, Moody stopped him and pointed out the drunk. The conductor gently quieted the man, bathed and bandaged his eye, then led him back to a seat where he could fall asleep.

After reflecting on all this for a while, Moody turned to his companion. "Towner, this has been a terrible rebuke for me! I preached last night to that crowd against Pharisaism and exhorted them to imitate the Good Samaritan. Now this morning God has given me an opportunity to practice what I preached, and I find I have both feet in the shoes of the priest and Levite." Moody included this story against himself in his messages during the rest of the tour.

In an age when fathers exercised an often tyrannical authority in the household and children existed to be commanded, Moody endeared himself to his sons, Will and Paul, by his easy playfulness and by acknowledging his weaknesses. His daughter-in-law remembered, "Oh yes, he had a quick temper, but my husband's and Paul's great memory of their father was when he had lost his temper with them, and after they had gone to bed they would hear those heavy footsteps and he'd come into their room and put a heavy hand on their head and say, 'I want you to forgive me; that wasn't the way Christ taught.'"

Moody was a man of enormous drive who built churches, seminaries, and training schools, sponsored conferences, and managed to unite quarrelsome church groups for great evangelistic endeavors. A riddle of the time went, "Why is D. L. so good? Because he drives so fast the devil can't catch him." But unlike many charismatic religious leaders who see their every enterprise as *de facto* God's will, Moody remained sensitive to direction. When the devastating Chicago fire of 1871 destroyed his church and mission school, Moody did not assume the typical posture: "This is the devil's attack on my righteous cause." He tried to listen more carefully. Later he recalled,

> The Chicago Fire was the turning point of my life. I had become so mixed up with building Farwell Hall and was on committees of every kind of work, and in my ambition to make my enterprises succeed because they were mine I had taken my eyes off from the Lord and had been burdened in soul and unfruitful in my work. When the Fire came, as a revelation, I took my hat and walked out!

Moody the celebrity managed to stay teachable; he wanted to keep learning. A friend once noted that Moody "seems to carry about with him now a little library; how he can have time to read, I cannot think." One of Moody's favorite phrases was, "We must grow or go to the wall."

In his travels, noted one biographer, Moody "always soaked up information on local background and personalities, pumped people about their families and work and interests." He read the daily papers faithfully, being deeply interested in political and international affairs. But unlike many of his contemporaries who glibly pontificated from the pulpit on issues they knew little about, Moody refused to press his opinions. He said he simply couldn't study enough to make legitimate public comment.

Moody the teachable proclaimer remained so until the end. Instead of dominating the annual General Workers' Conference he had labored so hard to create, Moody invited the best men he could find to teach. A colleague recalled that after introducing a speaker, Moody would leave the platform and sit at his feet, "always with his Bible open, always with a pen or pencil in his hand, and if anything was said which was particularly good he noted it and used it without hesitation." A seminary president fondly remembered, "When I opened to him the Bible which was so precious to him, the tears would come to his eyes and he would say, 'Say that again, Doctor.'"

Moody was continually awed by the transformations he saw God work in people's lives. He never reduced the Almighty to moldable size; he always remained himself a moldable mover and shaker.

When a group of ministers were debating which speaker to have come to their proposed meetings, one suggested they invite D. L. Moody. Another was a bit miffed: "Does Moody have a monopoly on the Holy Spirit?" His colleague replied, "No, but the Holy Spirit has a monopoly on Moody."

Charles de Foucauld also remained teachable. A brilliant monsignor twelve years his junior once dropped in for a visit and advised, "Do not neglect or despise the rich. Their amelioration is good also for the poor, and their sincerity is less doubtful." The man had other counsel also on baptizing (de Foucauld shouldn't do it too soon) and building (he shouldn't do too much). Instead of becoming indignant that a mere church official should try to correct a saint, Charles thought over the monsignor's advice at length, saw the problem, and decided to alter his evangelistic techniques.

LIGHT HUMILITY RESULTS in people who are unencumbered, content, teachable. These are admirable qualities, but they can leave us with the impression that light humility is a rather passive virtue, something tailored more for the hermit than the CEO. The humble and meek have a reputation for getting walked over on the road through life, rather than walking confidently down it. "You first" reflexes are said to leave people standing still. That's certainly a possibility. The passive can claim humility by default, but it's not light humility; it's not buoyant.

The difference between a pushover and someone infected with light humility is *identity*. Light humility gives people a strong identity. They're happily related to a glorious God, part of His purposes. Pushovers don't know who they are and consequently go with the prevailing flow, elbowed this way and that by more persistent egos. They can't say no to bad or exploitive people because they are desperately looking for identity in their peers. With their sense of self dependent on the shaping done by others, they make themselves shapeless to fit in.

Light humility focuses our lives toward God, giving a sense of direction. The humble are focused, not passive. They're secure enough not to be shoved arbitrarily, but also secure enough to step aside when necessary. They don't have to react defensively, because they are defended. They can be servants, not like those scrambling for a crumb of recognition, but like those fulfilling their high calling. They can give selflessly without being pushovers.

One Sunday three dirty, ragged men came to the Poor Clares in Jerusalem, where Charles de Foucauld was staying, to beg for charity. He promptly gave his tunic to one and promised his coat to the other two. Certain alterations were necessary to make the divided coat fit properly, however, so Charles talked one of the sisters into sewing up the garment. "It's urgent," he said, "because the three unfortunates are coming back tomorrow morning."

Next morning the trio of beggars arrived in the parlor and received their clothing. But then they demanded to be fed as well. When the sisters refused, they made a lot of threatening noises. Charles happened to arrive at that moment, and without a word grabbed one of the beggars and propelled him outside. He came back in and did the same with his two companions.

Recovering his breath, Charles told the nuns sheepishly, "I'm afraid I probably shocked you."

"No," they replied, "you delivered us. Thank you."

EXPANDING IN THE JOY OF OTHERS

In 1981 my father built a house by an Illinois cornfield, settled into his final years as a college professor, and married Barbara. They had an even bliss for four months—each morning waking up with a rush of thankfulness that they had found each other, each evening sitting on their porch in the fading light and watching autumn leaves blow.

Then one morning Dad's life stopped in mid-sentence. He sat on the bed, hands frozen to the top button of his shirt, staring desperately out the sliding glass doors toward the naked oak trees lining a pond.

Barbara wondered why he'd stopped speaking, walked over, put a hand on his shoulder, then saw the look in his eyes.

At the hospital they said he'd had a massive stroke. Several times they thought he was beyond hope, and his three sons came to save him or say goodbye. Barbara hung tough. He survived, partially paralyzed, and had to learn to speak again, reading first-grade books with enormous effort.

Barbara had occasion to be bitter: four months of happiness and then this. And she had waited so very long for those four months. Her first husband had darkened over the years into a jagged personality—dishonest, then unfaithful, then unbalanced. Before that there was her father who designed bridges, and one day crossed over one and didn't come back. The little girl who had so much love to give received only a few letters from him over the years. Now, finally, after a lifetime of male disasters, she'd found a good man, and made the most of it—for seventeen short weeks.

But Barbara avoided the inevitable consolations of bitterness and self-pity. She rose to the occasion, cheering every inch of Dad's improvement, every new syllable he could get his tongue around, and nursed him back to health one forgetful muscle at a time.

It has always been difficult for me to describe Barbara. She is so different from my brothers and me, who grew up expressing affection by hitting each other, and who absorb only with great difficulty words spoken sweetly. Barbara serves others as naturally as plants seek light. It would take enormous effort to construct a situation in which she could not find a way to be helpful. Some people might pass her off as a pushover, but I see light humility as plain as day. Barbara is never burdened down by some low-status mindset as she washes dishes that others have left to watch TV. Status is an incomprehensible word in her world. What one sees is a great capacity to enjoy other people's enjoyment. She expands instinctively, wraps around the needs of other people—and takes good care of herself in the process.

This woman's light humility expresses to me her earnest bowing of life before God. Sure, Barbara might not make a good used-car salesman, but she's no pushover. There's no black or gray humility in her bones. She's a highly valued administrative assistant who takes care of business.

I never get a sense that Barbara is stuck, that life has hemmed her in. Proud people would have folded long ago. The selfish would have knocked themselves hard against the walls. So many would have ended up so miserable after taking her blows. But Barbara is fulfilled she has a good life of her own.   Light humility.

6

DESERT DWELLERS
& LIVELY SAINTS

THE BIBLE SHOWS US light humility as a grand theme, something worthy of human life, and it gives that quality a specific shape— especially in New Testament teaching. The church down through the ages has also tried to express the ethic of humility in a variety of ways. Just as in art there are different schools—classical, romantic, realist, impressionist, and so on, which contemporary artists look back on and react to—so believers have a tradition of goodness to reflect on.

We want, of course, to take our ideals from what Scripture tells us, but it's also useful to get our bearings in the history of virtue. That may help us say something more useful in the present world, and to progress, if possible, beyond what has gone before. Romanticism or realism can turn into a rut; the original inspiration for any style can become dull imitation. We need to avoid religious ruts as well.

The story of humility in the church—how believers in the past have related to the self—is both a disturbing and an inspiring tale. Some of the first highlights we pick up from ecclesiastical history seem positively forbidding. There were early saints who made a spectacle of their humility, like Simon Stylites, born in A.D. 389. As a novice he tied a rope about his waist so tightly that it cut a deep gash and could scarcely be removed. His abbot dismissed him and warned others about this dangerous maverick. But Simon's fame grew among believers.

He took to fasting for the whole forty days of Lent, once chaining himself to a rock and standing for days at a time in furious prayer. But he could never get enough self-punishment. Pillar-dwelling was a fad among hermits at the time, so Simon constructed one five yards off the ground and dwelt on it four years. Pillar after pillar followed, built by enthusiastic disciples, each pillar a bit higher than the last. Finally Simon got himself forty cubits in the air on a six-foot-wide platform. He resided there for forty years, dressed in animal skins, taking charity from pilgrims and haranguing them about usury, injustice, and "the horrible custom of swearing." Between sermons he bobbed about a great deal, kneeling and genuflecting repeatedly in a frenzy.

It was a time when the faithful brandished a picture of revolutionary fervor against the self. Bible texts about mortifying the body and the wickedness of the flesh predominated. Many revered saints of the day abandoned as much of human life as possible and exiled themselves to desert hideaways to pray and abuse their bodies.

Simon and other desert dwellers were celebrities, not ordinary believers. But their ideal of mortifying the flesh pervaded the early church. Tertullian tells us: "Christian sinners spend the day sorrowing, and the night in vigils and tears, lying on the ground among clinging ashes, tossing in rough sackcloth and dirt, fasting and praying." He recalled that a penitent adulterer was "led into the midst of the brethren and prostrated, all in sackcloth and ashes...a compound of disgrace and horror, before the widows, the elders, suing for everyone's tears, licking their footprints, clasping their very knees."

Often, the more religious a person, the more he or she engaged in total war against the self. A devout woman named Paula founded a monastic community in the Holy Land where nuns were advised to pay little attention to dress: "A clean body and clean clothes betoken an unclean mind." She preferred to sleep on the ground and never took a bath unless dangerously ill. The great translator and ascetic Jerome presented as an ideal model for young women a girl named Asella, who at the age of twelve had dedicated herself to virginity and later lived in a cell, working with her hands and fasting strenuously.

LIKE CORPSES

In medieval times, the dark, savage picture of humility became more elaborate, and highly decorated in both ceremonial and theological ways. Here's the Franciscan theologian Bonaventure commenting on the Christ child's exile to Egypt: "It is fitting that perfect humility should be adorned and accompanied by three other virtues: poverty in fleeing from riches which are spurs to pride; patience in bearing insults with composure; obedience in following the bidding of others."

Humility was more carefully defined and subdivided. At times it took on a life of its own. The humility of St. Francis merited such marvelous honor, it was said, that God Himself "inclined to his wishes." The Almighty "repulsed the obstinacy of demons at his command, and held in check voracious flames at his mere nod."

Bonaventure applauded one who was "aroused to insult his own body out of true self-contempt" and admired such men as holy ones "inflamed with the spirit of true humility." Making a show of utter meekness, shouldering one's humility in public, was considered quite a heroic virtue by many believers.

The disciples of Loyola (the Jesuits) traveled around Europe begging for alms and seeking to do good. Many had renounced eminent learning and influential positions. Once three Jesuits were offered beds for the night at a hospital. The sheets were filthy and spotted with the blood of recently deceased patients. Two of the men jumped right in. The third, horrified, sought a cleaner place to lay down. The next day, however, he felt terribly grieved that he had shirked in the battle against self and reprimanded himself for his weakness. He wanted badly a chance to redeem his shameful act. At the next village hospital only one bed was available—the last occupant had died in it. The bedcovers were full of lice from the corpse. But the repentant father quickly removed his clothes and slid between the sheets. The lice pinched and stung him all night, making his body smart till it sweated, but he had "won the victory," and his deed would go down in Jesuit history as an act of honor.

Such acts were clearly removed some distance from Paul, who learned contentment in all circumstances. Now people were seeking the most disagreeable circumstances in order to spite their egos. And in the process the self was again made the center—as the thing constantly and deliberately despised.

The cult of total humility entailed a belief in total passivity. Saint Francis took this view to its logical conclusion. When asked to describe a truly obedient person he proposed a dead body as the best example:

> Take a corpse and put it where you will! You will see that it
> does not resist being moved, nor murmur about its position nor
> protest when it is cast aside. If it is placed on a throne, it will
> not raise its eyes up, but cast them down. If it is clothed in
> purple, it will look twice as pale. This is a truly obedient man.
> He does not judge why he is moved; he does not care where he
> is placed; he does not insist on being transferred. If he is raised
> to an office, he retains his customary humility. The more he is
> honored, the more unworthy he considers himself.

Ignatius of Loyola likewise wrote that men in his Society of Jesus "ought to be like a corpse, which has neither will nor understanding; or like a little crucifix which is turned about at the will of him who holds it, or like a staff in the hands of an old man who uses it as may assist or please him. So ought I to be under my religious rule, doing whatever service is judged best."

FULL-COLOR DEVOTION

In contrast to the pious corpses which such teaching attempted to inspire, a Carmelite sister named Teresa of Avila gives us a pleasant picture of a whole human being supremely devoted to Jesus. Teresa's mystical nature led her into ecstatic visions of a beautiful, fiery Christ who ravished her with His love. But she proved to be much more than a comtemplative. With thirteen like-minded sisters she took on the task of reforming her Carmelite order of nuns in the 1560s, because the convent in Avila had become a social center for women who desired an easy, sheltered life with few responsibilities.

Creating a new order of Carmelites dedicated to a more devotional and service-oriented life proved to be hard work. Her reforms brought on violent opposition from comfortable fellow nuns, a suspicious nobility, nervous magistrates, and the aroused citizens of Avila, who feared the order might become a financial burden. Teresa endured a great deal of slander and some outright persecution, but her calmness and consistent spirit of devotion in all this began to win her admirers. With deep roots in her Redeemer, this sister was secure enough to put criticism to good use. After one particularly heated attack a friend asked how she could hold her peace. "No music is so pleasing to my ears," she answered. "They have reason for what they say, and speak the truth."

Teresa wanted nothing more than to live out a quietly useful life admiring God. She would later look back with great fondness on her first experiment in reform: "I there enjoyed the tranquility and calmness which my soul has often since longed for....His divine Majesty sent us what was necessary without asking, and if at any time we were in want (which was very seldom) the joy of these holy souls was so much the greater."

When the need arose to establish other reformed convents Teresa could be a tough-minded conqueror of great difficulties. She arrived in Toledo to found a convent with only four or five ducats on hand—and succeeded. "Teresa and this money are indeed nothing," she wrote, "but God, Teresa and these ducats suffice."

Teresa demonstrated such skill in leading her nuns that she was asked to help in reforming other orders. In one convent which church officials deemed distastefully lax, Teresa had to take charge of sisters who had no intention of obeying her stricter rules. Some even became hysterical at the idea of a more disciplined, contemplative life. But Teresa managed to win them over, saying she'd come not to coerce or instruct but to serve and learn from the least among them.

A most unusual saintly commodity, Teresa was a reformer with a sense of humor. The sisters under her care didn't think of her as a strict disciplinarian, though the discipline she imposed was strict. Instead they saw a woman of sweet temperament, affectionately tender toward them, always able to maneuver them through difficulties with her lively wit and fertile imagination. Teresa made all their burdens seem light. Bonded heart and soul to Jesus, her own enormous responsibilities became light as well.

Teresa lived what most of us would consider a narrow, cloistered life, but she managed to create a balanced, full-color portrait of devotion. She was an earnest soul seeking only to be lost in Christ, yet she could stand up if need be to the highest civil and ecclesiastical authorities of her time. She was an individual mystic constructing her own "Interior Castle" who willingly submitted all her writings to the judgment of her confessor.

Teresa remained on joyfully intimate terms with the One who made her complete. After receiving communion on her deathbed, she exclaimed, "O my Lord, now is the time that we may see each other!"

Both in medieval times and earlier there were others, too, who found themselves rather than abused themselves in Christ. Augustine gives us a sense of his profound satisfaction in the fullness of God. In his *Confessions* he told God,

> The enticements of the wanton claim the name of love; and yet nothing is more enticing than thy love, nor is anything loved more healthfully than thy truth, bright and beautiful above all...no being has true simplicity like thine, and none is innocent as thou art...what sure rest is there save in the Lord?...thou art the fullness and unfailing abundance of unfading joy...who can deprive thee of what thou lovest? Where, really, is there unshaken security save with thee?

In Thomas à Kempis one gets another glimpse of a human being enjoying the complete God:

> Trusting in Thy goodness and great mercy, O Lord, I draw near, the sick to the Healer, the hungering and thirsting to the Fountain of life, the poverty-stricken to the King of heaven, the servant to the Lord, the creature to the Creator, the desolate to my own gentle Comforter.

Nicholas of Cusa, writing in his *Vision of God,* had a similar perspective: "Thou uncoverest the fountain whence floweth all that is desirable alike in nature and art." Catherine of Siena understood herself as one of the creatures God had made "most lovingly in His own image and likeness." She wrote of looking

> into the abyss of charity, and there saw how He was the sovereign and eternal Goodness, how for love He created and then redeemed us by the blood of His Son, and how this same love was the source of all His many gifts to us, whether sufferings or joys. All comes from love, and all God does is ordered toward the salvation of mankind.

EVERYTHING FOR THE LOVE OF GOD

From the Reformation on, the self ceased to be as dramatically abused as in earlier ages. Protestants, at least, no longer believed they could gain merit from deliberate suffering. But many still regarded the self as something "totally depraved," a hotbed of carnality where one could relax only at eternal peril. Believers after the Reformation had a better understanding of the basis of salvation, but as far as relating to oneself, the dominant theme often remained a wearying war against sin.

Still, there were men like Blaise Pascal, who pushed through his chronic, painful illness to a contemplation of God, getting far beyond himself to an intense enjoyment of the infinite. And there were women like Julian of Norwich, who advised fellow believers,

> It is quicker for us and easier to come to the knowledge of God than it is to know our own soul. For our soul is so deeply grounded in God and so endlessly treasured that we cannot come to knowledge of it until we first have knowledge of God, who is the Creator to whom it is united.

An especially unforgettable picture of existing completely toward God was provided by a seventeenth-century Carmelite lay brother named Lawrence. Brother Lawrence lived a consistent life of quiet service and seemed to his contemporaries a phenomenon of contentment and unbreakable joy in all circumstances. They wanted to know his secret. "It is not necessary to have great things to do," he once explained.

> I turn my little omelette in the pan for the love of God; when it is finished, if I have nothing to do, I prostrate myself on the ground and adore God, Who gave me the grace to make it, after which I arise, more content than a king. When I cannot do anything else, it is enough for me to have lifted a straw from the earth for the love of God.

Lawrence's ambition to express something wonderful with all his actions made the most unglamorous thing a potential work of art. He noted that many believers were trying all kinds of spiritual techniques to get themselves into God's presence. "Is it not much shorter and more direct," Lawrence asked,

> to do everything for the love of God, to make use of all the labors of one's state in life to show Him that love, and to maintain His presence within us by this communion of our hearts with His? There is no finesse about it; one has only to do it generously and simply.

Lawrence was spiritually intense, but he bore no burdens. Whenever he sinned he confessed: "I can do nothing better without You. Please keep me from falling and correct the mistakes I make." Then he proceeded, seeking His Lord's presence without more guilty introversion. After spiritual successes Brother Lawrence thanked God sincerely, acknowledging His grace.

As he lay dying at the age of eighty, Lawrence was given a few moments alone for reflection. When his friends returned to his bedside, they asked how he'd spent the time. He replied that he'd been doing just what he'd be doing for all eternity: "Blessing God, praising God, adoring Him, and loving Him with all my heart. That is our whole purpose, brothers, to adore God and to love Him, without worrying about the rest."

Other devout men and women were dominated by a very different type of reflection. Some sincere believers in the Puritan and Reformed tradition turned self-examination into an endlessly depressing exercise. Never quite assured that they were among the chosen of God, their lives were often dominated by a strained searching for evidences of election to that mysteriously select group. A righteous life obviously was a key. But who could say they were righteous enough? Enthusiastic transports also seemed to point to genuine conversion. But then, religious rapture—especially if it got too intense—could be attributed to the devil. And of course, if a person sunk too low after such experiences, as often happened, that also appeared to be the work of the enemy. The sober Christians who agonized in this way probably seemed quite humble, but worry over the state of their souls overshadowed admiration for the God who loved and accepted them in Christ.

However, other inidividuals in that same tradition managed to produce quite different canvases, dominated by the light of admiration. The Puritan divine Richard Baxter exhorted believers,

> Love as much as thou canst, thou shalt be ten thousand times more beloved. Dost thou think thou canst over-love Him?

> What! love more than Love itself?…Is it a small thing in thine
> eyes to be beloved of God?…Christian, believe this and think
> on it. Thou shalt be eternally embraced in the arms of that love,
> which was from everlasting, and will extend to everlasting.

Reading George Whitefield's journals, one gets the sense of a man keenly and gratefully aware of God's gracious acts around him, rather than someone obsessed with his own frailty. "How sweetly does Providence order things for us!" he wrote. "Oh may I constantly follow it as the Wise Men did the star in the East."

Nineteenth-century Anglican chaplain Forbes Robinson wrote in a letter, "It is glorious to be made in His image, and to be sure that all one's highest yearnings are a reflection—however broken, partial and unsightly—of His own marvellous life. We have indeed cause to be grateful for our 'creation.' "

ALL GOD'S GIANTS

Hudson Taylor represented a style of Christianity based in the "holiness movement," a style that took "resting in the Lord" and depending completely on Him as a primary objective. Such believers sought to become cleansed and emptied vessels into which God could pour His Spirit. Taylor in particular championed "the exchanged life," a full identification with Christ, exchanging one's will for His.

We might expect a man majoring in such an ethic to become a passive wimp. Taylor, however, was anything but that. He boldly walked into innermost China in 1854 and took on the forbidding task of evangelizing its unreached millions, who remained suspicious of all "foreign devils." Through his faith venture, the China Inland Mission, Taylor almost singlehandedly brought about a revolution in modern missions.

Taylor's exchanged life made him highly adaptable. He wore Chinese clothes, ate Chinese food, and adopted Chinese customs as far as possible—things many other missionaries of the time thought scandalous. But Taylor wanted to raise up a Chinese church free of foreign accessories and led by Chinese pastors worshiping in a "thoroughly native style of architecture." So this man gave himself up to a great goal: "to plant the standard of the Cross in the eleven provinces of China hitherto unoccupied."

By identifying himself with Christ and trying consciously to depend on Him for every aspect of his work—from finances to physical survival—Taylor was moved to accomplish more, not less. He once wrote, "How many estimate difficulties in the light of their own resources, and thus attempt little and often fail in the little they attempt! All God's giants have been weak men, who did great things for God because they reckoned on His being with them."

Taylor reckoned on this truth even in the worst of times. When riots broke out against two mission stations and lives were being threatened, a colleague found Taylor softly whistling his favorite hymn: "Jesus, I am resting, resting, in the joy of what Thou art." There were many emergencies and many occasions in which friends marveled at his calm courage under pressure.

"Resting in Christ" did not empty Hudson Taylor as a human being; it led to a grand quest that gave meaning to his life. In one letter he wrote, "I cannot tell you how glad my heart is to see the work extending and consolidating in the remote parts of China. It is worth living for and worth dying for."

Taylor had met something bigger than himself. His life was centered, not leveled. That became apparent to a young visitor at mission headquarters who was quite unimpressed with Taylor's appearance and bearing until he heard the man pray. "I had never heard anyone pray like that," the guest recalled. "There was a simplicity, a tenderness, a boldness, a power that hushed and subdued one…he spoke with God face to face."

UNEASY TRUCE

In more contemporary times Christians have developed a modified mixture of what has preceded us. Religious folk are basically mild; they laugh a little, cry a little, have fun a little, worship a little—nothing too extravagant. We've called a truce in the all-out war against the self, but we're still uneasy with it. No great devotion has replaced the old battles, so many believers have existed in a kind of limbo, without a burning center to their lives.

Others do find a wholehearted relationship with a God they can admire, and slip gracefully into light humility. In this light Harry Blamires remembers his literature tutor in the 1930s, the Oxford don C. S. Lewis. In their book-lined chambers, dons existed to pursue the scholarly life, not primarily to teach. Students tried to pick up whatever crumbs might fall to them by tagging along behind the tutor wrapped up in his own intellectual pursuits. Many dons, in fact, were notoriously lax, practicing golf strokes on the carpet or catching up on correspondence while the student read his essay to the furniture.

But Lewis, Blamires recalls, "discharged his teaching obligations with punctilious care and thoroughness." Students learned from a man who showed consideration, not someone looking down on them from the heights of his considerable accomplishments in English literature. Whenever Lewis needed to point out a serious flaw in some essay, he would try to combine it with praise for some other virtue in the piece.

Humility enabled Lewis to teach well. He had no memorized lines about how unworthy he was and he didn't pursue humiliation. He lived as a respected intellectual. But he bowed with his whole heart and mind before the holy God of Scripture, and in his admiration he became humble. One senses a light humility in the pleasure Lewis took in pointing out George MacDonald as the inspiration for many of his allegories, and in his warm praise for his contemporary Christian writer G. K. Chesterton.

Lewis could also enjoy his own successes as much as those of others. Blamires remembers him digging out the French edition of *The Lion, the Witch, and the Wardrobe* and delightedly pointing out how the French illustrator had captured a facet of his mythical characters different from that created by the English artist. Lewis took special pleasure in the praise the Narnia chronicles gathered from a wide audience. All this served not to prop up a fragile ego, but to deepen his sense of gratitude.

Blamires makes special note of Lewis's quality of contentment. After mentioning Lewis's rather demanding mother and alcoholic brother, Blamires writes:

> What an astonishing man he was at putting up with things! Childhood in Ireland, schooldays in England, war service in France were all marked at times by miseries which many a literary man would have turned into material for agonizing protest fiction. Yet how rarely is the note of grievance heard in Lewis' output! His own griefs and trials were mentioned only when mentioning them might help someone else to bear theirs.

C. S. Lewis is the man of our age who perhaps has best exhibited the winsomeness of light humility. It was reading his thoughts on the subject in *The Screwtape Letters* some years ago that started me on the trail of that quality. In the search I've discovered that the humility coming to us from Scripture is not some flat leveling of the soul but a great collision of two enormous facts: The self must be killed, and the self must be cherished in Christ. Both facts are powerful and neither can be watered down. Balance is important. "We have this treasure in jars of clay."

Those men abusing themselves in the desert were trying to express something important: Crucify the self. Their strange works are understandable as protest art echoing around the edges of complacent Christendom. Their harsh strokes on the canvas are something to remember. But we must add the other colors as well: God's assurances of our infinite value in His eyes. Both crucifying and cherishing are needed to fill out the picture. We don't want to fall into the old trap of black humility, but neither do we want to settle for some airhead grace that takes God's benediction without looking at its cost.

TODAY THE PENDULUM may have swung too far away from those ancient saints mortifying the flesh. The cult of indulgence has certainly wiped out any remains of the cult of suffering. We're properly embarrassed now by forefathers unable to enjoy life's pleasures, but perhaps we've lost their sense of a high and holy calling as well.

How can we express the sovereign God today? What new form can we give in our world to the invisible virtue? As soon as it becomes a banner over us, it shreds into thin air. But down in the groundwork of spiritual life, we find it to be an essential foundation. Without secure humility, the structure of our good life will tilt awkwardly and eventually collapse.

The Second Virtue

HARD
HONOR

7

THE SHIELD WE
MUST DEFEND

ONE OF THE MOST FASCINATING lights human beings have allowed to guide their lives is the idea of honor. It comes to us as a long tale with a varied cast of characters.

In the West the tale begins among barbarian tribes working out their hierarchies in the forests, determining who belonged among the worthy and who did not. They created a primal honor of the strongest, the bravest, the most fertile. Being kinless or "ill born" always excluded one from the ranks of the honorable (as reflected in an old French peasant saying: "There is more pity shown to a clod than to an orphan"). The deformed were looked upon as God-cursed.

Honor flowered in the age of chivalry when knights developed their codes of behavior. Poet and jouster Ulrich von Lichtenstein left this creed amid the romantic narrative of his adventures:

> Knights who seek for honour, you should make sure
> Of serving, when you're armed, ladies of worth;
> If you wish to use your time
> In knight's ways, with honour,
> Pay court to fairest women.

> Your courage should be high as you bear shield;
> You should be polished, bold, blithe and gentle.
> Serve knighthood with all your skill
> And be glad, set love high;
> Thus you shall win high praises.

MY HONOR, MYSELF

The medieval church turned this warrior ideal into the Christian knight who defends the faith. It broadened the obligations of honor beyond merely defending one's clan. For example, there were those infidels over in the Holy Land to consider. Knight could be turned into crusader by an appeal to his honor: The heathen had insulted him by taking over and defiling his sacred sites, and he must respond.

Other knightly adventures at home took on spiritual overtones, like those epic quests for the Holy Grail that captured the popular imagination. But these were pursuits only an elite could afford. It took a great many peasants to give the knight the means to live an honorable life.

The knight of chivalry also dedicated himself to the pursuit of a high lady's affections. Sir Lancelot and Queen Guinevere are the archetypical example. In these romances, honor predominated; the intense devotion hung on special status. The lady was enshrined as an almost unobtainable trophy. The knight's progress was measured by how well he distinguished himself in tournaments and how skillfully he wooed the woman.

Chivalry typically makes us think of elaborate courtships. But for centuries, violence remained the most characteristic expression of honor. The Norse hero Beowulf told King Hrothgar,

> Better is it for each one of us that he should avenge his friend, than greatly mourn. Each of us must expect an end of living in this world; let him who may win glory before death, for that is best at last for the departed warrior.

To win glory meant to avenge, to humiliate the enemy.

Military action was regarded as morally purifying. Geoffrey of Monmouth had the legendary Cador of King Arthur's court complain,

> When it is obvious that men are no longer using their weapons, but are instead playing at dice, burning up their strength with women...then without any doubt their bravery, honour, courage and good name all become tainted with cowardice.

One's reputation mattered above all else, even a posthumous one. Xenophon defended the glory of warriors this way: "And when their fated end comes, they do not lie forgotten and without honor, but they are remembered and flourish eternally in men's praises."

Traditional honor always goes back to this warrior ideal. In 1811, John C. Calhoun replied to John Randolph (who cautioned against fighting the British) by exclaiming, "Sir, I here enter my solemn protest against this low and 'calculating avarice' entering this hall of legislation." Peace with submission, he declared, was "only fit for shops and countinghouses," and this nation was "never safe but under the shield of honor."

Warrior types, of course, weren't the only ones negotiating their lives in the currency of honor. Humanist scholars of the Renaissance had broadened the definition beyond loyalty to clan and military valor; they included the prestige and virtue of learning, especially legal expertise and service to civil government. The ideal of honor evolved and came to include more recognizable virtues. Archaic honor was modified. Loyalty to clan became loyalty to country. Primitive boasts turned into condescension toward inferiors. Revenge evolved into more abstract concepts of justice. The knight of chivalry eventually dissolved into gentility, the ideal of the Christian gentleman.

But the center remained the same: to define and maintain one's position. Only the means to that end changed. Honor was still essentially a possession one must defend; it was, paradoxically, a shield one has to protect. You must always be on the lookout for insults and slights. Men resorted to duels to defend their honor, absolving their good name even at the cost of killing someone.

The making of oaths was always an important ritual among the honorable. They helped identify the people who counted, who were in the inner circle. Blacks in the American South, for example, were ineligible for oath-taking and thus could not serve as witnesses in the trials of whites. (Since the heart of traditional honor is one's standing in relation to others, there had to always be a group of the dishonored to help establish a place for the honored; the elite usually distinguished themselves by rejecting the lowly, the alien, the shamed.)

Honor was also how people tried to achieve self-worth. Norfolk, in *Richard II*, declared: "Mine honour is my life.…Take honour from me, and my life is done." The Roman Antony put it more succinctly: "If I lose mine honour, I lose myself."

Qualities like forgiveness and repentance find little room where the ideal of honor holds sway. The whole point of honor, after all, is to defend the self, not accuse it. In the South after the Civil War many Confederates refused to take their defeat as a judgment on their cherished institution of slavery. They felt rather that their honor and collective self-esteem had been trampled upon and that somehow the South would rise again. Soon after Appomattox, a fiery nationalist named Edmund Ruffin shouted, "With what will be my last breath, I here repeat and would willingly proclaim my unmitigated hatred to Yankee rule—to all political, social and business connections with Yankees, and the perfidious, malignant and vile Yankee race." Then he shot himself in the head. Admirers carved his last statement on his tombstone. It expresses the essential drive of the honorable: death before humiliation.

In the game of honor, those who conquer expect the defeated to be penitent, their valor having triumphed. But the same honorable valor forbids them to repent when conquered.

Shame, not guilt, was the great fear in cultures that put a premium on honor. A woman could be socially destroyed by rape, even though she was morally guiltless. The shame of being "soiled" doomed her to social isolation. At the same time men might carry on private affairs and still keep a grip on their honor. Only if adultery became a public scandal did shame enter the picture and threaten a man's position.

More recently, honor has become much more of an individual thing. People could make up more of the rules themselves about what constituted honor. The artist Gustave Courbet once refused the ribbon of the Legion of Honor bestowed by France's minister of fine arts because it belonged to the monarchical order and he cherished republican sentiments. In turning down the award he declared, "I honor myself by remaining faithful to my lifelong principles; if I betrayed them, I should desert honor to wear its mark."

It's nice that Courbet had principles. But one gets the picture of a self-important man elevating his tastes to moral imperatives. He's defending a possession, this time a very private one.

Too Proud to Sin

Honor isn't all bad, of course. It has been used to uphold virtues. And it probably helped for some time in the West to keep gross immorality more or less at bay. In some ways it remains a secular way to be good. People hope their honor will keep them from shameful sins. But it tends to break down when the heat is on. When honor is a possession I'm defending, it can't stand over me too high. Possessions can't make too many demands on us.

A girl is traditionally supposed to "defend her honor" if tempted by a seducer. But when there's little shame attached to giving in, there's little threat to honor. It's easy to give up that possession anyway. Virtue centered on personal honor boils down to a hope that we'll be too proud to commit certain sins. But of course many temptations make it quite easy to be humble.

Honor also bends with whatever group is bestowing it. West Point remains a bastion of traditional honor. It cultivates a uniformed, titled elite who cherish their membership in the clan. A West Point "master of the sword" declared, "Here in everything we do, we talk of honor." Cadets must live by a code of honor, pledging, "I will not lie, cheat or steal, nor tolerate those who do." This ethic reinforces the unity of the elite.

West Point does promote some healthy virtues. But out in the battlefield, the pressures of the group are different. Senior military leaders, many of whom were West Point graduates, became infamous for their inflated "body counts" in Vietnam. Deception became part of the honor of the group. Traditional honor doesn't hold up well under such heat because it's soft; it bends with whatever principles you choose to claim as possessions or with whatever the group is adhering to at the moment.

Honor is fading fast as a guiding light. It has always been deeply flawed; we're probably more tolerant and less bellicose in its absence. Yet we ache without it. There are holes left.

Human life has a grander shape with honor; it means something. Just making up the rules as we go along sounds great in a fast-moving movie plot, but in real life it runs into that old nemesis, human cruelty. We flail about wildly without a strong structure around us, and people get hurt, sometimes maimed for life. Self-acceptance becomes a hot topic. Best-sellers hover around it, and therapies bulge with suggestions on how to get more. We learn all the techniques, but something's still missing.

It's hard to hold together without honor. We constantly talk about discovering who we are, a question that never occurred to our ancestors. We can't accept their archaic honor, hacking a self out of the hierarchy of the clan, excluding the lowly in order to be included with the noble. And yet we long for the identity that got lost in the shuffle. Just making up our own is not enough. We're isolated and alienated enough as it is.

This is our dilemma. Can we have a human life without honor? Can we find an honor that doesn't war against human life?

LOOK, SIMPLY LOOK

One of the best examples of a society based on honor was England in the last half of the nineteenth century. Honor had become respectability in the very class-conscious Victorian world, and a great deal of commendable behavior resulted. Basic decency could be expected of gentlemen. Moral scandal was to be avoided.

But the frailties of traditional honor were also apparent. The upper classes clung to their privileges as the elite who could make up many of the rules. Citizens in the growing middle class clung to their good name, pursuing that position primarily through avoidance. They avoided sexual suggestiveness, of course (as the twentieth century incessantly reminds us), but they also avoided crudeness in general—and that included vast numbers of the population: the lower classes. Soberly dressed ladies and gentlemen promenading London's streets in elegant carriages politely turned their gaze from the filthy, illiterate urchins in the alleys. They generally considered it bad taste to discuss the miseries of those beneath them.

The Industrial Revolution was drawing multitudes from farm to factory, where machines promised regular wages—but demanded twelve-hour-a-day drudgery. The destitute could apply to workhouses for refuge, but conditions there were kept so bad that all who could move their bodies fled to work of any kind.

As usual, the children of the poor suffered most. In a prospering, relatively enlightened land, their options were pitifully limited. Many were worked to death in factories. Many had to flee homes where desperate straits bred alcoholism, prostitution, and deadly epidemics. These homeless children created the world Charles Dickens would expose—orphanages where they could subsist under the stern rule of their betters, and the mean streets where petty crime could keep them alive a few more days.

These poor were the honorless. They had no social place, no leverage. In this unspeakable underworld they were kept in their place by the honor of their superiors.

In such a society Charles Haddon Spurgeon grew up as a typical middle-class Victorian from a respectable family. He was a good boy who liked to study. His brother James recalled, "I kept rabbits, chickens, and pigs and a horse; he kept to books." At the age of fifteen Charles had become familiar with the Puritan theologians.

This deeply sensitive lad began to wrestle with the problem of sin and guilt. The "universal requirements of God's law" weighed on him night and day. He knew he had committed transgressions against Almighty God. He was lost. What could he do about it?

Charles visited church after church trying to get a clear answer.

> One man preached Divine sovereignty, but what was that sublime truth to a poor sinner who wished to know what he must do to be saved? There was another admirable man who always preached about the law, but what was the use of ploughing up ground that needed to be sown? Another was a practical preacher…but it was very much like a commanding officer teaching the maneuvers of war to a set of men without feet… what I wanted to know was "How can I get my sins forgiven?" and they never told me that.

One Sunday a snowstorm drove Charles into a small Primitive Methodist church where a layman was preaching. This obviously unlettered man stumbled through a talk on one text: "Look unto me, and be ye saved." He explained, "Now lookin' don't take a deal of pain. It ain't liftin' your foot or your finger; it is just 'Look.' "

Charles saw a glimmer of hope in the crude exposition. The layman portrayed Christ as saying, "Look unto Me; I am sweatin' great drops of blood. Look unto Me; I am hangin' on the cross." He kept hammering away at his point: We must look, simply look.

For Charles this suddenly unlocked the mystery. He had been longing to do fifty things to gain salvation—making a pilgrimage, scourging himself, anything that might give him assurance—but here he discovered the one single act that mattered: looking at Jesus on the cross in faith. It struck Charles as a revelation: "I could have risen that instant, and sung with the most enthusiastic of them, of the precious blood of Christ, and the simple faith which looks alone to Him." The revelation sank in: "I was an emancipated soul, an heir of heaven, a forgiven one, accepted in Jesus Christ, plucked out of the miry clay and out of the horrible pit."

Charles was overwhelmed by the realization that God did not look at him as he was, a convicted sinner, but as someone emancipated, accepted in Jesus. The good news emerging from the Cross broke over him with exhilarating power. It was to become the central theme in his long ministry in London as the "Prince of Preachers."

The evangelical gospel shaped Charles Spurgeon's theology, gave him a burning mission, and enabled him to become something more than a typical Victorian gentleman. He could not, for example, pass off the wretchedness of the lower classes as something inevitably beneath him. He saw every human being as an object of God's grace.

A Right to Grace

A look at his many-faceted ministry at the Metropolitan Tabernacle shows us just how seriously he took that grace. The Tabernacle constantly bulged with activity—volunteers sewing clothes for the children at the orphanage, preparing bouquets for the sick, and learning how to help expectant mothers. Others busied themselves with the Blind Society, the Female Servants' Home Society, the Gospel Temperance Society, the Loan Building Fund, the Christian Brothers' Benefit Society, and the Tract Society. Still other Tabernacle members went out to minister to the destitute in some forty missions scattered around South London, to teach street children at "Ragged Schools," and to sell inexpensive books and pamphlets to the population. Spurgeon's gospel-driven energy inspired Tabernacle members to move beyond occasional acts of conventional charity and create a peripatetic body of grace aimed at transforming lives.

Spurgeon built an orphanage very different from the usual institutions that children like Oliver Twist endured. He determined to avoid barracklike quarters, uniforms, and all the other things that reminded kids that they were objects of charity. He had individual homes built, each with a name, each with a matron acting as mother to fourteen boys or girls. He built a gymnasium and swimming pool. The homes formed a quadrangle enclosing a grassy playing field broken up with flowers and shrubs. There children who'd been cramped in filthy hovels and narrow streets could expand their lives.

Whenever Spurgeon dropped by, the children thronged around him. He made it a point to know all their names and to have a penny for each one. These children from a variety of backgrounds—black and white, Jew and Gentile, Anglican and Catholic—mingled in a healthy atmosphere, all objects not of charity but of grace, all redeemable.

Spurgeon also tried to help their older brothers, many unemployed or working long hours for pitiful wages. Without education they had virtually no chance of improving their lives, so the pastor organized evening classes at the Tabernacle where young men could study free of charge. He also enabled a great many impoverished young men to get through his Pastor's College.

Since the biggest event in his life was the day grace came to Spurgeon the undeserving, he knew how to give graciously. When he once noticed that a student's clothes were badly worn he stopped the young man and asked him to go on an errand. He was to deliver a note to a certain address and wait for the reply. The address turned out to be a tailor's shop, and the message required the tailor to supply a new suit and coat for the boy.

Spurgeon didn't just ignore class differences; he rammed his fist through them. He also battled larger prejudices. When Indian nationalists led a small revolt against British rule and were mowed down, Spurgeon called for a service of national humiliation. This was a time when Englishmen boasted of India as the jewel of their vast empire on which the sun never set. Imperialism would not become a bad word until the next century. But Spurgeon spoke on behalf of the Indian people against the actions of his government, reminding all that "only righteousness could exalt a nation." He took up an offering to assist those wounded in the revolt.

On another occasion Spurgeon met a black man who'd escaped from slavery in South Carolina and asked him to talk about his experiences at an evening Tabernacle service. This brought strong criticism from America, which was then heading toward civil war. Believers there, who'd become avid readers of Spurgeon's sermons, demanded that he state his position on the matter clearly. Spurgeon did: "I do from my inmost soul detest slavery...and although I commune at the Lord's table with men of all creeds, yet with a slave-holder I have no fellowship....Whenever one has called upon me, I have considered it my duty to express my detestation of his wickedness."

For Spurgeon, all human beings have a right to the grace that had overwhelmed him in his darkest hour. No man could be declared beneath redemption, whether Indian revolutionary, black slave, or street urchin. All must be regarded in the light of the Cross.

FROM NOUN TO VERB

In this remarkable man and his London ministry one sees that old noun *honor*—encrusted with knightly coats-of-arms, hoary with clannish loyalties, propped up as respectability—suddenly becoming a spirited verb. Spurgeon escaped the confines of conventional honor by honoring.

And in his honor we find a skillful revelation set against the somber hues and dignified patterns of Victorian England. Grace erupted like a flood of red and yellow paint all over the grim slums of South London; defiant colors braved the most depressing miseries huddled under an endless factory smoke haze. Gray human lives blossomed, shining out of hopeless conditions—redeemable, yes, and objects of grace.

Spurgeon's humor had a special place in the composition. He was a great orator who drew huge crowds into the Metropolitan Tabernacle, but he managed to sidestep the stuffy propriety endemic to most good men in his position. In the midst of one of his dead-serious lessons on preaching at the Pastor's College, Spurgeon could launch into side-splitting comedy. A student recalled:

> Then came those wonderful imitations of the dear brethren's peculiar mannerisms; one with the hot dumpling in his mouth, trying to speak; another sweeping his hand up and down from nose to knee; a third with his hands under his coat-tails, making the figure of a water-wagtail.... By this means he held the mirror before us so that we could see our faults, yet all the while we were almost convulsed with laughter. He administered the medicine in effervescing draughts.

Enveloped in rock-solid grace, Spurgeon could afford to take himself lightly. And also to not take petty criticism so seriously. When someone reprimanded him for slipping humorous remarks into his sermons, he afterward remarked, "He would not blame me if he only knew how many of them I keep back."

GRACE PROPELLED this artist of the Spirit. It enabled him to keep creating in spite of the debilitating pain brought on by rheumatic gout in his later years and in spite of the severe depression that followed. It enabled him, above all, to honor.

The one closest to him knew that best. Susannah Spurgeon, like her husband, suffered from serious illness. She remained a semi-invalid most of her life. But Charles never regarded her as a burden. Most driven men maintain only a token presence with their families, but the Spurgeon household knew they were cherished. When this prince of preachers died, one of those watching at his bedside with Susannah recalled her prayer: "We were touched beyond all expression…to hear the voice of the loved one, so sorely bereaved, thanking God for the many years that she had had the unspeakable joy of having such a precious husband lent to her."

8

BETTING ALL HIS
RIGHTEOUSNESS

CHARLES SPURGEON'S VENTURES in Victorian England show me a compelling alternative to traditional honor: honor as a verb, the extension of God's grace. Instead of falling back into the time-honored rut of carving out a respectable niche for ourselves, we concentrate on carving out a place for other people. Honor becomes something we give rather than something to defend as a possession.

Spurgeon's gracious regard of England's most unpromising citizens grew directly out of the way God regarded him, the particular regard called justification. God honored Spurgeon the sinner in a life-changing manner, so he honored other people in the same way.

His evangelical emphasis on justification by faith may seem a bit old-fashioned these days. We don't go in for elaborate theological definitions, and attaining right standing with God in the courts of heaven isn't a burning question for most of us—even for most religious people. But the Atonement is the key that turns honor inside out. It is revolutionary in more than just a theological sense.

THE TRAGIC FLAW
To help us understand the profound difference God's special regard can make in human life we can go back to one of the influential myths that has shaped humanity's view of itself. The story of Achilles, from Greek mythology, still echoes in our world today.

According to legend, Achilles' mother, wanting to bestow immortality on her son, took him to the River Styx and plunged him in its waters. As a result his entire body became invulnerable to mortal blows—except for one spot, the heel by which she had held him in the water.

Achilles grew up to become a great hero. The ancient poets recounted a series of noble exploits involving the siege of Troy. Achilles defended Iphigenia, a young princess condemned by a soothsayer to die as a sacrifice. But the princess refused to let him risk his life for her. When King Agamemnon wronged a valiant warrior, Achilles bravely drew his sword against him, and was restrained only by the goddess Athena. During the long siege of Troy his entry into battle saved the day for the retreating Greeks; the rival Trojans trembled before this mighty son of the gods. Achilles was also pictured mourning dramatically and honorably when his friend Patroclus, to whom he gave his armor, was killed.

Later Achilles received armor more glorious than any yet worn by mortal man. He slew innumerable Trojans, who leaped into the River Xanthus like locusts driven from fields on fire, and then drove the survivors up against the gates of Troy. He spotted his nemesis Hector and pursued him, wielding a massive spear, his armor glowing like fire. Hector fled, but at last Achilles drove his weapon through the warrior's neck.

The most enduring version of this tale describes how Achilles fell in love with a daughter of Priam and came unarmed to the temple of Apollo to be married to the princess. But there the treacherous Paris gave him a mortal wound in that one vulnerable spot, his heel.

Thus the Greeks gave us an enduring image: Achilles' heel, the tragic flaw. The great hero involved in so many noble exploits was defeated by that one point of vulnerability. The exposed heel became a symbol for a character blemish—something like pride, for example —that proved to be the downfall of more than one Greek hero.

The idea of man the noble creature defeated by some unfortunate shortcoming is a perennial theme in literary tragedies. It's also part of the self-portrait to which most of us cling in everyday life. If it just weren't for that little problem with booze, or that occasional outburst at home, or that accidental detour of lust, everything would be fine. The myth has been absorbed as part of humanist orthodoxy, which proclaims that mankind is essentially good, evolving toward an ever-higher destiny, but still tripped up by certain tragic elements in the plot.

A FLASH OF FAITH IN THE DARK

Scripture presents us with a very different way of understanding ourselves. Its history of the plan of redemption turns the tragic flaw on its head. When Jehovah decided to form a special nation to preserve His truths in the ancient world, He did not select as first citizen some Achilles with blazing armor, massive spear, and a résumé of noble exploits. He chose a man who could be nudged into an open-ended odyssey. Abram followed God's call, not knowing where his final destination lay.

While settling in Canaan, Abram had good days and bad. He could be generous with nephew Lot and empathetic toward wicked Sodom. He could also lie repeatedly to the authorities about his wife in order to protect his own neck. Graciously hospitable to strangers, he acted cruelly toward Hagar, the woman he took as concubine.

When making offerings to God on those stone altars, Abram could lift up only a mixed bag of achievements. God could have easily focused on his flaws. His penchant for lying to get out of a tight spot, for example, could have become the central theme of the story, his Achilles' heel leading to a tragic downfall. But Jehovah intervened and maneuvered Abram around the potential tragedies. That's not the way He wanted the story to end.

God chose to focus on a single, promising quality. One night Abram couldn't sleep; he'd been thinking about Jehovah's promise to make a great nation out of him. He was getting old now, wife Sarai had long since passed child-bearing age, and still they had no heir. How could the promise be fulfilled? Abram whispered a complaint heavenward: "You have given me no children."

God's reply was to invite him out of his tent and under the stars. Gazing up at the vast, speckled sky, Abram heard God promise, "So shall your offspring be."

Jehovah was trying to tap into a certain trait in His man, that same quality that had moved him out of the comforts of Mesopotamia and into an adventure with the Divine. And Jehovah found it. Abraham responded; he believed his Lord would do the impossible.

Then Jehovah responded, too. He looked down at this aging nomad under the stars, stretching on the tiptoes of his faith, and He saw an Achilles covered in resplendent armor. God counted Abram's faith as moral heroism: righteousness. He chose not to look at the flaws but to focus entirely on this one flash of faith in the dark.

Thus would Abram become Abraham, the father of faith, the one in covenant with God. Abraham would stumble; his flaws would tumble out; he would make serious mistakes. But God kept regarding him as Abraham, the one who'd accepted His promise, His covenant, in faith.

Because Jehovah kept working on that one redeemable quality instead of the tragic flaws, it did become heroic. The faith God had awakened and nurtured bore fruit. On Mount Moriah, Abraham lifted a knife in his trembling hand above his son Isaac, bound on an altar of sacrifice. He stretched faith to its outer limits, clinging in terror to the hope that God would supply the sacrifice or else raise his boy from the dead. Abraham, the man who must communicate the faith to a nation, felt for a few moments something of what God the Father would feel looking down on the sacrifice of His Son. The patriarch who must share the covenant truth experienced its sacrificial heart.

Abraham's encounter with Jehovah paved the way for other encounters that would spotlight the same theme: God looks for the quality He can redeem into righteousness.

Another patriarch, Jacob, started out miserably as a deceiver, tricking a blessing out of his blind father, fleeing from the brother he'd betrayed. But Jehovah didn't abandon him as tragically flawed. He showed the fugitive a ladder leading to heaven. Redemption was still possible.

One night Jacob found himself wrestling with an angelic visitor. Though wounded, Jacob refused to let go and pleaded for a blessing. In that gesture God saw a man stretching out in faith, and He blessed him. Jacob became Israel, the man who struggles with God (not just with his flaws). His life as a redeemed human being could begin.

Much later, when several Hebrew spies sneaked into Jericho to check out the city's formidable defenses, a prostitute named Rahab decided to hide them in her home. She'd heard about this God of heaven who dried up seas and flattened adversary armies, so she asked that her family be spared when He came to town.

This woman is commended for her faith in the book of Hebrews. God did not focus on her sordid profession or pick apart her motives. He grabbed hold of that one small gesture as something redeemable. He looked at her through that quality, and she and her family escaped the destruction of hopelessly corrupt Jericho.

David presided over Israel's golden age, but he also possessed some disastrous flaws. His callous appropriation of Bathsheba and termination of her husband formed just one of the dark spots. He could be incredibly vengeful and murderous. He made tragic mistakes with his children. During long periods of his life he could easily have been written off as a criminal. But God kept looking for a better ending.

When the prophet Nathan bravely pointed his finger at David for his adultery and murder, the king didn't lash back but repented in sackcloth and ashes, seeking God in prayer. David was crushed by his sin. He pleaded for divine forgiveness not just to straighten things out, but also because he couldn't live without it.

Jehovah saw David stretching out, and He grabbed hold of that redeemable quality. Here was "a man after God's own heart." Jehovah used this capacity for repentance to great effect, helping David reconstruct his life.

GOD'S NARROWED GAZE

Throughout the epic stories of Scripture we find people encountering a God who wants to redeem them, who works to find a way to regard them as righteous. Tragic flaws are not the theme. We don't see noble creatures moved through a series of heroic deeds and then prostrated by some kink in their characters. We find ordinary people moved because God regards them through some gesture of faith. He redeems them, then nurtures them toward heroism.

At the end of a long line of such adventures, we come to Paul's clarifying exposition: God justifies the ungodly, honoring those who reach out in faith. Paul best articulated this good news in his epistle to the Romans.

Chapters one and two of the book present an insurmountable problem: Humanity's habitual cruelty is acted out in front of a Creator who is uncompromisingly just. How are people ever going to find the union with Him essential for ultimate survival if their deeds are a continual rebuttal of His holiness? No matter how uprightly secular or ceremoniously religious we try to be, our integrity never adds up to what the law requires. We fall silent looking at the wide gap between what we know to be right and what we do.

Having outlined the apparent checkmate our moral failures place us in, Paul introduces God's winning move in chapter three. It is God's leap of faith (not ours). He promises to justify us on the basis of faith in Christ alone, apart from our moral performance. He's willing to bet everything on that one gesture, that one glimmer of redeemability.

He can do so only because of Christ's performance, which climaxed on the cross. In the definitive act of honoring, Jesus became our legal substitute. He stood in our place as the one condemned, unyielding before the taunts of enemies and the betrayal of friends, steady beneath the crushing weight of the Father's abandonment. Those who accept this honor of the shed blood are counted as forgiven and are "accepted in the Beloved."

In chapter four Paul builds on the case of Abraham, who looked up at the stars that night and accepted God's promise of countless descendants. Paul explained that God chooses to honor our faith as His righteousness. In the gesture He sees the whole. Reaching out to touch the passion of Christ, we are enveloped in it and counted as part of it.

This is the perspective that rescues us. God narrows His gaze and looks only at our faith, not at our countless errors and chronic mistakes, focusing with holy intensity on some gesture rather than the vast sickness within. Faith is only a gesture, but it becomes a handle God uses in snatching us out of our fate.

In chapter five Paul seals his argument and makes explicit God's remarkable act of honor. The "abundant provision of grace" and the "gift of righteousness" flow to the unworthy through the "one man, Jesus Christ." Yes, "through the obedience of the one man the many will be made righteous."

This righteousness, this right standing with God, comes to us as a gift. It's grace, unmerited favor, unconditional acceptance—these definitions remind us that we have done nothing to deserve our privileged place. But it's also important to remember that God does seek something to value as he counts us righteous. Justification is not God's saying, "You're a complete jerk, but I'm going to pretend you're wonderful." That kind of regard is just a highly refined put-down, a formal generosity that makes the unworthy feel all the more painfully indebted. Justification is God's declaring: "You've joined yourself to My Son; I regard you as I regard Him. I'm going to treat you as what you can become."

VALUE VERSUS MERIT
Our redemption is a legal transaction involving the payment of a debt, but it also involves the passion of the Father and Christ on the cross. They weren't playing pretend on Golgotha. An immeasurably intense devotion drove Them to sacrifice all for us. They see something of value even among the indifferent spectators at the cross, something redeemable, something worth saving. So They are willing to regard even the most unpromising applicant for grace as a full-fledged member of the fraternity of the saved.

We have value, but we don't have merit. A great many Christians down through the centuries have tripped over that fine distinction and tumbled into theological warfare. Some want to emphasize God's sovereign act of grace and so define the sinner as a depraved wretch who possesses not a speck of worth in his whole sin-saturated being. Others want to emphasize our cooperation with God's act of grace and identify the sinner as someone who can attain merit and make himself worthy, or worthier, of that grace.

Both points of view are only partial truth. We have value; however far we may have strayed, we bear the imprint of God's image within us. No human being is worthless. When we reach out in faith to Christ, that's something of value. It is precious; it is promising; it's a piece of the whole. Faith is not a zero.

But faith is not merit. It doesn't deserve anything. We may have something of value, but that still doesn't measure up to the glory of God, to His character.

Faith is not a down payment on a costly salvation to be followed by regular payments of good works the rest of our lives. Making a promising gesture and measuring up to God's standards are completely separate things. The former is something within us on which God graciously focuses. The latter is something Jesus Christ accomplishes totally apart from us.

All this relates back to black humility—trying to squash mankind into the mud in order to exalt God. We don't need to build this caricature of wretched-worm humanity to demonstrate that we fall short of God's requirements. He is far above our best. His perfect law throws our good works into shadow. We consistently come up short even of our own mediocre moral expectations.

Only God's act of honoring overshadows our tragic flaws. He still hopes. He's still willing to bet all His righteousness on us. He's still able to count as whole those who make that first gesture of faith.

Justification can appear to be the most esoteric of Christian doctrines, an elaborate legal fiction perpetrated to please some unfathomable divine necessity. But it really lies at the center of God's self-revelation. It spotlights something fundamental in God's character: His gracious regard. And that can transform human life.

It's often said that all theological doctrines revolve around the Cross. Our moral life revolves around it as well. God's honoring us in the Atonement is the fountain from which all our relationships must take their inspiration. It splashes color on that tepid word *love* that we've tried to make carry so much ethical weight.

All the richness of God's character is involved in His honoring. The source spills over to its object. This is what we must express. This is how we come to hard honor. It's based on two beams of wood impaling the earth, firm, unshakable. God regards us graciously though we mock Him, beat Him, and gamble for His garments as He suffers in hell.

Hard honor doesn't go with the flow or depend on the trend. It doesn't look for tragic flaws or reasons to exclude. It counts every human being as redeemable. It never turns away but constantly looks for some promising quality, some crack through which grace may find an entry.

The Cross turns honor the possession into honor the gift. All the richness of traditional honor—its uniforms, codes, titles, coat-of-arms, and privileges—is uprooted and bestowed. The believer's honor is in honoring, regarding others with the Redeemer's unchanging grace.

A FASCINATING TRIANGLE

Scripture has its own tale of honor, a story dramatizing just how radically different our Redeemer's point of view really is. All those knights in shining armor find their counterpoint in the courts of King Saul, where one day two rivals met: Jonathan, son of the king; and a rising military hero named David. One stood in line to the throne while the other had been anointed by the prophet Samuel to occupy it. But instead of jealousy and the struggle for "rightful honor" one would expect, a heroic friendship sprung up between them.

David's exploits against the Philistines grew to mythic proportions and began overshadowing the majesty of the king himself. Saul fretted. David's spiritual claim to the throne, via the same prophet who had anointed Saul for kingship, became evident and ate away at Saul's fragile ego. One day the king hurled a spear at his harp-playing warrior, and David fled into hiding.

Thus began one of the most fascinating triangles of Bible history. Saul, the increasingly obsessed monarch, was losing his grip on the throne and on reality. David, the anointed shepherd, understood his calling but would not slay the king for it. Prince Jonathan stood between them. The prince was bound by blood and royal tradition to his father, and his whole future was on the line—on Saul's side. David presented him quite a different bond. The two young men had recognized a spirited faith shining in each other's eyes.

This was a time of moral backsliding in Israel. For the Hebrews, facing belligerent Philistine armies, the God of Abraham, Isaac and Jacob had shrunk. And their leader had abandoned prophetic guidance. But David and Jonathan somehow escaped the erosion of faith all around them and clung to identically spunky beliefs.

When David had brought bread and roasted grain to his soldier brothers in the Valley of Elah and peeked over the ravine toward the enemy troops, he didn't think of how well-armed they were. He wondered at the inactivity of the "armies of the living God." When Goliath, the Philistine robo-warrior with his massive weapons, stepped out (as he'd done for forty mornings) and issued his make-my-day challenge, David didn't tremble with the others. He was appalled that this man should defy Jehovah.

After getting a relieved go-ahead from King Saul, David walked down the ravine toward a mocking Goliath and picked up five smooth stones. The lad informed his adversary that he was coming against him "in the name of the Lord Almighty." The same God who had delivered David the shepherd from lions and bears on the hills near Bethlehem enabled him to down the Philistine hero with one shot to the forehead. The invading army fled.

Not long before this, Jonathan had his own solo adventure against the Philistines in a mountain pass at Micmash. He talked his armor-bearer into sneaking up with him to the enemy camp in a crevice between two cliffs. Jonathan believed that "nothing can hinder the Lord from saving, whether by many or by few," so he ventured out to test that proposition.

Jonathan asked the Lord for a sign. He would show himself to the men in the outpost, and if they said "Come up to us," this would indicate God approved the mission. Never mind how outnumbered the two might be or how suicidal the mission appeared on paper; the only thing that mattered was whether the living God was with them.

Jonathan and his armor-bearer popped out from behind a rock, waved at the Philistines, and received the requested invitation: "Come up to us and we'll teach you a lesson." Hearing this, Jonathan urged his friend, "Climb up after me; the Lord has given them into the hand of Israel," as if the outcome had already been decided. As it turned out, Jonathan's plan worked well. The two Hebrews killed about twenty men and sent the rest of the Philistine army into a panic.

Try to imagine what it must have been like for David and Jonathan to meet one another, each an isolated oasis of courageous faith in a vast desert of stunted belief—to finally find the same fire in another's eyes after nurturing it alone for so long. No wonder their souls were knit together.

Jonathan's commitment to David as the rightful successor grew, but so did his father's rage. Saul wanted David dead and tried to pressure Jonathan into cooperating. At dinner one day he tried to pound some sense into the youth: "You idiot, don't you know that as long as you side with David you will never be established as king?" Jonathan wanted to know what wrong David had done to deserve death. Exasperated, Saul grabbed a spear and hurled it at his son. Jonathan left the table unscathed, but broken with shame at what his father had become.

Jonathan secretly met with his soul-mate and managed to keep him out of harm's way. At the same time he would not completely deny his father. He went with him into his final, doomed battle on Mount Gilboa, where both were killed.

There is one moment in the extraordinary relationship of Jonathan and David that, for me, speaks of the whole. In that time and place of disintegrating relationships, Jonathan especially wanted to make a covenant of loyalty. This prince took off his royal robe and placed it around David's shoulders. He gave him his tunic and belt, his sword and his bow. Jonathan was, in effect, crowning the future king, the man who would take his place in history. And he did it without any sorrow, but with enthusiastic devotion. To find someone whose soul burned with the same faith—this meant everything. He would honor it above everything else, even his own future.

Here we have the knight in shining honor, the prince distinguished by heroic deeds bestowing the emblems of his honor on another. The royal robe and the gleaming sword that had vanquished the enemy were not possessions to defend, but means to honor a friend. The Bible turns the knight of chivalry upside down. Honor gallops out of the castle and becomes a verb. The armor we've kept polished for centuries as our honorable emblem becomes clothing for the needy.

ABOVE REVENGE

A little later in the narrative we find a story that takes on the theme of revenge, archaic honor's oldest and most trusted companion. All those aggrieved twosomes pacing off in opposite directions for a duel should stop a moment and look at a Hebrew fugitive.

David, running about the desert of En Gedi trying to keep at least one rocky hill between himself and Saul, had plenty to avenge. He, the rightful heir to the throne, had to live like a fugitive. His persecutor had forfeited his kingship by disobeying Samuel and now clung to power only by fierce, neurotic will.

One day David got his golden opportunity. Saul had marched into En Gedi with three thousand choice soldiers selected from all Israel. This time he wasn't going to let wily David get away. While his men rested near the Crags of the Wild Goats, Saul went into a cave to relieve himself—the very cave where David and his band were hiding. There he was, this usurper, alone and pathetically vulnerable. David's men urged him to get satisfaction and avenge his slandered name. Surely this was God fulfilling His promise to "give your enemy into your hands."

David crept forward in the dark and drew his knife. But he could not bring himself to harm Saul. Instead he cut off a corner of the king's robe and crawled back to his men. They were flabbergasted, no doubt whispering fiercely, "Why didn't you kill him, for God's sake?"

But David replied, "The Lord forbid that I should do such a thing to my master, the Lord's anointed." He had to restrain his men from going after Saul themselves, and the king walked out untouched.

There in the cave David had seen something besides his persecutor, something besides a man perversely obsessed. He saw a person whom God had once anointed, just as he himself had been anointed. He saw a king who early in his reign had heroically rescued the city of Jabesh, accompanied by "valiant men whose hearts God had touched."

David even felt bad about laying a hand on Saul's royal robe, perhaps remembering the princely garment that had been placed so graciously on his shoulders. This fugitive had to honor the one whom God had once chosen. He would not lift his hand against him; surely somewhere there must be something redeemable left in the man.

David walked out of the cave with his men and, seeing Saul, called out, "My Lord the king!" He prostrated himself before Saul and then made his appeal, lifting up the piece of royal cloth that Saul now realized, white-faced, was missing: "See, my father....I have not wronged you."

David's eloquent act of honor had its effect. He did strike something redeemable. Saul broke down and cried out, "You are more righteous than I....You have treated me well, but I have treated you badly." He acknowledged David's right to rule Israel, summoned his three thousand crack troops, and went home.

Later Saul's demons would overwhelm that moment of redemption, and he began pursuing David again, not really stopping until he met his end on Mount Gilboa. But David's act of honor shines out no matter what the ultimate outcome. It was artful goodness at its best. David reversed the long and proud tradition of revenge. Instead of wresting satisfaction from the recalcitrant foe, David honored him as the anointed. He saw him through his original calling.

For a while this young king-to-be stopped in its tracks the endless convulsion of assassination and counter-assassination that so often moved people to and through the throne. His act of honoring raised up a wall against it. Toward the end of Israel's history we see the terrible spectacle of people killing to be king. How invaluable David's act of honoring must have been during the golden age, before that protracted fall of the chosen!

BESTOWING PURITY

Scripture also takes on the honor of the pure maiden in her ivory tower who defends her untouched image like real estate—chastity used as a coat of arms, a status symbol. We get the Bible's perspective in the classic romance story of Ruth and Boaz. A wealthy landowner of Bethlehem, Boaz, was out checking on the barley harvest one day when he spotted a young woman working the edges of his field. He watched her work hard all day, picking up stalks the harvesters had left behind. Boaz asked about the girl and heard the remarkable story of Ruth, a widow from Moab who had left her country to come and care for her aging mother-in-law, Naomi.

During a break in the work one afternoon, Boaz approached the girl. As an impoverished foreigner working alone, Ruth was vulnerable out in the fields. So Boaz extended his protection. "My daughter," he said, "don't go and glean in another field. Stay here with my servant girls....I have told the men not to touch you. And whenever you are thirsty, go and get a drink from the water jars the men have filled."

Surprised by this act of kindness, Ruth asked, "Why have I found such favor in your eyes that you notice me—a foreigner?"

Boaz replied that he admired her faithfulness to Naomi and her courage in coming to this new land. He said, "May you be richly rewarded by the Lord, the God of Israel, under whose wings you have come to take refuge."

Boaz was a powerful man in his community. It would have been easy for him to take advantage of this attractive widow. But he treated Ruth with courtesy and respect. He didn't see an unclean alien or a servant girl beneath his class, but a woman with a beautiful character.

As the harvest progressed, Boaz continued to show kindness to Ruth. He instructed his men, "Even if she gathers among the sheaves, don't embarrass her. Rather, pull out some stalks for her from the bundles and leave them for her to pick up, and don't rebuke her."

Naomi began hearing about the man's attentions to her daughter-in-law and realized he was a relative, a kinsman-redeemer, one who could marry the widow of a deceased relative in order to produce children who could carry on the relative's name. Naomi understood that Boaz was attracted to Ruth, and Ruth spoke warmly of him. It was the custom for the widow to make the formal proposal to the kinsman-redeemer, so one day Naomi carefully instructed Ruth on how to present herself to Boaz.

That evening Boaz was alone after threshing barley near his fields. A steady breeze blew in from the Mediterranean during the hours before sunset. The chaff had been blown away and the day's harvest lay in a neat pile of grain. Boaz lay down to sleep. He would be there all night, guarding the barley.

As he slept, Ruth approached quietly in the dark. She lifted his blanket and lay down at his feet. This was a symbolic gesture; among the Hebrews, marriages were solemnized by the man throwing his robe over the woman. Boaz woke up and peered into the dark. "Who are you?" he said.

"I am your servant Ruth," came the reply. "Spread the corner of your garment over me, since you are a kinsman-redeemer."

Boaz enthusiastically answered, "The Lord bless you, my daughter. This kindness is greater than that which you showed earlier." He added: "Don't be afraid. I will do for you all you ask." Ruth had thrown herself at his feet, but Boaz didn't gloat over his conquest. He spoke of the kindness she had shown, and thanked her as a "woman of noble character." Knowing that people might get the wrong idea about her visit, he kept the circumstances a secret.

This story has many of the ingredients found in tales about a gallant knight winning the beautiful virgin. But all of Boaz's protective courtesies were directed at a widow, not some virgin enshrined in a lofty tower. He honored an impoverished gleaner who was burned by the sun and smudged by the soil. He treated her with all the delicate consideration one would give the fairest, most innocent maiden. The important thing for him was not moving into prime real estate no one else had touched, but honoring Ruth and respecting her good qualities.

The old emphasis of sexual honor was in defending turf, carefully regulating property values, as it were, so that a supply of untouched women would be preserved for knights who wanted to settle down. But biblical honor *bestows* purity. To a certain extent, purity is something we can give. In the eye of the beholder, it helps create the worth that women especially covet.

THE WORLD RETITLED

In the book of Acts we find a story that challenges all the titles and privileges that were so essential in the old world of honor: the resplendent uniforms of the elite, the elaborate deferences, the choice banquet positions. The Bible, in effect, retitles the world. A man named Ananias leads the way.

He was waiting in Damascus for the coming of a persecutor. Everyone had heard of the brilliant young Saul of Tarsus who'd carried out a campaign of harassment against believers in Jerusalem. This man had been given authority by the Sanhedrin to take into custody any followers of Jesus he might find in Damascus.

Ananias and the other believers surely prayed earnestly that somehow this grand inquisitor might be stopped. And he was. News spread through the city that Saul had stumbled into town completely blind, a soldier leading him by the hand. Instead of ferreting out Christians, he was holed up in the house of Judas on Straight Street. Ananias was of course overjoyed. The enemy had been struck down. That was the good news. But then Ananias had a vision. God instructed him to go to that very house, lay his hands on Saul of Tarsus, and restore his sight.

The command seemed incomprehensible. Ananias reminded his Lord that Saul had come to town "to arrest all who call on your name." But the Voice told him to go anyway and informed him that

Saul was now "my chosen instrument" who would spread the gospel to the Gentiles.

Impossible! Saul, the Pharisee of Pharisees, rising fast on his track record of vigorously contending for the faith of his fathers—this man was now a Jesus evangelist? Most of us would have demanded proof, or at least a probationary period. After all, there was so much to forgive. This man had the blood of saints on his hands.

But Ananias chose the perspective of faith; he focused on God's statement that Saul was a chosen instrument. He walked over to Straight Street, knocked on the door of Judas (yes, the name that shouted of betrayal), was ushered in, and placed his hands on Saul just like that. And he said, "Brother Saul…"

I'm impressed that Ananias prayed and Saul was healed, and that he prayed for the Holy Spirit to fall on Saul and baptized him. I'm also impressed that Ananias and other believers spent several days teaching Saul all they knew about Christ. But I'm most moved by those first two words Ananias uttered. He called the grand inquisitor "Brother Saul" just on the strength of God's honoring the man as a chosen instrument.

In that word of welcome I see all the titles and trappings and uniforms of the world absorbed. "Brother" becomes a title that supersedes all others. It was a title Ananias courageously gave away. Christ has laid down His life, the world is turned upside down and inside out with redeemability, and we can become children of God forever and say the word "Brother" as a welcome into fellowship with Him. The world is retitled.

PRECISELY HONOR

In the narratives of Christ's life we find examples of an honor honed to curative precision. Out of the whole populace of Capernaum, shoving and clawing its way close to the Miracle Worker as He made His way slowly through them, Jesus felt that one timid, desperate touch from the woman who'd been hemorrhaging for twelve years. He stopped the town in its tracks, singled out the woman and confirmed her healing as a personal, moral act: "Take heart, daughter, your faith has healed you."

When the disciples tried to move some runny-nosed kids out of the way for more important visitors, Jesus honored the undervalued not with some condescending pabulum about how sweet they looked, but by pointing out a quality of guileless faith their elders needed to imitate: "Unless you become like little children…"

Jesus' contemporaries argued endlessly about who might qualify as a person's neighbor. There was no question the Gentiles were not, so no obligations toward them existed. But what about a person who was ceremonially unclean? What about those of the Samaritan sect?

Here was traditional honor at work. How can the elite behave in a way that maintains their position? Jesus turned this question on its head. He answered the question of who is my neighbor by telling the story that emphasized how to be a good neighbor. The Samaritan honored someone who would have walked on by had the tables been turned. The issue was not how may I maintain my honor, but how may I honor?

In His discourses Jesus leaped above the law to artful goodness. Does it say not to murder? Hard honor compels us to avoid insulting another; that's a type of murder—we've written him off as unredeemable. We cannot judge another; a critic isn't looking for that window of redeemability, he's looking for Achilles' heel. Jesus pushed honor to specific extremes: If someone slaps you on the cheek, turn to him the other one. If you have a sworn enemy, pray for him. The radical nature of this ethic demands that in any and every circumstance we must honor our neighbor. There is no conceivable situation in which we're justified in dismissing another human being as outside of grace.

Here we have a different knight indeed, one whose battle is to defend not just those fair maidens in an ivory tower, but also those stuck in the mud at the bottom of the moat. Here we have a different kind of tough marine whose uncompromising code of honor demands that one resist hatred to the last, no matter the cost.

REACHING FOR THE REDEEMABLE

The apostle Paul was embedded in the hard honor of the Atonement, God's will to mercy, that immovable rock of grace that refused to budge on Golgotha when humanity pressed its ugliest face against it. And he consistently honored all the imperfect, troublesome individuals under his care. It's one thing to profess love for humanity in general and applaud the abstract idea of brotherhood. But when it comes to the menagerie of personalities you rub against at work or in church, love seems quite different; it is immediately deglamorized. The lovely poster proverbs are difficult to apply. Soft honor falls apart when put up against the specific. Hard honor begins to shine.

I see Paul's honor best amid the deafening roar of a mob in Jerusalem. He'd been seen near the temple with a Greek friend, and people assumed he'd brought the man inside and "defiled this holy place." Some Jews from the province of Asia began shouting that Paul was going all over the world slandering everything the Jews held sacred. Word spread through the streets, and people came running.

They dragged Paul out of the temple, quickly shut its gates (as if to keep it from further pollution), and began pounding on the man viciously. Fortunately the Roman commander in Jerusalem heard about the commotion and hurried to the site with his soldiers. Seeing him coming, the rioters stepped back from the man they were about to beat to death.

The commander quickly arrested the troublemaker lying in his own blood on the ground, and bound him with two chains. He then asked the mob what crime the man had committed. They began yelling out a mass of accusations with such ferocity that the Roman officer thought they'd better take Paul into the barracks. But the mob wanted their victim dead now, and the soldiers barely managed to shove their way through the mob carrying Paul as countless arms and legs tried to get a piece of him.

Finally they reached the steps of the barracks and relative safety. Before they could go in, Paul revived himself enough to make a request. He wanted to speak to the crowd. He had narrowly escaped a brutal death and he was just about to be rescued, but now he wanted to turn toward the contorted faces screaming for his blood and have a few words.

For some reason the commander gave his permission. Paul stood up on the steps and motioned to the crowd. When they quieted a bit, he said, *"Brothers and fathers, listen now to my defense."* The crowd fell silent; Paul proceeded to tell the story of his conversion, and through it made an appeal to his countrymen.

The bruised and bloodied apostle saw more than the faces of rage; he saw people who could be redeemed. This was no abstract humanity in the distance, easy to honor in theory. This was a mass of contorted faces, specific pieces of rage eager for his blood. But hard honor would not let him retreat from that spectacle. Paul reached for the redeemable human being behind the frenzied caricature. And for a few moments at least, he touched the mob.

9

PERFUME POURED
OUT BEFOREHAND

PATRIARCH, PRINCE, AND PROPHET set before us the epic tale of hard honor—one of those values that turn the world upside down. And that story too points us toward the New Testament epistles, where the quality is given explicit authority. "Outdo one another in showing honor," says Paul; "Build each other up." Peter commands: "Honor all men. Love the brotherhood." Husbands are to be considerate, "bestowing honor on the woman, as the weaker sex, since you are joint heirs of the grace of life."

In Ephesians, Paul declares that a man is to look on his wife as if he were Christ looking on His church, giving Himself up for her. We're to honor our wives as the chosen; we're to see more than rollers and wrinkled weariness opposite us at the breakfast table; we must see our wives as the chosen. Women in turn are to see Christ in their husbands and to affirm that potential—not just seeing the slouch on the sofa watching a playoff game. We are to submit to one another out of reverence for Christ. In other words, something external to the particulars of the relationship inspires our honor.

Paul continues: Children, honor your father and mother. Parents, honor your children by disciplining them without anger, as those entrusted to you by the Lord. Servants, do your work as if for the Lord. Masters, give up threatening; be impartial; regard slaves not as slaves but as brothers and sisters in Christ. See more than just a laborer.

Honor is the first and last word in the way we relate to other people. Listen to Peter: "To sum up, you should all be of one mind living like brothers with true love and sympathy for one another, generous and courteous at all times. Never pay back a bad turn with a bad turn or an insult with another insult, but on the contrary pay back with good."

New Testament teaching gives this hard honor a functional shape. It suggests the components it is made of, and what it accomplishes.

John defines love as God sending "his Son as an atoning sacrifice for our sins." His blood covers a world full of terrible transgressions. Hard honor begins from this point; it's the love that covers a multitude of sins, sweeping away the garbage.

Hard honor is immensely useful as a clearing agent. It eliminates all kinds of conditions and expectations that people huffing and puffing indignantly erect as barriers. Just as light humility gets us past all the useless baggage an insecure ego can pile up inside us, so hard honor gets us past all the petty faults that can hang us up in relating to others.

A NEVER FLENCHING WELCOME

Just inside the vestibule we peered cautiously at the long pews and smattering of saints, not at all sure our faded jeans and unkempt hair would find a welcome. After all, this was Tulsa, Oklahoma where the solid folk croon along with "Proud to Be an Okie from Muskogee." But the Baptist chapel seemed our only alternative.

Soon an elderly lady came over and invited us to sit down for "Reverend Johnson's talk." We scooted into the pew at the back of the small church and listened to the reverend deliver his Sunday vesper message with simple, unadorned conviction. Behind him, on the bare white wall, hung a tiny picture of Jesus.

After smiling our way through greetings at the end of the service, we explained our problem. On the way back from a summer Christian training conference in Dallas, our bus had broken down and was towed to a filling station nearby. Most of the youth had taken a Greyhound home; five of us had decided to stay and try to get the bus fixed. Unfortunately, we'd discovered that the mechanics at the gas station were dishonest.

The church folk were eager to help, especially a Mr. John Reed, who had a mechanic friend. "Why, we'll have 'er runnin' in no time," he said cheerfully. "Ralph can fix most anything."

After a phone call, Ralph the mechanic came by and opened up the hood. Ron, the other driver, and I tried in vain to recall meaningful symptoms for him: "Well we were driving along the highway and —it quit—just died."

Ralph climbed into our venerable yellow school bus and turned the key. The engine responded with a token groan. After he poked around under the bus for a while it became clear that our vehicle wouldn't be fixed that night. But Mr. Reed—slightly balding, open-faced, and freckled—had an idea: "Listen, you all can come over and stay at our house. We've got plenty of room. We'll get this thing goin' in the morning."

The five of us couldn't come up with any of the polite refusals that customarily keep strangers from barging in. There was just our suddenly retired bus and the empty night. So we gratefully climbed into Mr. Reed's 1961 stationwagon.

We made our way to a modest suburban home in a blue-collar neighborhood, and John and Evelyn Reed made room. The house had seen a lot of living and showed no traces of luxury, but in some mysterious way Mr. Reed and his wife made the thought that we were imposing slip from our minds. It was as if we were their kids home from college. A sofa here, a few cots on the screened porch there, and everyone was settled.

It took a good part of the next day to find engine parts. John drove us around, pointing out the sights of Tulsa. Other men from the church came in the evening. They joked together, drank Evelyn's coffee, and installed the parts, while we collegians stood around feigning assistance. Finally our bus started in earnest. The men cheered, had a final cup, and departed in the night.

Tuesday morning, after a savory meal of biscuits, scrambled eggs, and grits, we boarded our purring vehicle and thanked the Reeds profusely. We had nothing to give but thanks; they had provided everything else. As Chris, the lone girl in our group, cried half-cheerfully, we waved from the windows and pulled out.

After a couple of miles through the suburbs our bus began to screech. The clatter reverberated from different places, cleverly disguising the source of the problem. Ron and I jumped out and opened the hood. We stared at the engine for what seemed a respectfully long enough time, poking around, commenting sagely to each other, "Yeah, that's the radiator all right."

Pulling up noisily at the now familiar blue frame house, we smiled sheepishly at John Reed and explained, "It started making awful noises."

This time it took two days to fix. But the Reeds remained gracious: "Great, you kids can come to prayer meeting with us."

At the little Baptist chapel a warbling organ cranked out hymns that I had always thought rather dull. But that night, singing among those square jaws and weathered faces, I caught a new warmth from the old, familiar phrases.

Reverend Johnson asked if we would get up and "testify" about the Lord's blessing at our conference. The five of us went up to the creaky wooden platform one by one and talked about what we'd learned. John and Evelyn, looking like proud parents at a graduation, beamed at us as we mumbled our words of witness.

Afterward, everyone enthusiastically thanked us. We had said little, but they called it a "wonderful blessing." Our Okie friends felt as if their small, isolated congregation was now bound to the larger body of Christ.

Thursday morning brought another tearful farewell. Our bus lumbered along amiably for an entire two blocks before falling fast asleep in third gear. It couldn't be coaxed awake. A highway patrolman dropped by. We tried to explain that friends just down the road could help us in just a few minutes, but he insisted our bus had to be towed off the narrow road immediately. He radioed a truck, and we were hauled across town to Ace Garage. I got on the phone: "John, it's me again."

"Well, I'll be. How far did you all get this time?" John wasn't upset. His voice sounded as affable as ever. "You sit tight, hear? We'll be over in a jiffy."

The five of us feasted on fried chicken, green beans, and corn on the cob. In the afternoon Chris looked at old photo albums with Evelyn, and the rest of us touched up the front siding and helped the Reed's twelve-year-old boy feed his rabbits. It felt good to be just family.

Friday morning. "This is going to be it," we said confidently. We waved to "Mom" and "Papa" Reed again through the bus windows, and they stood for a long time on their narrow crabgrass lawn.

At the outskirts of Tulsa, our crotchety yellow vehicle started hinting—little groans here and there. All was not well. The motor misfired; the hinting grew more persistent. Ron and I grimaced at each other and finally decided to turn around. There was no way we'd make it back to Illinois.

What would the Reeds say this time? Surely they wouldn't believe it; surely we'd catch a hint of tension in their faces. But no, Papa was out on the lawn waving as soon as our telltale sputtering could be heard coming up the street.

We apologized lamely, but John wouldn't hear of it: "Glad to have you back."

During our entire stay in Tulsa we never saw a trace of the wearying strain that must come from having five extra people camp out in your home. The Reeds always managed to make us feel we were honoring them, not they us. Tested to the limit, their welcome never flinched.

One guy in our group was black. The neighbors imperfectly concealed their distress about his sleeping in their midst. But John told me quietly he was proud to be sheltering the young man.

We had popped out of the alien world of protesting, drug-infested universities into their Okie land of country music and the flag. Yet our two mutually intangible cultures presented no barriers. Mom and Papa Reed always treated us as a blessing. They valued us for our fellowship and accepted us—extra toothbrushes, sleeping bags, dirty socks and all.

Saturday arrived, our fourth attempt at departure. We embraced our adopted family and said hopeful, sad goodbyes. This time Chris's tears were not shed in vain.

POURED FULL

The following Christmas my family took a trip south to Texas. We were passing by Tulsa on a Sunday when I suddenly remembered the chapel close by the freeway and talked my parents into stopping for a few minutes.

When I stepped inside the chapel, the worship service was almost over. Reverend Johnson was preaching with the same conviction as before. During the closing hymn he and I exchanged excited glances.

Meeting outside under a high noon sun, the church folk's happiness rushed over me. Before then, I don't think I really knew what it meant to be greeted. Papa Reed kept telling my dumbfounded parents what a tremendous boon we students had been to their church.

Those people's delight just because I was present struck at something deep inside me. John's youngest, a seven-year-old, had been away at summer camp during the broken-down-bus episode. The girl had never laid eyes on me, but she rushed over anyway and hugged my waist earnestly as if for a long-lost brother. At that moment I felt I was poured into being. All the marketable qualities I subconsciously relied on to make me feel valuable—the with-it clothes, the clever lines, the flashy personality—all seemed insignificant and were brushed aside in the warmth of the moment. I had nothing with which to recommend myself. I became empty, illuminatingly so, and in that sudden vacuum I experienced the grace of being poured full by their jubilation.

That church may not have been a spiritual powerhouse. From the inside it may even have felt rather dry. Perhaps Sunday by Sunday the believers gave their sincere but drowsy assent to the sermon. A casual visitor might not catch a lot of excitement from the group. But a potent honor simmered in that aged stone building squatting diffidently by the rush of interstaters. That congregation disclosed to me "the grace of the Lord Jesus Christ," banners blowing. Their act of honor filled me to the brim with that same great stream of grace that flows through Scripture.

HARD HONOR is tough enough to break through barriers. It creates a way to regard someone with grace even when there are no apparent grounds for it. When Jesus' act of honor is paramount and His retitling of the world with the words *sister* and *brother* predominates, the whole gaudy scaffolding of differences collapses.

Paul took hard honor to its logical and revolutionary conclusion: "There is neither Jew nor Greek, slave nor free, male nor female, for you are all one in Christ Jesus." Christ is all in all; His sacrifice trivializes all other human distinctions. Paul told the Corinthians, "For Christ's love compels us, because we are convinced that one died for all." Christ's death allows us to look on the world in a totally different way; He has placed a supreme value on each individual in it. "So from now on," Paul continued, "we regard no one from a worldly point of view." The reconciliation is what determines perspective now. God is already reconciled to sinful human beings because of Christ's act of honor. Any alienation people may experience is strictly their doing, their choice.

God's act of honoring also makes available a rich source of identity; His creative regard finds many echoes. Hard honor bestows meaning—that is another its essential components. It can pour unexpected significance into even the most aimless, dreary lives.

Lifted Up as Emblem

Jesus and His disciples were reclining before a special festive supper six days before Passover in the home of Simon, a leper whom Jesus had healed. This was Bethany, the town of Martha, Mary and Lazarus, Christ's devoted followers. The town's inhabitants were finally making a big deal out of the Nazarene rabbi; they sensed His ministry was heading toward a climax at Jerusalem. Word had spread among the crowds pilgrimaging toward the holy city that one of Jesus' followers had at one time been a corpse. Everyone wanted to see the man, and his healer. The Nazarene's enemies, their hands tied temporarily by the admiring multitudes trying to catch a glimpse, circled for the kill.

In this tense excitement Simon hoped to honor the great Teacher and give Him a restful Friday evening. All was proceeding as planned, with Jesus and Lazarus reclining in honored places, when suddenly the guest room filled with a pungent fragrance. The nostrils of Judas were the first to identify and quantify it: pure nard, very expensive. He and the others who'd dropped their bread saw that Mary had crept in and was pouring an alabaster vial of the perfume on Jesus' head, as if anointing Him. Then she moved down to remove His sandals, rubbed His dust-streaked feet with the remainder of the nard, and wiped them off with her hair.

Judas did some quick calculating. That was three hundred days' wages evaporating into thin air. Noting the disturbed look on the faces around him, he declared that this perfume might have been sold for a good price and the proceeds placed in his fund—for the poor, of course. Most of the disciples agreed. It did seem to be a costly gesture, even a tragic waste.

They were perhaps even more disturbed that a mere woman should be so forward. Was it proper for her to be anointing the spotless rabbi? What business did she have interrupting their pleasant, relaxed evening? Several voices joined in Judas's criticism. Some reprimanded Mary directly. Her face flushed. She was about to beat a hasty retreat when Jesus silenced the guests with a sharp rebuke: "Leave her alone." He knew that her awkward act flowed out of a wealth of devotion.

Jesus informed His indignant companions that this woman had done something beautiful. Then He immortalized her act by linking it to His coming passion. "She poured perfume on my body beforehand to prepare for my burial," He said. Jesus was about to place Himself in the hands of His enemies, endure a mock trial, suffer greatly on the cross, suffer much more in the terrible dark away from His Father, then lie cold and bloodless in a tomb. The climactic confrontation of His life was approaching. But His disciples couldn't grasp it; they offered no real companionship during that most difficult of journeys toward Jerusalem.

Jesus transformed this woman's stumbling gesture of blind devotion into a companion piece, a part of the spectacle of His Atonement. Jesus seemed to say, Only this woman among you all has echoed ultimate truth; only she is identified with Me in the great ordeal ahead.

Jesus lifted up Mary's act as an emblem for all the redeemed down through the ages who would come to honor His sacrifice with twenty-twenty hindsight as much as she honored it now impulsively. The soundly rebuked woman heard these words: "Wherever the gospel is preached throughout the world, what she has done will also be told, in memory of her." Jesus honored the dishonored one by giving her meaning. His insight into the significance of her gesture redeemed her from the shadows. Mary could take home her alabaster vial, now fittingly empty, and walk tall amid the gossips of Bethany. She was part of the Messiah's sacrifice, and no one could ever take that away from her.

Hard honor carves meaning out of the rough stone. It's Michelangelo seeing an angel in the shapeless mass of rock. It thrives on a certain kind of insight that finds great meaning in the clumsy gestures toward the light we all manage on occasion.

By getting past exteriors, hard honor creates personhood. The apostle Paul's fruitful ministry was based on the premise that a believer stands before the righteous God "holy and blameless and beyond reproach." He liked to assure his listeners, "In Him you have been made complete." He also tried to extend such generous divine grace in his own relationships. He labored with all his energy to "present every man complete in Christ." The wholeness that God makes possible must seep into the innermost being.

People are much more fragile than we usually think, especially in their inner sanctum where self-worth struggles to bloom. Macho quarterbacks and beauty queens, as well as pimpled nerds and business failures, desperately need a sense of value that goes beyond accomplishments. It needs to be separate from what we do or don't do. Hard honor creates such personhood.

GESTURES THAT TRANSFORM

I walked into room 307 with three clean sheets and a plastic bag, not knowing exactly what to expect. It was the first night I'd received Mr. Griffin's patient care card. A nurse's aid told me he'd had a stroke. I hoped the man could at least roll over for his bed bath.

Griffin lay still on his back in the semiprivate room. As he breathed slowly, the sheet undulated over his large belly. I figured he weighed close to 180 pounds.

He was my last patient. I wanted to get through with him fast so I could have some time to finish reading the last chapter of *The Biblical Meaning of History*. It had been a long evening of hustling bedpans and drawsheets. Too many little red lights had flashed above patient's doorways. Too many incontinent bowels, gurgling throats, crabby cardiacs, and moody post-operatives. I was ready for the big recliner in the orderly lounge.

After quickly checking Griffin's pulse and temperature, I began tucking the sheets under him. As I moved to roll him over he tried to speak. I leaned close. He lifted his eyebrows, nodded his head, twisted

his lips, flayed with his tongue—but no words came out. A few sylla-
bles and a pointing of his wide eyes, however, got the message across.

"Okay," I told him, "the john."

It was terribly hard hoisting his torso up into a sitting position.
He was dead weight. I popped out in the hall; the other orderlies
were busy. Just my luck. Well I wanted to get this over with fast
anyway.

There was an aluminum walker in the room; maybe that would
help. "Mr. Griffin can you use the walk—oh, never mind." I placed it
beside the bed. Pulling his slightly mobile left arm over my shoulder
and encircling his waist, I grunted and heaved the man upright.

Griffin leaned toward the walker, tottered on his stiff legs, and
collapsed in my arms. Make that 200 pounds. The back of his hospital gown flew open and his bare buttocks pressed against my thigh.
Forget the walker. Taking a deep breath, I locked my arms around his
chest and dragged him roughly across the room to the bathroom
door. His dry, flaking feet slid lifelessly over the green tiles.

My patient struggled to move his good arm, trying to be of assistance, but I just kept dragging. In the heat of my exertion, I silently
cursed his bulk and nearly dropped him while swinging his back
around to the toilet. But we made it down all right. I shut the door
and left him for a while.

Time for a break.

Only much later did I realize I had acted dishonorably. Mr. Griffin had become for me a bag of meat, a task requiring the shortest
distance between bed and toilet. I didn't sense that he was already
distraught over his seemingly healthy limbs that refused to budge on
command. He didn't need some impatient orderly to emphasize his
helplessness. In my hurried round of patient "care," I had forgotten
that those pale cheeks could flush with shame like any man's. The
intelligence and pain reflected in his eyes escaped me. I could not
take time to honor such things in my hurry to get back and discover
the true biblical meaning of history.

That incident, however led me into one of my first introductions
to the meaning of honor. Mr. Harvey existed in the geriatric ward,
one of those patients who lay immobile in a no-man's land between
the living and the dead. They told me he was only about fifty, but his
pale skin stretched taut across a gaunt face. His mouth hung open
and his breathing was hardly perceptible. Once in a while his heart
was moved to beat regularly. Although at times his eyes moved,
Harvey seemed unaware of his surroundings. The doctor once said
something about schizophrenia. Harvey's many ailments kept him
shuttling between county and state hospitals.

On many days I drew him as a patient, one of the "bed baths." It wasn't easy rolling him around on the bed and changing the sheets underneath him. His unbroken silence and occasional look of discomfort made it harder. I always wondered what was happening inside the man's head. Who could really know? Harvey's inscrutable expression always got to me somehow. His countenance suggested an odd combination of Dick Tracy and concentration camp survivor. I decided to try an experiment.

I began talking to the man—no conversation, just a few words each day after checking his reticent pulse. I would shake his hand firmly, lean close, and ask, "How are you doing, Mr. Harvey?"

I continued sending my greeting into the vacuum of his face for about two weeks. He remained incommunicado, but I didn't mind. It felt good speaking and being respectful when there was no obvious reason to do so.

Then one day after I had changed his gown, recorded his temperature, and spoken my greeting, Mr. Harvey looked right at me and mumbled, "How — ah — you." He squeezed my hand ever so slightly.

I stared back, speechless for the moment, witnessing a little crack in the open-and-shut case of schizophrenia. I felt as if we'd crossed a great distance and finally met face to face. My efforts had been only a gesture, and I received only half a gesture in return, but that proved to be one of the most exciting dialogues of my life.

In acts of honor we are able to help form each other. We create better things than the meager materials inside most of us might suggest. We nurture personhood. And we are asked to nurture it even in those who hurt us. God tells us to love our enemies and pray for those who misuse us; He can ask this because He did it so well on Golgotha. In Romans 5, Paul reminded his readers that Jesus died for them while they were quite happily sinning against Him. It's rare enough for anyone to give his life for another man; a few heroic types might die for a noble person, but to die for the obnoxious, the ungrateful, the unpromising—that falls off the end of the equation. That's hard honor.

Paul learned it. He could never stand apart in judgment from even the worst. He was always involved because of God's overshadowing grace. To the Corinthian believers who'd struggled with everything from incest to lawsuits among themselves, he exclaimed, "I do not say this to condemn you; I have said before that you are in our hearts to die together and to live together." It is this hardest kind of honor that has the most potential to transform people.

KILLER AND SON

Frank and Elizabeth Morris were driving Tommy Pigage back to jail after one of his MADD (Mothers Against Drunk Driving) speaking engagements. Tommy began talking about the Bible study course the Morrises had introduced him to and how he felt strengthened by it. Soon it became apparent that the young man had made a commitment to Christ.

Frank asked him, "Have you been baptized?"

"No, but I'd like to be," Tommy answered.

The three were just about to pass the Little River Church of Christ, where the Morrises were members. They pulled into the parking lot and stepped inside. Lay members of this congregation could perform baptisms, so Frank led Tommy up to the front of the sanctuary, draped him in a white robe, and waded into the frigid baptismal pool.

As Elizabeth watched her husband raise his arm over Tommy's bowed head, she recalled an almost identical scene several years before when Frank had immersed their son, Ted, in the same pool after his commitment at age eleven.

There was one big difference, however. Tommy was no earnest adolescent but a convicted killer. And the person he had killed was the Morrises only son. After drinking himself into a stupor one night in 1982, he'd climbed in his car, swerved down a road, and smashed head-on into 18-year-old Ted's car.

The Morrises were consumed with grief and rage. Frank followed the legal proceedings religiously, living for the day when Tommy would be found guilty. Elizabeth, when not contemplating suicide or crying her heart out on Ted's pillow, fantasized about throwing the electric chair switch herself at his execution.

Shocked by the depth of her hatred, she began praying for a way out of it, haunted by Christ's words on the cross: "Father forgive them." One day Tommy spoke at Ted's high school as part of his rehabilitation, and Elizabeth mustered enough courage to speak to him afterward. Then, finding that no one ever visited the youth in jail, she decided to go see him. Seeing an utterly desolate young man behind the bars, Elizabeth felt a surge of warmth.

After a bit Tommy blurted out, "Mrs. Morris, I'm so sorry. Please forgive me."

For a moment everything froze as she stared at the man. She thought of the Father who lost an only Son, of His incredible act of honoring on the cross, and everything became clear. She forgave Tommy sincerely and asked his forgiveness for the hatred she'd nurtured for months.

The Morrises joined in Tommy's rehabilitation and were able to convince him that God could help him kick his eight-year addiction to alcohol. Frank Morris had found the strength to help, but he still wrestled with forgiving Tommy.

Then came that spontaneous moment of baptism. When Frank lifted Tommy out of the water, the youth begged, "Please, I want you to forgive me, too," and embraced him desperately. The bereaved father said tearfully, "Yes, I forgive you."

Tommy's initial chances of rehabilitation weren't good. He bore the psychological handicaps of growing up in a troubled family and had been addicted to alcohol from the age of sixteen. But he did succeed in finding sobriety, a steady job, and a strong sense of purpose in serving the Lord, largely because Elizabeth began calling every day and Frank asked him to help with outdoor work around the house. The grieving couple found their way to hard honor, counting the killer as their son.

VICTORS

Deep in the rain forest of Ecuador, a small group of Americans and Auca Indians gathered at dawn on a sandbar of the Curaray River. Kimo, an Auca pastor, began explaining the meaning of baptism to four teenagers—Steve and Kathy Saint and two Auca youths. He reminded them that their immersion in the water was a witness of the death and resurrection of Christ.

As the low, fiery tropical sun cast long shadows, Rachel Saint watched her children file into the river. Her husband, Nate, could not be there to share in the event. He had bled to death on this same sandbar some years before, when his kids were small. Four other missionaries had died with him, speared by a group of Aucas that included Kimo. The man who stood now in the Curaray raising his hand solemnly over fourteen-year-old Steve had once raised his weapon in fear and anger against the boy's father and helped kill him.

Nate Saint and his companions had been longing for some time to reach the isolated, greatly feared Aucas. In 1667 a Jesuit priest had attempted to introduce the faith to Aucaland and been quickly dispatched. Two hundred years later, rubber hunters entered the forest and burned Auca homes, raped the women, and killed or enslaved the men. If the Aucas had been unneighborly before, they had much more reason to be so now.

Nate and his companions began dropping gifts to the Aucas from an airplane. They called out friendly phrases and got a few smiles and waves in response. Finally they decided to chance a face-to-face encounter and selected a sandbar they nicknamed Palm Beach for a landing. The men knew it was risky. One of the group, Jim Elliot, told his wife, "If that's the way God wants it to be, I'm ready to die for the salvation of the Aucas."

All the signs had been good, but something went wrong during that first encounter between Kimo and his companions and the missionaries. The Indians' deeply rooted fear that foreigners came only to kill and destroy compelled them to shed blood.

Remarkably, the five missionary widows did not beat a hasty retreat from what most would regard as a land of savages. Instead, they remained in Ecuador with their children and continued attempts to reach the tribes in the forest. These women had a hold on a hard honor that insisted, against the odds, that these people were redeemable.

An Auca girl who'd left the tribe after her father was killed was converted, and went back to her people to tell them about Jesus and His great sacrifice. One month later Rachel Saint and Elisabeth Elliot hung their hammocks with the Aucas. They began living out their forgiveness day after day and pointing to its source in the Atonement of Christ. Kimo was one of the first to see in Christ's blood a means of spiritual cleansing.

And so they'd come to this dawn on the banks of the Curaray. Those two fatherless teenagers also knew about hard honor; Kathy and Steve Saint had chosen Kimo as the one who would usher them symbolically into the arms of a heavenly Father.

After the baptism, Rachel Saint, Kimo, and the four teenagers walked over to the graves of the five martyrs. Together they sang the hymn those five men had sung just before departing to meet their fate:

> We rest on Thee, our Shield and our Defender;
> Thine is the battle, Thine shall be the praise;
> When passing through the gates of pearly splendor,
> Victors, we rest with Thee through endless days.

THESE ARE MASTERPIECES of honor, artful goodness at its best. They belong on large canvases dominating our gallery walls. They embody the act of atonement, the will to mercy, making it powerful and vivid over our pedantic landscape of tepid loves and gaudy hates.

It's only fitting that the climactic scene in these acts of art involved baptism. In baptism a new believer accepts publicly a wildly improbable honor: identification with Christ's heroic death and resurrection. He is retitled, reclothed, recounted as a person with all the rights and privileges of the beloved Son who marched confidently into heaven and into God's throne room after a triumphal *tour de force* on earth.

The Saint family and Elizabeth and Frank Morris managed to honor other people as they had been honored by God. That's the primary ethical thrust of the New Testament, a call to arms that echoes beneath all other admonitions. Hard honor anchors us irrevocably to God's act of atonement, that greatest of artistic spectacles played out on a hilltop against dark, rolling clouds, flashes of thunder, earthquake, and a large cast playing humanity at its best and worst. We must express that act, flesh it out. We must make our own canvases out of the Atonement.

10

SPLENDID ROBES
& SPECIAL SERVANTS

FROM THE EPIC of honor in Scripture and its functional shape in New Testament epistles we turn to the story presented us by the church attempting to reflect this quality.

The tradition of honor begins brightly in the first century: "How these Christians love one another!" was the first pagan response (quoted by Tertullian) to the Christian movement. From the beginning Christians made it a point to honor those least likely to receive benevolent regard. Funds were regularly collected, Tertullian wrote,

> to feed the poor and bury them, for boys and girls who lack
> property and parents, and then for slaves grown old and ship-
> wrecked mariners; and any who may be in the mines, on the
> penal islands, in prison... they become the pensioners of the
> confession.

The good news about God's grace paved the way for a new way of looking at the disadvantaged. They weren't objects of God's curse, but people capable of redemption. Most of the early Christians did an exceptional job knocking down barriers of class and race that got in the way of honor.

The Emperor Julian, writing to his pagan clergy about the influence of Christians, complained, "The impious Galileans support not only their own poor, but ours as well; everyone can see that our people lack aid from us."

A severe famine once persuaded many pagans that the gods were angry and demanded elimination of the "atheists" in their midst. Yet these followers of Jesus awed everyone by their selfless caring for the victims of famine, pagan and Christian alike.

Women especially benefited from Christian honor. Treated as equals in the eyes of God, they took on important roles in the church. Husbands were told to treat their wives with as much consideration as Christ showed His bride, the church.

It's important to remember that all the lofty ideals we hear about from the philosophers of Greece and Rome applied only to society's elite. Their ethic was for aristocrats only. But those moved by Christ's honor brought a different social order into the world. They extended grace and dignity to all human beings—even to their most ruthless enemies. Echoing the words of Paul, the *Epistle to Diognetus* stated that Christians "

> love all men, and are persecuted by all. They are poor, and make many rich. They lack everything, and in everything they abound. They are abused—and they bless. They are reviled, and are justified. They are insulted, and they repay insults with honor.

Some Christians under torture would not reveal their names or social class, home or place of origin. They simply said they were Christians who belonged to a universal church, and refused to claim any other identity.

Delivered from Blindness

Toward the end of the fourth century a fifteen-year-old son of wealthy property owners in Britain was captured by Irish pirates and taken back to Ireland, where he labored as a slave tending sheep. After six years he managed to escape. He made his way, with great difficulty and providential help, back to civilization.

This experience traumatized the lad, who'd grown up sheltered on his father's comfortable estate. One wouldn't expect him to express any fondness for those who had enslaved him during the best years of his youth. And yet this boy, Patrick, ended up returning and spending his life in Ireland, laboring to bring its people from paganism to Christianity.

During his years of captivity, Patrick had discovered God as a very present helper in times of trouble. He had apparently been quite indifferent to religious matters before, but he began fervently worshiping his Lord in Ireland. Later he would look back on those six years not as tragic captivity but as a great deliverance from spiritual blindness. He wrote, "Before I was humiliated I was like a stone that lies in deep mud, and he who is mighty came and in his compassion raised me up and exalted me very high and placed me on the top of the wall."

The experience of finding in God a deliverer, both physical and spiritual, when no human help was available, gave Patrick a profound appreciation of redemption; it made justification by faith graphic. So when the call came to minister in Ireland, Patrick went, propelled by hard honor. Those people up north weren't just barbarians; they were people whose lives had been rendered invaluable by the shed blood of Christ. Patrick set off to become a good shepherd for the redeemable.

The gospel-proclaiming church had introduced a new way of honoring, of seeing every human being primarily through Christ's act of honor. But gradually other kinds of honor crept in that compromised this principle. Virginity, for example, became something of a status symbol in the church, a higher level of spirituality which the married could not attain. All the glory of mystical union with Christ, which every believer is entitled to, was focused on the cult of virginity. Many church leaders believed that only the celibate could be spiritual in the deepest sense.

Others who had suffered persecution and torture for their faith also came to occupy an upper niche in the church. These "confessors" sometimes lorded it over other members, and most occupied prominent positions. Less distinguished believers reverenced their heroic accomplishments.

It's commendable, of course, to admire those who suffer for their faith or who forgo marriage to dedicate themselves to Christian service. But when they attained a certain exclusive status in the body of Christ, hard honor was fractured, and the old honor of reputation crept in.

During the Middle Ages, extending the gospel and thus Christ's honor didn't occupy center stage. Honor was further compromised by the increasingly high status of the clergy. Those who made that mystical sacrifice of Christ's body during Mass took on cosmic size above their congregations. Believers were obliged to pay homage to men in splendid robes, and also to holy relics in splendid shrines. The outward trappings of holiness often obscured more redeemable inner qualities. But there were still radicals around who majored in *honor*, the verb.

While riding through the plain below the town of Assisi, a youth named Francis encountered a leper and was horrified by the man's appearance. Determined, however, to be a knight of Christ, he slipped off his horse and ran toward the man, who extended his palm to receive some alms. Francis gave him a few coins—and a kiss.

Later, according to Bonaventure, Francis would live with a group of lepers, for a time "serving them all most diligently for God's sake.

He washed their feet, bandaged their ulcers, drew the pus from their wounds and washed out the diseased matter; he even kissed their ulcerous wounds out of his remarkable devotion, he who was soon to be a physician of the Gospel."

There were quite a few saints who took on the challenge of Christ's honor in earnest. Contemporaries of Joan of Orvieto used to say, "Anyone who wants Sister Joan's prayers should do her a bad turn." Ignatius walked many miles out of his way in winter to nurse a man he heard had fallen ill—the same man who'd stolen his small store of money a few weeks before. Saint Spiridion interrupted a gang of thieves attempting to make off with his sheep one night, but set them free with a gift of a ram "lest they should have been up all night for nothing."

The Reformation pushed out considerably more room for honor by championing the priesthood of believers and by spotlighting its theological source: justification by faith. But in the fierce battles over this and other doctrines, honor was often trampled. Theological opponents did not often seem redeemable, especially when they remained unmoved by one's arguments.

The circle of honor did not yet include Jews. Protestant preachers could wax eloquent about the Christ who opened His arms to those who remained indifferent to His sacrifice, the One who would not curse even those who mocked it. But many in the church called for harsh penalties against the Hebrews who remained indifferent in the present.

Some in the Reformed tradition began to draw lines all too visible between the elect and those not elected, the chosen and those on the outside. Puritan preaching at times implied that the poor were undeserving—after all, God had made them that way. Those who prospered economically took success as a sign of God's blessing—and election. Eventually, only upstanding, hard-working citizens could claim the possibility of redemption. In many Christian minds, God was no longer looking for an opportunity to save, but working rigidly through the unfathomable machine of predestination.

RECOGNIZING JESUS

By the nineteenth century, Christ's honor was diffused into middle-class respectability. Charles Spurgeon's peers could draw boundaries between themselves and the unwashed masses. William Booth could not. His Salvation Army regulars, like Spurgeon's Tabernacle volunteers, sought out the unlikeliest candidates of grace in the slums of the Industrial Revolution.

The great revivals of the eighteenth and nineteenth centuries created an awakening of Christ's honor and gave birth to the modern missionary movement. Some missionaries allied themselves with imperialism and the political interests of their home country. They didn't honor, but patronized, and sometimes exploited. Those most propelled by the gospel, like the Moravians, were the most likely to truly honor the peoples they worked among and to look for aspects of their culture that were redeemable.

There have been extraordinarily sensitive missionaries who upheld Christ's honor, like David Brainerd among the American Indians, Adoniram Judson among the Burmese, Hudson Taylor among the Chinese, and, in the twentieth century, Don Richardson among the Sawi people of Irian Jaya. Richardson discovered a cannibalistic culture that had somehow developed an ethic of crafty betrayal and murder as its highest ideal. But he still found something to honor among the Sawi: their concept of a Peace Child. He made this bit of Sawi culture blossom into the hard honor of Christ.

Honor has had its skillful champions at home, too, like Paul Tournier, the Swiss physician ministering to the whole person. To read his accounts of patients with serious psychological problems brought to wholeness as he offers personal wisdom from his own devotional life is to watch a remarkable healer in action. Tournier consistently wrested the redeemable from psyches twisted by neurotic guilt and bitterness.

We also see a wonderful kind of honor in the ministry of an Albanian nun named Mother Teresa, who labors cheerfully among the poorest of the poor in Calcutta. She has chosen to concentrate on those least likely to win assistance in a bottomless ocean of poverty where only a few promising souls can be rescued. Mother Teresa cares for the destitute and dying. She and her sisters (the Missionaries of Charity) trip off through the slums in their blue and white saris each day to pick up emaciated bodies lying in the street and take them back to a shelter where they can die with a measure of dignity, assured of God's love, surrounded by gentle hands, looking up at a smiling human face.

Teresa's work does not follow the prescription of triage. It has no great economic impact or strategic value. It's a work of art; as Teresa would describe it, "a beautiful work for God." But her ministry has become one of the most forceful statements made in the twentieth century. Hard honor. Mother Teresa expresses it so well because she sees much more than disease-ridden, filthy bodies amid the refuse of Calcutta. She sees Jesus in disguise, the One who said, "Whatever you did for one of the least of these brothers of mine, you did for me."

She really does feel she is touching Christ when she caresses some nameless face brought in off the streets barely breathing. She accepts each day as a challenge to discover Jesus up close again in one of His many improbable disguises. She once wrote this prayer for herself:

> Dearest Lord, may I see you today and every day in the person of your sick, and, whilst nursing them, minister unto you.
> Though you hide yourself behind the unattractive disguise of the irritable, the exacting, the unreasonable, may I still recognize you, and say: "Jesus, my patient, how sweet it is to serve you."

THIS IS OUR HERITAGE of artists. We can learn from the way believers have tried to express the grace of Christ down through history. They leave us a gallery of canvases, some plain, some badly composed, some achingly beautiful. How can we build on this tradition? We have the challenge of fleshing out Christ's honor in our present world. We must always get our bearings and our inspiration from the hard honor given clear shape in the New Testament. But those who have gone before us also urge us on to express that eternal quality, to create from it something new that will be compelling for our contemporaries.

The Third Virtue

OPEN
ALLEGIANCE

11

AFRAID OF A PLACE
TO STAND

THE LEADERS of the Khmer Rouge looked out over Cambodian rice fields and felt a growing need to do something about the chronic poverty of their countrymen. Pockets of wealth among the merchants and officials in the capital city of Phnom Penh seemed to produce only decadence. Socialism was chosen as the obvious solution, but the Khmer Rouge went further, refining their communist doctrines into an urgent mandate for immediate change that they called "pure revolution."

In 1975 they began implementing their truth. The Khmer Rouge turned Cambodian society upside down. They emptied the capital and drove its inhabitants out to the countryside to work in communal farms. Everyone would be equal. No more exploitation. No more city decadence.

But the pure revolution required the sacrifice of those who couldn't be pressed quickly enough into the new mold, and there were many who erred against the Khmer Rouge program. Farms run by soldiers of the regime turned into killing fields where millions of uprooted men, women, and children starved or were executed. The new era of absolute equality dawned among vast pyramids of skulls. When news first leaked out about the number of casualties, it seemed preposterous. Most people couldn't fathom a tragedy so vast in the name of reform.

On the other side of Asia from Cambodia's horror, Iran's Shi'ite Moslems felt a growing need in the 1970s to somehow fight against the Western decadence that was tearing many of their countrymen from the faith of their fathers. Iran's powerful Shah had brought some measure of prosperity to the country, but his policies also produced unwanted side effects: increased alcoholism, drug abuse, prostitution, and a general turning away from God to materialism. Time for reform.

Led by the Ayatollah Khomeini, Muslim fundamentalists created a revolution in 1979, bringing the nation back to faith, truth, and morality. Iranians gathered in enthusiastic crowds around their new, charismatic, authoritative leader, and feverishly chanted slogans until they became an all-enveloping truth.

Iran made a stand against the tide of Western amorality, against evil. Its people began to believe in something. Tehran was cleaned up. No more addicted teenage girls roaming the streets. Far fewer drunk husbands carousing with other women on weekends. But the Ayatollah's moral revolution required the sacrifice of countless enemies. Summary trials and executions of nonconformists abounded in the early days. Intolerance came to be nourished as official doctrine.

The new morality required constant enforcement: Revolutionary Guards roaming the cities began checking up on women not covered from head to toe. An exposed lock of hair or rolled-up sleeve warranted a lecture or even arrest. Repeat offenders were beaten. One of the familiar sayings plastered on buildings in every city read, "Whoever fights against the truth shall be defeated." Truth had to be defended at all costs. Its enemies were everywhere. America, that old exporter of moral decay, became Satan. A troublesome neighbor like Iraq was transformed into the embodiment of evil, and Khomeini declared a holy war against it. Turbanned clergymen promoted martyrdom among teenage boys. These youth became fervent *basij*, volunteers for the endless war who were often asked in battle to form a human wave, moving ahead of regular soldiers to distract the enemy and clear the ground of mines.

Defending the pure faith required a fountain of blood. There was an inspirational reminder of that in the town of Mashhad. At its center stood a three-tiered fountain bubbling water dyed a deep red. Behind it loomed a portrait of the Ayatollah, and below him were photographs of his many loyal dead.

ACHING, YET AFRAID

These days it's no wonder we're gun-shy of those shouting for one truth and one faith and calling for absolute allegiance. Behind the people who take the strongest stands against evil, we seem to always see the shadow of the guillotine. Those willing to die for the truth are usually willing to kill for it, too. That's scary. We conclude that maybe it's better just to keep absolute truth out of the picture. Maybe we should scale down our allegiances to something more manageable.

What I feel. What I believe. What I like. These seem less dangerous objectives, and most of us have adopted them with relief and even a sense of self-righteousness. The circle of truth has constricted around the borders of the self. We won't talk loudly about right and wrong; we won't call for anyone's blood.

But sometimes the world aches for someone to take a stand and declare a great allegiance. Evil is still out there, and its victims multiply. At times our silence can seem painfully loud. There's an increasing tendency in public life to downplay tragedies in favor of preserving the flow of planned events.

Israeli athletes were murdered at Munich during the 1972 Olympics. What should we do in response to this live, televised outrage? After deliberating, those in charge decided the games must go on. To stop would be to acquiesce before terrorism.

A prize fighter's wife committed suicide in despair over her husband's career. He vowed to proceed with his upcoming bout and go into the ring for her—yes, for her. The fighter was applauded by sportswriters for going on in spite of his heartache.

Twelve people were trampled to death by a crowd shoving their way into Cincinnati's Riverfront Stadium for a concert by The Who. What should we do? Go on with the concert. Canceling it might incite the crowd to further violence.

These decisions aren't all bad, of course. Sometimes canceling an event does give in to evil. But the tide appears to be flowing in only one direction: Don't stop the action, don't interrupt. You begin to wonder if the loss is really counted, really absorbed. Have we become incapable of making statements? Don't we ever need to make a clear stand against evil, even if it's costly?

Almost all the Germans in the 1940s who passed by columns of starving, ragged, Jewish fellow countrymen marching off to death camps did not take a stand against Nazi authority. They would not ask questions. They averted their gaze from the hollow eyes and sunken cheeks, constricting the self and their allegiances to safe boundaries. This was not happening to them; it was not their responsibility.

Almost all American whites in the 1950s who passed by ramshackle schoolhouses where black people were forced to try to educate their children did not take a stand against the hallowed tradition of segregation. This was not happening to their children. Their well-defined circle of selfhood did not include those of another color.

People find it hard to make stands against evils that aren't happening to them, to oppose lies that don't sully their reputations. But declaring our allegiance to the truth, making a stand against evil, is essential in our world. We don't live in a garden where we can wander about picking any old flower and simply enjoy the fragrance of whatever we feel, whatever we choose to believe. Thorns are everywhere. Cruelty and human suffering abound. Our kids grow up in a sea of drugs. They can't just drift; they'll drown if they do. They have to resist at some point. Any businessman who's going to retain a sense of decency in a competitive marketplace has to damage his competitive position at some point by being honest.

This holds true in any field of work, from the televangelist tempted to stretch the truth in his fund-raising letter to the nurse who doesn't want to care for an AIDS patient. Stands against the tide are essential, not optional. They keep our heads above water. We have to declare some higher allegiance or evil will completely dominate us. Without making a stand, we're more amoebas than human beings.

When you get right down to it, it's frightening to think there's no truth on the horizon bigger than our individual selves. The self ends up absorbing all truth. We're constantly urged to "find your truth" and assured that ultimate answers and "god" are in some inner recess of the heart. It's all within you. I don't find that very comforting. In a world where truth has no separate existence, it's almost impossible to make courageous stands. How can one be expected to make sacrifices? There's nothing more important than me out there.

Yet most of the stands against evil we see in the world today aren't comforting either. Belligerent crowds chanting out their fanatical allegiances and revolutionaries devising some pure doctrine that justifies genocide turn truth into a bloodthirsty threat.

That's our dilemma. We need to give our allegiance to something bigger than ourselves, but we don't want to be swept up in it. We ache for a meaningful place to make a stand in the world, and we are afraid of finding it.

MOMENT OF TRUTH

Europe in the beginning of the sixteenth century badly needed someone to take a stand. But the very church that had unified society in the Middle Ages and served as its moral resource seemed to make a meaningful allegiance impossible. Christendom had been corrupted from the top down. By most accounts, negligence, ignorance, absenteeism, and sexual immorality were endemic to the clergy. They had become a privileged class wielding cosmic power over the laity. Warrior Pope Julius II's ventures had required a ghastly shedding of blood. His successor, Pope Leo X, earned this description from one historian: "Elegant and as indolent as a Persian cat. His chief preeminence lay in his ability to squander the resources of the Holy See on carnivals, war, gambling, and the chase."

The church under the Renaissance popes clenched the keys to the kingdom tightly, brandishing its power to excommunicate over the unruly, gullible masses. It dictated truth, jealously guarding its exclusive right to read and interpret the Scriptures. It amassed wealth, coming to rival the states of Europe in its temporal power.

Almost everyone acknowledged clerical abuses and the sorry state of religious life. Many voices raised the cry for reform, but no one could find the leverage to move a colossal religious power off its vested interests. The basic problem was that Rome profited immensely from the "mechanical religion" into which Christianity had degenerated.

Rome's corporate portfolio included a piece of Moses' burning bush, chains that had bound Paul, Saint Veronica's napkin with a portrait of Christ, and countless other hot properties translating into a great treasury of merit that could be drawn upon by the many visiting pilgrims. One of the coins paid to Judas for betraying Christ held great potential merit; it had been ruled that a visit to that relic alone could result in fourteen hundred years being taken off someone's sentence in Purgatory. Crawling up Pilate's Stairs, the Scala Sancta, on hands and knees while repeating a Pater Noster at each step could release a soul from limbo outright.

By the sixteenth century, the accumulated merit of the saints, available through such relics and rituals, had been quantified as indulgences. Procuring an indulgence meant the transfer of merit from the surplus fund to some needy sinner with a meager account.

In 1510, two monks were sent to Rome to consult with the Pope and settle a dispute that had arisen in their Augustinian order. One of the monks was named Martin Luther. He considered it a wonderful privilege to be able to visit the Eternal City. Here was a grand opportunity to appropriate the enormous spiritual benefits available, so Luther set out to celebrate Mass at sacred shrines, visit the catacombs and basilicas, venerate the bones of martyrs, pray at their shrines, and adore as many holy relics as possible.

But slowly this monk became disillusioned by the corruption he saw in the church. The Italian priests he met seemed almost flippant about their duties. He was shocked by stories of gross immorality among the clergy; some considered themselves virtuous because they confined their sexual exploits to women.

At that point, this lone monk in a vast city of holy places began to doubt. He wondered whether a sacred shrine or relic could actually convey merit. Luther was climbing up Pilate's stairs on his hands and knees, repeating the Lord's Prayer at every step and kissing each one, when suddenly, having arrived at the top, he raised himself and exclaimed, "Who knows whether it is so?"

Martin Luther had come up against the whole elaborate system of merit-earning that greased the wheels of the church, and he found it wanting. But his doubt was at first only a despairing thought: If these means of merit prescribed by the church couldn't really bestow grace, what hope was there?

In response to this moment of truth Luther could have dropped back into cynicism, exploiting the institution he no longer believed in, like so many of his contemporaries. Instead he continued to anguish through six-hour confessions, feverish good works, penitence, and mystical theology in search of some assurance of acceptance with the holy God. And he finally found it—after he was assigned to the chair of Bible at the University of Wittenberg. He began studying and lecturing on the book of Psalms and discovered many verses foreshadowing the life and death of the Redeemer. Luther's thoughts turned more and more to the Christ who takes on Himself our iniquity. Then he took on Paul's epistle to the Romans and there discovered the truth of justification by faith with all the excitement of a man beholding a new continent. The justice of God, which had always seemed a terrifying obstacle, now reshaped itself into "the just shall live by faith." "I grasped that the justice of God is that righteousness by which through grace and sheer mercy God justifies us through faith," Luther wrote. "Thereupon I felt myself to be reborn and to have gone through open doors into paradise. The whole of Scripture took on a new meaning."

A TIME TO SPEAK

For Luther, Paul's gospel threw a sharp light on the mechanical Christianity around him. One day an experienced indulgence vendor named Tetzel paraded into town, preceded by dignitaries, a cross emblazoned with the papal arms, and a bull of indulgence borne on gold-embroidered velvet cushion. Tetzel planted the cross in the marketplace and proclaimed that a special indulgence had been issued by his holiness the pope to defray the expense of rebuilding Saint Peter's basilica. Subscribers would enjoy a complete and perfect remission of all their sins.

The time had come to speak. Luther did so; on the eve of All Saints, he posted on the door of the Castle Church in Wittenberg a proposal to debate ninety-five theses. They proved to be of more than academic interest. The Augustinian professor's theses were surreptitiously translated from Latin into German, passed on to the press, and quickly became the hottest topic in Germany.

People had protested against financial exploitation like Tetzel's for over a century without much to show for it. But Luther was impelled to strike a more resounding blow. Carried along by the momentum of his new-found allegiance to justification by faith, he blasted indulgences as a blasphemy against the mercy of God, declared that the saints have no surplus of holy credit to bestow, and affirmed that Christ's "merits are freely available without the keys of the pope."

Pope Leo X heard of these dangerous views and quickly decided to "smother the fire before it should become a conflagration." He first exerted pressure on Luther's Augustinian order to have him censured. But at their triennial gathering in Heidelberg, the professor of Bible defended himself effectively.

His enemies boasted that he would burn within a month. But Luther didn't budge. This painfully sensitive monk who'd spent years groveling after deeper penance, continually begging his superiors for some additional burden of good deeds, had found a place to stand. Clinging to the rock of the gospel in order to save himself, he'd found, quite unexpectedly, enormous leverage. He discovered the strength to face down the whole medieval system of legalism.

While church authorities threatened, Luther was further radicalized by his studies. The Latin translation of Jesus' call to "repent" in Matthew 4:17 was "do penance." But Luther saw from Erasmus' Greek New Testament that the original had the sense of "be penitent," literally, "change your mind." This undercut the church's highly evolved sacrament of penitence.

Threatened with excommunication, something that always paralyzed medieval man with fear, Luther calmly replied, "Only God can sever spiritual communion. No creature can separate us from the love of Christ."

When a Dominican named Prierias issued an official written reply to Luther's views that emphasized the authority of the universal church, the reformer wrote back with words that would become his most telling protest: "You cite no Scripture. You give no reasons."

Next, Luther was summoned to appear before the papal legate, Cardinal Cajetan, in Augsburg at a session of the imperial diet, or legislative assembly. With the pope, emperor, and cardinal against him, Luther saw little chance of escaping the stake. He was not yet the champion of an aroused German nation against papal abuses, but merely a lone Augustinian who'd incriminated himself regarding heresy. But still he stood firm.

At the session, Cajetan urged Luther to recant and be reconciled to the church. Luther said he wished to be instructed regarding his errors. Cajetan replied that he'd denied the church's treasury of merit. After a bit of delicate maneuvering around the issue of what a certain papal bull had actually stated on the matter, Luther came out bluntly: He would not hold a papal statement on indulgences above the many "clear testimonies" of divine Scripture. The cardinal reminded the defendant that Scripture itself has to be interpreted, and the pope is the one authorized to do so for Christians. Luther retorted: "His Holiness abuses Scripture. I deny that he is above Scripture."

The next challenger who stepped forward was a professional disputant named John Eck, who arranged for a formal debate with Luther at the University of Leipzig. During the long and heated discussion Eck accused his opponent of "espousing the pestilent errors of John Hus," the Bohemian heretic burned at the stake. Luther took the opportunity to speak on behalf of an authoritative Word and human conscience: "No believing Christian can be coerced beyond holy writ. By divine law we are forbidden to believe anything which is not established by divine Scripture or manifested revelation."

Eck pressed Luther with an attack others had frequently repeated: "Are you the only one that knows anything? Except for you is all the church in error?" It is difficult for us in this secular age to understand how powerfully that argument must have struck the Augustinian professor. The church had been for him mother and conscience and truth. It made the world coherent. Luther was still profoundly devoted to it; he did not wish to be a schismatic. But he couldn't fall back among the countless other would-be reformers who'd become part of the exploitive, legalistic system. He couldn't forget his allegiance to those many clear testimonies from Scripture. No one had refuted them. And so he told Eck that he had to confess what he believed to be true, that he was willing to defend the truth with his blood, and that, after all, "God once spoke through the mouth of an ass."

In between debates and the complicated legal maneuvers that kept him ahead of the stake, Luther put together a thorough program of reform in an "Address to the German Nobility." He called for an end to clerical elitism: All believers should have the same legal rights. He objected to the pope's exclusive claim to interpret Scripture. Didn't the Bible promise that any layman could understand the mind of Christ? He wanted the papacy to curtail its vast income-generating machine and rediscover apostolic simplicity.

Again and again Luther contrasted the corruption and decadence of church leaders with the humble servanthood of Christ. Luther's call shook Europe out of its complacency. A great number of people finally sat up and took notice of the radically different ideal for the church apparent in God's Word. Those protecting their power, however, dug in their heels. Luther's books were publicly burned in

Rome, and a papal bull condemning him was printed, notarized, and disseminated.

Luther still stood firm, issuing his trademark reply: "This bull condemns me from its own word without any proof from Scripture."

'HERE I STAND'

The big showdown occurred before an imperial assembly at Worms. The setting is justly famous. Enthroned in pomp and splendor sat Charles, the Holy Roman Emperor, glorious symbol of all the medieval unities, culmination of a line of legendary Christian sovereigns going back to Charlemagne. Around him were representatives of papal power in their imposing robes. And before them all stood a former monk, a tin miner's son, with no shred of authority, but with a growing faith in the sufficiency of God's Word.

Luther did not come before his chief examiner, the archbishop of Trier, cockily. When first asked whether he would repudiate his writings, his reply was barely audible. But Luther's trepidation was due less to the august assembly than to his conviction that all present stood before Almighty God and must give answer to Him. Later, in a speech explaining the purpose behind his various published works, Luther found his voice. He spoke for the many in northern Europe who now struggled to reform the church fundamentally: "Universal complaints testify that by the laws of the popes the consciences of men are racked."

"No!" the emperor interposed.

Luther went on unruffled, "When Christ stood before Annas, he said, 'Produce witnesses.' If our Lord, who could not err, made this demand, why may not a worm like me ask to be convicted of error from the prophets and the Gospels? If I am shown my error, I will be the first to throw my books into the fire."

The archbishop asserted that Luther had no right to call into question "the most holy orthodox faith" confirmed by "sacred councils" and "so many famous men." Then he demanded, "Do you or do you not repudiate your books and the errors which they contain?"

Asked to choose between what appeared to be certain death and a betrayal of what he saw as the plain, repeated teaching of Scripture, Luther chose the latter: "Unless I am convicted by Scripture and plain reason—I do not accept the authority of popes and councils... my conscience is captive to the Word of God.... Here I stand, I cannot do otherwise."

Here is a picture to remember. Before the pageantry and ceremony of medieval authority, one man stood as an iron wedge lifting it off dead center—a plain, thick-featured wedge driven against a colossus that wielded nonnegotiable decree and inquisition. He declared his unconditional allegiance, and Christendom tumbled over into Reformation. Eventually the church itself was moved to recognize that forgiveness had become a growth industry and abuses of clerical privilege scandalous to the laity. Partly as a result, church leaders initiated the Counter Reformation.

LUTHER WAS NOT a particularly elegant artist of the spirit. It's his persistence against the odds that makes the picture striking. Out of the monolithic stone of medieval authority he carved out a place for an individual believer enlightened by God's Word. He kept presenting the truth of the gospel against all that would distort it, until finally its inherent authority broke through.

≡ • ≡ • ≡ • ≡ • ≡ • ≡ • ≡

12

INTO THE CLUTCHES
OF THE WORD

MARTIN LUTHER SUGGESTS TO US that God's Word is where we can make a meaningful stand against evil. His reformation, at least at first, was based on allegiance to the moral authority of Scripture, not human decrees backed by the sword. In the Word we find a Truth big enough and important enough to overshadow that omnivorous self.

'THIS IS IT'

The Bible compels. Even people who run into the Word out of the blue are often captured by the way it speaks with authority. I discovered this while teaching Bible classes in Japan. Most of the college students and young professionals in our English school had no reference points for the God Who is There. Transcendence had to be carved out of a pure-blind secular mindset. Yet when they did wander into Bible classes to practice English, many were caught by the Word. Its truths had an unexpectedly adhesive power, and they couldn't easily shake off its call to goodness. I saw totally unprepped, only slightly interested individuals fall into the clutches of this authority. And those who at length did willfully extricate themselves often found it quite difficult to live outside its verities, even though they'd done so rather comfortably before.

The Word packs quite a punch. Sometimes its big, all-inclusive Truth hits people instantly. A Japanese youth walked into an evangelistic meeting, heard Christ's words—"A new commandment I give you: Love one another. As I have loved you, so you must love one another"—and immediately made a life-changing commitment: "This is it, this is everything I've been looking for."

A young Jewish intellectual sat reading a New Testament for the first time, wedged among chickens, turkeys, babies, and singing passengers in steerage aboard a ship plying the Mediterranean. He got caught up in the drama of Jesus clashing with the Pharisees over a woman caught in adultery. His pulse quickened as they pushed Jesus up against the wall with the law, demanding this woman's death. For a moment Arthur Katz paused, wondering what Jesus could possibly say in return, and then read the words, "Let him without sin cast the first stone." Katz gasped: "A sword had been plunged deep into my being. It was numbing, shocking, yet thrilling because the answer was so utterly perfect....It cut across every major issue I had ever anguished upon in my life....I knew that what I had read transcended human knowledge and comprehension. It had to be Divine."

The Word strikes deep because it is God speaking, not just nice religious literature. It presents itself as God-breathed, inspired revelation, the will of God. It comes to us from outside, from an absolute perspective. That's why it speaks with authority.

The Word is compelling force; events are said to occur in order that it may be fulfilled; history is ushered into shape before it. Scripture, the "living and active" Word, has to happen. It is not a suggestion, an option, a possible scenario. It is divine necessity penetrating the artless, formless world. It will speak, or the very rocks cry out.

If we relate honestly to this kind of compelling Word, we are inspired to something called open allegiance. We want to open ourselves completely before its claims; we want God's voice echoing in our innermost selves. We give the Word our unconditional loyalty— willing to listen to whatever it says and go wherever it clearly directs. Open allegiance presents a whole human being to the whole Word.

However, if we present only a piece of ourselves to the Word or listen only to an agreeable portion of it, we're likely to fall into the misfortune of closed allegiance. We select some pet point of view and cling tightly to it as the whole. We close off other perspectives in the Word and build detours around them. Closed allegiance attempts to finalize rather than broaden God's voice.

The book of Revelation begins with a word of blessing to all who read its words and take them to heart, and it ends with a stern warning to those who would delete any of its passages. The Word is not to be played with; it exists to speak to us, not we to it.

A manipulatable Word is no help at all in a world aching for a meaningful allegiance. If we're standing over it, declaring what may be taken seriously and what ignored, the omnivorous self has just found one more victim to absorb. Nothing's happened to move us. We simply remain safe in our sphere of closed allegiance. Paul warned Timothy about such a state in which people can no longer stomach "sound doctrine" and gather around likable teachers who tickle their ears with undemanding fables.

But God's Word arrives on the scene as (to reapply Barth's phrase) the Wholly Other. When presenting the gospel, Paul insisted: "I did not receive it from any man, nor was I taught it; rather, I received it by revelation from Jesus Christ." Peter broadened the point: "For it was not through any human whim that men prophesied of old; men they were, but, impelled by the Holy Spirit, they spoke the words of God." The prophets passed on messages that sometimes only future generations would comprehend, profound truths into which "even angels long to look."

To the Rescue

Open allegiance expresses the fact that Scripture is bigger than I am; I cannot contain it, exhaust it, or mediate its message. In Scripture, the self at last runs up against something that can't honestly be consumed, an authority beyond its reach that names the demons and labels the goods. "All Scripture is God-breathed and is useful for teaching, rebuking, correcting and training in righteousness." That transcendent Word comes close to correct and reprove. It is quite directive in a world of fragmented and chaotic impulses, giving us hard-nosed principles (law) and mystical secrets (spirit) to create something meaningful out of randomness. Coherence doesn't form around us by itself. The law of entropy is at work; energy decreases, disorder increases in the moral sphere as well as the physical. We don't naturally evolve toward holiness; we stumble into habits. And so the Word must actively rescue us in our entropy.

Open allegiance accepts the often pointed direction of Scripture. It is willing to have the Word come in and upset things, even favorite habits or cherished notions. Open allegiance listens when the Word becomes a sword of the Spirit battling against evil, even when the blows fall close to home, and that's why it can take a stand in the world.

The assumption underlying the ideal of taking a stand is this: The world in general isn't sailing toward nirvana but careening off course. The whole moral order is out of whack. Therefore, to exist meaningfully on this planet is to make protest. Here is where the impetus of the Word is essential. It speaks from outside the self-supporting echo of our culture; it is an uncompromisingly moral voice above us.

Secular points of view have to more or less go with the flow. It's hard to escape that flow when talking of morals if we're making up the rules as we go along. In fact, the basic idea of right and wrong apart from what society thinks doesn't make much sense without an external authority. The Word helps us buck the tide.

Scripture forces people against the issues that matter most; it pushes people one way or another. We don't need to uncover who's out and who's in or track down "enemies of the truth." Jesus once told a group of Pharisees trying to corner Him with their sons-of-Abraham credentials that they were sons of someone else, trying to kill him because "you have no room for my word," and refusing to believe Him precisely because He was telling the truth. They shied away from the light because their deeds were evil. The prophet Zechariah once lamented those who had to make their hearts "hard as flint" in order not to absorb the oracles of the Lord Almighty. Being either within or without the Word is no casual matter; it's a life-and-death issue, a double-edged sword cutting to the marrow, "to dividing soul and spirit," where we make moral choices affecting our destiny.

The Truth is not quite as amiable a guest as the contemporary mood suggests. It does not step politely around all our cherished furniture and sit down only where directed. When taken to heart as the Word of God it can wreak havoc, overturning our pet theories, piercing our best defenses. The Word has the authority to arrest us even in the privacy of our own "sincere beliefs" and shove us out into that light the Pharisees found so appalling.

This unique authority from above has deep roots in the earth. It is not a disembodied, purely mystical voice. It's about things seen and heard and touched here; it emphasizes eye-witnessed events. God not only imparted the inspiration of ideas, but He also inspired with His actions. God acted, and men took notes. The Bible is intertwined with real empires, geographical details, biographical facts, personal encounters. That's another reason the Word enables us to make a stand. It's not just a private, psychological truth, something that affects only me. It's a truth that's there, imbedded in the facts of history and in the physics of the world. It's a truth about what happened, what's really there, what's really important, and what's going to happen to the things that are important and the things that aren't. Meaningful truth has got to stand up to the world's falling apart. Some "truths" are going to melt away in intense, apocalyptic heat, and others are going to endure for eternity.

SOLID GROUND

Few of us are compelled to stake our lives on likes and dislikes. Great stands against evil are not inspired by personal preferences. But subjective truth always comes down to that: what I feel, what I like. Objective truth, however, does offer us a worthwhile allegiance, some solid ground to stand on: Jesus born during the reign of Caesar

Tiberius in the town of Bethlehem, touring Nazareth, Bethesda, Capernaum, Jerusalem; crucified under Pontius Pilate; resurrected, according to skeptics who placed their hands on His wounds—this is how the Word creates a definite place for us.

Open allegiance remains pliant before objective facts and propositions; our own opinions are kept relative to the authority of the Word. Closed allegiance hardens around whatever subjective "facts" it discovers; the Word is kept relative to one's absolute opinions.

Open allegiance responds to God's Word as a rock-steady point of reference that will never betray us. "The grass withers and the flowers fall, but the word of our God stands forever." It is *the* place to stand, no shifting, no illusions. Reliability comes from being accurate almost all the time; authority comes from being accurate all the time, and from being always relevant. Theories rise and fall, statistics play games with each other, scientific studies point this way and then that —they are all useful, yet limited. But the Word is unlimited in its usefulness, a deep well where we can always draw up more of that elusive, life-giving substance called Truth.

Let's try to define it. Truth in general involves the facts in general and faithfulness to the facts, being ever-ready to tip our hats to reality instead of swerving around it or dressing it up or down. Truth capitalized involves the most important facts, faithfulness to the facts that are eternally true. This is what the Word is about. Jesus, when praying to the Father, said, "Your Word is truth." Here we have , something that is factual all the time in every place, something that stands above the flux.

People who accept such a Truth best express it with open allegiance, investing their lives in its wholeness. There *is* something transcendent to express; more than just the details, the moment, the passing fad, the perimeters of this particular place, the bent of this particular age. Something stands forever, its principles on the mark despite all other moving targets.

The Word's special kind of veracity is the antithesis of the crowd chanting slogans and claiming power with the guillotine. At first it may seem just another scary truth that people can exploit to carry out some horrifyingly "pure revolution." But a close look at the Word itself gives us a very different picture of authority.

We start with the prophets. The dominant picture they present is naked, moral authority cast against the corruptions of Israel's king or priest or people. They were lone, often lonely voices crying out in an idolatrous darkness. Usually they were ignored or censured. Some were beaten, thrown into pits, or sawn asunder. The great majority possessed no official position, no legal or military leverage, nothing except an earnest "Thus saith the Lord." That was how they made a stand and hoped to change society.

When we come to Christ the picture crystallizes. Christ above all "taught as one who had authority." How? By lining up a squadron of Roman soldiers behind Him? By negotiating for a Sanhedrin endorsement? No. By piercing people's hearts with the Truth. His words compelled. He is the quintessential Word and the quintessential reformer, the meek-looking rabbi utterly without legal or political pull who swayed the multitudes with His powerful Word.

The apostles, enlivened with Jesus' Spirit, carried on that tradition. Paul was careful even to refrain from using eloquent oratory to manipulate his hearers. He believed he was called to present the gospel "not with words of human wisdom, lest the cross of Christ be emptied of its power." He and all his colleagues made a stand before Jew and pagan, before influential priest and autocratic Roman ruler, wielding only one thing: the gospel. No other defense, no other support, no other authority. They simply sought to win people to the Word.

Any other kind of authority betrays the real one. The minute people take up the sword or organize an inquisition to enforce Truth, they deny the authority of the Word. They assert that human beings must be compelled by some other means, and they cut themselves off from the voice of prophet, apostle, and Christ. This is closed allegiance—fastening on some piece of the Word as a club instead of encouraging others to open up before it.

GOD'S IDEAL IN OUR HANDS

The Word of God can certainly be misused. Its words can be quoted for all manner of ends. People have twisted it into an instrument of abuse all through history. So some suggest that we water down its authority a bit to make it a less potent weapon. But not taking its authority seriously is precisely the problem. Those wielding it as a club are not standing under it. They aren't spoken to by the whole as much as yelling through its disjointed pieces. They close tight around some point that the self takes a fancy to, instead of opening up to the Voice that pierces to the marrow. Closed allegiance is the problem.

Open allegiance comes from standing under the Word as well as on it. Under the Word we can lift up an authoritative voice against evil, but we also make sure it is the authentic voice of Scripture that persuades, and not some human pressure. We stand best on the Word's authority by stripping all our props away and relying exclusively on the power inherent in the Word.

Still, we have to admit that an authoritative Word does intimidate some people who see it as a restriction on life rather than a sure guide to life's essential form. And authority, divine or otherwise, often elicits the most opposition from the most creative. Art and authority seem to occupy two belligerent ends of a spectrum; one can increase only at the expense of the other.

That's probably true of the kind of authority most of us are acquainted with, the kind that has to deal with a great many uncapitalized truths, details, procedures, styles, and spheres of interest. The old wineskins of tradition only painfully make room for the new wine of the Spirit. But dealing with big Truth is what all artists have traditionally been about. The struggle of the artist has been to give expression to some form, some reality that he sees as most important.

The authority of the Word is primarily creative. After all, the entire created order in all its variety came about through "the word of God." In Christ's parable of the four soils, the Word planted in receptive hearts is capable of bearing fruit a hundredfold. When Paul was cut off from his field of work in a Roman dungeon he took comfort in the fact that "the word of God is not imprisoned." It was still out there in Asia Minor where he had left it, performing feats and overcoming adversaries. It still created new life, though the apostle's was coming to an end.

That's another reason Scripture can inspire open allegiance: It's the creative Word of God within which people grow and expand. Open allegiance keeps making discoveries in the riches of the Word; it keeps seeking to change. Closed allegiance, on the other hand, tends to see the Word as information to conquer. You finalize on the truth you see in it and then proceed to dig in and defend your position.

Open allegiance does see absolute truths in Scripture, but it also sees the challenge of applying them, expanding on them, expressing them in new ways. The Word must be continually spoken, its essential form continually fleshed out.

Scriptural Truth inspires profound expression. It tells us about the values that go deep. Creativity doesn't thrive in a vacuum; it gravitates toward a form; it wants to express something important, meaningful. The French classicist painter Ingres was moved to produce his masterful works at least in part by a belief that there is only one art "which has as its foundation the beautiful, which is eternal and natural." Robert Frost saw form as a healthy challenge; he once said that writing poetry without reference to rhyme or meter would be like playing tennis without a net. He couldn't see the point to it when there was good, honest prose around. Even a wild mystic like William Blake battling against the hold that the classical style of Joshua Reynolds had on England, labored to express "Ideal Beauty," "Innate Ideas in Every Man."

American sculptor Horatio Greenough set himself to capture the "majesty of the essential instead of the trappings of pretension" and spoke of it as a religious quest: "We shall have grasped with tiny hands the standard of Christ, and borne it into the academy, when we shall call upon the architect, and sculptor, and painter to seek to be perfect even as our Father is perfect."

This is not the sum of art, of course. But a long and highly fertile tradition in art demonstrates that absolutes, Truth, ideal authority, and creative achievements can be synergistic. Ideals move people to create, and the Word is God's ideal made tangible in our hands.

The Word has incited benign revolutions all through history. It is an agent for change, serving as a continual source of spiritual life in the midst of inertia and entropy. The living and active sword pierces to the marrow. Much maligned, sometimes burned, often neglected, misunderstood, misused—it's still there, speaking with a voice of authority. Those who truly hear it well want to give it expression.

FUMBLING THE TRUTH

Scripture itself provides its own illuminating epic about open allegiance to the Truth and making a meaningful statement in the world.

The patriarchs fumbled their way toward making a stand in the wildness of Canaan. Though caught up in the adventure of following after this high-minded, communicative Yahweh, the God of heaven, they still retained an adolescent penchant for wandering off course. It took them a while to learn the value of faithfulness under fire.

Abram choked while waiting out a famine in Egypt. He was sure his hosts would kill him to get his beautiful wife, Sarai, so he asked her to say she was his sister. Maybe he could protect her better that way, Abram rationalized. The rookie patriarch wasn't yet ready to take a stand on truth and let Yahweh take care of the consequences.

Pharaoh did take a fancy to Sarai, but when he found out Abram had deceived him he was deeply offended and sent the whole clan packing. Abram's cowardice brought reproach on the name of God.

After God renamed him Abraham (and Sarai became Sarah), he choked again while staying in Gerar with King Abimelech, telling him the same lie about his wife being his sister. The woman was actually his half-sister, but he neglected to come out with that little detail about their marriage. The patriarch still couldn't stand with both feet on the truth. Abimelech brought Sarah into his harem, and God had to intervene, telling the king in a dream he was about to take another man's wife. Abraham again slinked off from a near disaster.

His son Isaac took up the habit. He told Philistine neighbors that his beautiful wife, Rebekah, was his sister, afraid they might kill him on account of her. But those neighbors proved more upright than he. When the Philistine king found out Rebekah's marital status, he ordered that no one touch the woman on pain of death.

The next generation fell into the same mishandling of the truth. When Isaac was sick, almost blind, and about to die, his son Jacob impersonated brother Esau in order to receive the birthright blessing. After the deception was discovered, the family fell apart.

Taking a stand on the truth under pressure did not come easy to the founders of God's holy nation. But one man finally did it, with wonderful results. Betrayed by his own brothers, sold as a slave, separated from his beloved father, isolated in an alien culture, a youthful Joseph made a courageous stand. He refused to take the easy way up the ladder by sleeping with the boss's amorous wife. Wrong was still wrong, even in a world where no one had heard of Yahweh. His allegiance to principle remained the same.

Joseph stood upright even in the dungeon where his refusal of the woman's advances landed him. He served cheerfully, and when the chance finally came to get out of jail and into power on the strength of his gift of prophetic knowledge, Joseph still stood with both feet on the truth. He made plain to Pharaoh that it wasn't his own store of knowledge that enabled him to interpret the monarch's dream and peer into the future, but a revelation from the God who sees and knows all.

Joseph's loyalty under fire to God's truth ended up saving most of the world in general and the Hebrew clan in particular from starvation during a long famine. Yahweh's name was honored before the heathen.

A COURAGEOUS FEW

During subsequent centuries, when the nation of Israel hewed out a place for itself in Canaan, became a monarchy, prospered, divided, was reformed, and then decayed, one conflict dominated the history: the struggle against idolatry. It was always Yahweh against the idols of Israel's contemporaries, the truth about a God who rules over all in the heavens versus countless compromised editions, deities that pictured only pieces of God that one could manipulate and distort according to need.

Fertility cults majoring in sex, violence, local protection, and good crops proved to be strong competition for the God of atonement symbols and ten commandments. Prophets came on the scene to campaign on behalf of the truth, the whole truth, and nothing but the truth. Their "Thus saith the Lord" stood against every idolatrous rite. Amid the downward flow of Israel's moral life constantly

tripped up by those "high places" and altars to Baal, a few men
made courageous stands.

The prophet Elijah faced down majority opinion on the top of
Mount Carmel. At the time, the whole country seemed to be falling
down before Baal; his false prophets held all the political power
under Queen Jezebel. But the truth hadn't changed. Jehovah was still
the only One really up there in heaven who could speak. And Elijah
made His voice graphically inescapable to the crowds that had sold
out. He asked that fire come down from Jehovah and consume the
sacrifice drenched with water, and it did.

Prophets had to stand against the tide. They had to make statements about truth in the midst of loud choruses to the contrary.

In the third year of his reign, godly King Jehoshaphat of Judah
ventured north on a visit to morally dangerous ground and the
palace of King Ahab of Israel. Ahab had "sold himself to do evil in
the eyes of the Lord, urged on by Jezebel his wife." But more recently, in response to the gruesome death of the evil queen and some
pointed words from the prophet Elijah, he'd humbled himself before
God in sackcloth and earned a temporary reprieve. Jehoshaphat
probably wanted to see if Ahab had really been converted.

As the two kings talked, Ahab brought up the subject of Ramoth
Gilead, an Israelite city that had been taken by the king of Aram. He
proposed that the two join forces and recapture the town.
Jehoshaphat declared himself and his forces at Ahab's service, but he
suggested that they first "seek counsel of the Lord."

Ahab happened to have four hundred in-house prophets to call
on. They were ushered in and asked, "Shall I go to war against
Ramoth Gilead, or shall I refrain?"

The men responded unanimously, "Go…for the Lord will give it
into the king's hand."

Jehoshaphat was a bit suspicious of this prophecy dished out so
quickly from eager-eyed faces. How had Ahab, a recent convert from
years of Baal worship, managed to surround himself with so many
spokesmen for Jehovah? They all looked over-programmed.

The king of Judah wanted a real voice speaking real truth from
the real God. He asked, "Is there not a prophet of the Lord here
whom we can inquire of?"

Ahab groaned and replied that there was one man who claimed
the right credentials, but he had a very negative attitude. Micaiah,
son of Imlah, had never said one good thing about him.

Jehoshaphat thought the man should be summoned anyway, and
Ahab consented. While Micaiah was on his way, the four hundred

hired voices tried to be more convincing and worked themselves into a frenzy of positive reinforcement. "Attack Ramoth Gilead and be victorious," they shouted. One put on a pair of iron horns, danced around, and declared, "With these you will gore the Arameans until they are destroyed."

Meanwhile, the messenger who was sent for God's prophet gave him a pointed word of advice: "Look, as one man the other prophets are predicting success for the king. Let your word agree with theirs, and speak favorably." But Micaiah would not agree that truth can be established by acclamation. He looked the messenger square in the eye and said, "I can tell him only what the Lord tells me."

The two arrived on the scene, and Micaiah stood before the monarchs in their royal robes. Ahab turned wearily toward God's prophet and asked, "Micaiah, shall we go to war…or shall I refrain?"

Micaiah decided to test the man a bit. Mocking the other fervent prophets, he declared, "Attack and be victorious for the Lord will give it into the king's hand." Micaiah was saying in effect, "Do you *really* want to know?"

In the presence of his more upright colleague Jehoshaphat, Ahab maintained that he had always wanted the facts straight: "How many times must I make you swear to tell me nothing but the truth in the name of the Lord?"

So Micaiah gave it to him with both barrels: "I saw all Israel scattered on the hills like sheep without a shepherd." Ahab's resolve to hear the truth collapsed. He turned to Jehoshaphat with a didn't-I-tell-you look and complained: there was that negative attitude again.

But Micaiah kept going. Before the hundreds of disapproving prophets he told Ahab that they had become lying spirits leading him toward disaster. Their head man slapped Micaiah, but he stood firm. In the end, Ahab sent God's prophet to prison and stubbornly marched off to the predicted disaster.

Prophets stood against the tide, and sometimes even kings listened. The bright spots in Judah's history—Asa, Jehoshaphat, Joash, Hezekiah, Josiah—took stands on the basis of God's truth, the Word, the covenant, and tried to turn back the tide.

Josiah is a particularly illuminating example. Arriving on the scene when Judah was deep in decline, he decided to have Jerusalem's neglected temple repaired. While cleaning up materials that had accumulated on the premises, a priest named Hilkiah discovered the Book of the Law. It contained the old covenant, the moral transaction between Jehovah and His people, that created this unique entity called Israel.

Josiah had a scribe read the book to him. He listened to God's expectations for His people spelled out and heard the litany of blessings and cursings that finalized the covenant. The Word hit home. Its authority had not changed. Josiah felt anguish over the awful distance his people had come from their noble origins, and he felt the hot breath of judgment hovering over them. The king ripped his royal robes apart and wept as one who mourns a death. Afterward he sought out prophetic guidance.

Josiah took a stand. He initiated reforms, removed idols, reinstituted the Passover, and personally led the citizens of Jerusalem to make a commitment to "perform the words of the covenant written in this book."

SPEAK OR DIE

For the prophet Jeremiah, the Word was something he found and consumed. It became "a joy and the delight of my heart." But the Word was also a fire burning in his belly that would not let him rest. It was a strain holding it in; Jeremiah had to speak or die. And when he did speak, he made the loneliest, most courageous stand in the Old Testament. Jeremiah told his people they were resolutely heading toward oblivion, pursuing emptiness and becoming empty. He informed the good citizens of Judah that iniquity is a stain that can't be brushed away, and he grew more unpopular with each livid oracle he delivered. Corrupt priests and gutless kings tried to silence his disturbing voice on several occasions. But nothing could compromise the truth that propelled this man against the tide.

Jeremiah's irrepressible moral voice and Judah's decadence came to a head during Nebuchadnezzar's siege of Jerusalem, when his overwhelmingly superior forces threatened the city with destruction. Those prophets-for-hire were still mouthing their cheap good news: God would surely rescue His people and destroy Babylon. But Jeremiah had to lay out the cold truth from his Lord: "See, I am setting before you the way of life and the way of death. Whoever stays in this city will die by the sword, famine or plague. But whoever goes out and surrenders to the Babylonians who are besieging you will live; he will escape with his life."

To the Jews, the chosen people of God, those could only be the words of a traitor. Jeremiah must be palming shekels from Nebuchadnezzar. A prophet of Jehovah urging abandonment of the holy city? Impossible.

Persecution intensified, pressure heated up. But Jeremiah could not change the message. He even predicted that the temple would be as thoroughly destroyed as Israel's desolate Shiloh. The sanctity of the building could not somehow excuse the willful lack of holiness among those worshiping in it. This outraged the priests. Their temple was sacred, period, no matter what corruptions might slip into its courts. To surrender it to heathen hands seemed sheer blasphemy.

Jeremiah was threatened, imprisoned, thrown into a cistern, mocked, and treated as a traitor, but that didn't change his allegiance to the facts. The fire burned on. This prophet shows us not only great courage in his single-handed campaign for the truth, but also the terrible anguish of a sensitive man who is misunderstood and isolated. There's nothing glamorous about his stand. It was an exceedingly difficult position to take, but the truth gave him no alternative.

CLOSE TO FLAMES... AND CLOSE TO GOD

If Jeremiah's life shows open allegiance within a tragedy (pleading to the end with Judean refugees wandering off course toward Egypt), a prophet named Daniel gives us a more hopeful picture. He took a stand in the courts of the conqueror, Nebuchadnezzar, and it started out with something that might appear trivial. Daniel and three Hebrew companions had been selected for training in the king's personal service. As the new elite selected to govern Nebuchadnezzar's vast empire, they were fed from the king's table. Quite a privilege for exiled captives. But Daniel realized he could not eat this and obey the Hebrew dietary laws contained in the Word.

So Daniel took a stand by proposing a test. He told the reluctant steward: Let us eat our kosher food for ten days and then compare us to the other young men who are eating the king's morsels. Daniel didn't whine apologetically that he had to follow certain rules peculiar to his religion. He offered to demonstrate that God's way was best; it would stand up to the test.

In this first comparative dietary study, Daniel and friends did look healthier after ten days. Permission granted.

This faithfulness in the details of their religion led to faithfulness when the big test came—out on the plain of Dura, with thousands of emissaries from around the empire bowing down on cue to the statue of gold that Nebuchadnezzar had erected. Shadrach, Meshach, and Abednego could not agree with the majority. This personification of Babylon lifted high above them was not the kingdom to which they were looking forward. It was not the rock that would become a holy mountain and fill up the whole world. They could not bow down to this substitute.

Nebuchadnezzar's kind but firm words of advice didn't move them. The sight of blazing furnaces waiting to receive the irreverent didn't move them. Not even the flames up close and personal shook their resolve to keep standing when everyone else bowed to the lie.

This time tragedy gave way to a glorious deliverance. The three Hebrew youths stood upright in the furnace, just as they had before the statue of gold, and God came close.

The Old Testament story of Israel's stumbling over and over before idols manages to end on this triumphant note of three men ramrod straight no matter what the consequences. And it yields to God's great stand in Galilee. The long line of men and women expressing allegiance to the Word against the tide came to a climax in the Word Himself standing among us. The Word was made tangible, lived out at last in all its fullness.

SOMETHING GREATER

Jesus was the Word of God made flesh, its perfect embodiment. He magnified the law as a basis for artful goodness and contrasted it to a constrictive human tradition—a closed type of allegiance antithetical to His religion of excelling in the spirit of the law.

What's the law all about? Loving God with all your being, and your neighbor as yourself. No intricate ethical dilemmas here; the emphasis is on values that can take you a long way above the law. He understood primary principles, and He exposed whatever contradicted those values.

Jesus condensed the Word to its essentials, then expanded those essentials to something bigger and greater than the religious tradition around Him could encompass. The Word had been withered into a multiplicity of derivative details. Jesus brought it back to its original vitality.

Love, the abstraction, became the healing of lepers, care for the poor, a welcome for outcasts, deliverance from demons. The Word did things no one had ever seen before. A man born blind received his sight. Lazarus exited his own tomb, hale and hearty.

The temple stood for something as a house of prayer. But merchants and money changers had made it into a lie. The truth of the welcome God gives to sinners who come for mercy had been terribly distorted. Here Jesus acted most directly and violently against evil. With his bare hands He would force the temple to speak with an authentic voice. The exploiters fled and the needy returned, led by children's praises.

Jesus spelled out His open allegiance to the Word, all the while spied upon, interrogated, harassed, and criticized by the tradition that had usurped the truth. Finally Christ's enemies would test His allegiance to the limit on Golgotha by means of the horrors of crucifixion. There He made the most important statement of all time, welcoming all comers into the living Word until the end, creating a place where the weakest and most misguided can stand securely and become strong.

13

A WITHERED HAND
IN THE SYNAGOGUE

THE NARRATIVE of patriarch and prophet leaning hard on a Truth bigger than themselves leads us into New Testament teaching, where this matter of declaring our allegiance by taking a stand is nailed down. Paul declared: "We can do nothing against the truth, but only for the truth." His statement expresses both confidence in the ultimate sovereignty of God's realities and a resolve never to betray them. Believers are urged to cling to the Word, to loyally confess the faith, to be faithful until death. We are to stand fast in the "true grace of God," "stand firm and hold to the teachings," "stand firm in all the will of God," "stand firm in the faith." Paul told the Thessalonians that their valor meant everything to him: "For now we really live, since you are standing firm in the Lord."

Taking a stand matters, but this allegiance is not an end in itself. The place where we stand is what gives it value. We stand in God, in His will, His teachings, His grace. It's His revelation of Himself that gives us a meaningful statement to make in the world. We find a Truth that will stay put, and so *we* are enabled to stay put.

In the epistles, we also begin to see the essential components of standing firm in allegiance—how it works, what it produces. First, when we stand on the authority of God's Word, we automatically avoid standing in a lot of foolish places. Just as with light humility and hard honor, open allegiance clears away a lot of life's clutter. If we shout about what the Word typically shouts about and emphasize what it characteristically emphasizes, we won't get sidetracked into making big stands on little issues. There are a great many noisy battles that turn out to be mostly smoke when examined with a good dose of the Word, a great many battlegrounds that turn into mirages.

Those who maintain an open allegiance must be diligent work-men "handling accurately the word of truth." The Word is not a blunt instrument that we may grab most anywhere and use to pound against "error." It is a finely crafted tool, cutting more deeply than the sharpest sword, piercing and penetrating to do what nothing else can: "It judges the thoughts and attitudes of the heart."

The Word is powerful because it helps us get to the core of things. Surgically precise in its principles, it lays bare everything before it as it separates the benign from the malignant. The Word shows us what's vital, what's worth taking a stand on.

GOLD VERSUS STRAW

Gathered on this Sabbath day in a Galilean synagogue, the scribes and Pharisees kept glancing from the rabbi, draped in customary prayer shawl and commenting on Scripture, to a man with a withered hand seated in front. They were hoping Jesus of Nazareth, the itinerant teacher, would incriminate Himself before the law right there while attempting to explain it to them.

These men had caught Jesus' disciples in a transgression on the previous Sabbath. The twelve had been passing through a grainfield and, being hungry, plucked some stalks, rubbed the heads of wheat in their palms, and ate the grain. Technically this could be considered harvesting and thus an act of labor on the Sabbath. When the spying scribes objected, Jesus had replied, "The Sabbath was made for man, not man for the Sabbath."

To them this didn't seem at all like an explanation, and they determined to convict this rival teacher as a Sabbath-breaker. So they made sure a prime candidate for healing was seated prominently in the synagogue as Jesus spoke. Healing, in their minds, was also labor and thus was prohibited on the Sabbath.

After rolling up the scroll and putting it away, Jesus, sure enough, looked at the man with a shriveled hand and asked him to come and stand in front of everyone. Then He hurled His challenge at the heart of the legalistic religion that was choking the life out of His people. He stared at the Pharisees and asked angrily, "Which is lawful on the Sabbath: to do good or to do evil, to save life or to kill?"

Jesus' adversaries could not reply; they weren't prepared to deal with big principles, only to uphold the elaborate defenses they'd built around their religious territory. Jesus seemed to be reading their thoughts. Already they were pondering how to eliminate this uncontrolled, charismatic figure—and here He was about to save life from decay. "To save life or to kill?" For a moment they felt nailed to the wall. When Jesus asked the man to stretch out his arm and restored it to health, they could say nothing in rebuttal to the awed congregation.

Jesus took a stand. His acts spotlighted a religion of compassion and rebuked a religion of petty legalism. He demonstrated that the whole convoluted structure of regulations guarded by the Jewish elite stood in opposition to basic human and divine values. Simple acts of charity had been walled out of the Sabbath; what could be more ludicrous?

Jesus' stand was important because it embodied a vital principle: the priority of loving people. That's more important than religious conventions. Open allegiance to the Word points to what matters more. It must possess a degree of discernment — eyes trained to find that hidden treasure and the pearl of great price in the rough. By continual exposure to the "solid food" of the Word, those aiming for open allegiance "have trained themselves to distinguish good from evil." By not allowing themselves to be led astray from the primary values of Scripture, with "sincere and pure devotion to Christ" they are able to tell the difference between doctrinal edifices built of gold, silver, and costly stones, and those made of wood, hay and stray.

HOW TO STAND

Paul took a definite stand in the first century, one that is contentiously visible in several of his epistles. He championed the gospel of grace against all comers, giving a precise, theological shape to the revolution that Jesus had begun. There were quite a few people around the early believers who would have gutted the gospel— counterrevolutionaries, if you please, who wanted to keep certain Jewish traditions as a kind of security blanket. Circumcision, holy days and ceremonies assured them they were the chosen. Paul consistently rejected these external symbols of the old covenant, not because they were immoral, but because they were pointing people to the wrong kind of assurance. The Atonement of Christ had to be the center. Nothing must occupy its place. If the foundation stone of salvation by grace through faith was weakened, the enslaving legalism that Jesus had overturned would fall on them again.

So Paul fought and fought hard. He opposed certain Galatians who were trying to insert circumcision and the law between believers and grace. He opposed Colossians who were trying to insert asceticism between believers and grace. He opposed those in Rome who were under the illusion that possessing the law meant they would be justified by it instead of by faith alone.

Paul cried out for a pure gospel, and as a result he gave Christians down through the ages a solid and safe defense from the chronic plague of legalism. The apostle generally had to make his points on the run; there was always some fanatical group pledged to do away with this arch-betrayer of the fathers. He took a courageous stand, but it was based on an open allegiance. Paul took some big swings, but he did not swing wildly.

Notice, for example, how he dealt with the issue of food offered at pagan shrines. Some of the meat sold in the marketplaces of Corinth and other cities had been set before pagan idols. Christians wondered whether it was okay to purchase it. Was the meat somehow defiled or even dangerous? To those who had just come out of a world overpopulated with active gods and demons, the meat shouted idol worship. To other believers, it was just food.

Paul was asked his advice. One might expect this vociferous champion of a pure gospel to flail against any form of "compromise." Instead he exhibited a sensitive regard for the feelings of those concerned. He believed that pagan gods held no power over the worshipers of the one God. Food offered to them had no magical power to harm. But he also recognized that "some people are still so accustomed to idols that when they eat such food they think of it as having been sacrificed to an idol, and since their conscience is weak, it is defiled." Fear of this food offered to idols was a kind of weakness, a lack of maturity and of confidence in the gospel of grace. But it was not an evil to oppose. Paul advised, "Accept him who is weak, without passing judgment on disputable matters."

Above all, the apostle wanted empathy in matters where a person's subjective reaction was what made something healthy or unhealthy: "The man who eats everything must not look down on him who does not, and the man who does not eat everything must not condemn the man who does, for God has accepted him." Paul warned those who felt free to eat the sacrificed meat not to become a "stumbling block" to their more sensitive brothers, saying, in effect, my eating it can be perfectly fine for me, but if it's harmful for my brother, I'll avoid it out of courtesy.

Paul championed the cause of Christian freedom, but he dealt gently with those who hadn't yet let go of all their security blankets. When questioned about which Jewish traditions involving ceremonial foods and holy days one might still observe as a believer in the Messiah, Paul counseled, "Each man should be fully convinced in his own mind."

Here he seems totally opposite from the man waging war against "Judaizers," the man who opposed any compromise to the pure gospel as evil. The difference is this: Paul's battle cries were directed against men deliberately attempting to subvert the gospel, wolves in sheep's clothing who were seeking power in a congregation by imposing their own brand of legalism. They posed a clear and present danger to the gospel of grace that was just beginning to bear fruit in souls long hibernating in an arid religion of law. These men were not working out the problem of new wineskins for new wine but rather poisoning the new wine itself. They simply would not accept the cornerstone of justification by faith. This was an evil to oppose, and Paul gave his life proclaiming an opposite allegiance.

His words of understanding, on the other hand, were directed toward people who *were* struggling to work out the problem of new wineskins: What new religious practices will best express the new gospel of grace? Some were barely fumbling toward a faith that would rely completely on Christ's atonement. But Paul accepted that. He perceived that this was not compromise but growth, and he encouraged this growth gently and skillfully "like a mother caring for her little children."

Paul shows us how to stand, how to oppose evil. So many times we fight the wrong battles in the church. We pound on splinters as if they were the crossbeams of truth. We erect a superstructure around a few doctrinal gargoyles on the roof while the foundation of love, grace, and peace decays underneath us.

Paul opposed real evil. He clearly presented a Truth central in the life and death of Christ, and he clearly objected to those who deliberately undermined it. At times we have to meet evil head-on with a stubborn insistence that an important scriptural truth cannot be compromised. At times the Word asks us to go into battle. "Put on the full armor of God, so that when the day of evil comes, you may be able to stand your ground." Some have been moved by the Word to make strategic protests that have changed history.

ENERGY FROM THE WORD

William Wilberforce's powerful oratory won him election to England's parliament from Yorkshire in 1780. His prominent family and quick wit won him a welcome to London's elegant private clubs and scandalous parties. He was speeding on toward upper-class pleasures and political advancement when an old schoolmaster interrupted. The two were vacationing through the Swiss Alps together, debating the fine points of politics in their carriage, when the subject of religion came up. Wilberforce treated it flippantly at first, but the schoolmaster kept mentioning more serious concerns. Finally they did talk in earnest, and Wilberforce agreed to begin reading the Scriptures daily.

The Word took hold. In the midst of parliament's summer session and the whirl of London social life, Wilberforce couldn't help seeing things differently. He began to notice the corruption and oppression around him. Later, touring the continent again with his former schoolmaster, he delved into a Greek New Testament. The Word became a dominant preoccupation and finally led him to commit his life to Jesus Christ.

Wilberforce continued to serve in parliament, beginning each day with a time of prayer and Bible reading. But now he looked on the issues before him from a new perspective. He read a clergyman's impassioned account of the horrors of the slave trade and found his calling.

Wilberforce's open allegiance to the Truth compelled him to take a stand in parliament against a profitable trade that was enriching the British Empire. He began pouring out his powerful oratory on behalf of the black men, women and children who were bleeding, starving, and suffocating to death in the holds of British ships.

The opposition marshaled its forces. They assured the country that Africans were happy to escape the barbarities of their homeland. They warned that two-thirds of England's commerce would disappear if the slave trade were abolished.

For a time the claims of business drowned out Wilberforce's pleas for justice. But this sickly, diminutive orator would not stop. A small group gathered around him, men devoted to Christ and the abolition of the slave trade. They distributed thousands of pamphlets, spoke at public meetings, circulated petitions, and organized a boycott of slave-grown sugar.

They brought the slave question up for a vote year after year in parliament, never giving in to defeat. At one especially low point, Wilberforce opened his Bible and out fell a letter, written to him years before by John Wesley. It read in part, "Unless God has raised you up for this very thing, you will be worn out by the opposition of men and devils, but if God be for you who can be against you?"

Finally, after years of frustration, a bill banning the slave trade passed on February 4, 1807, at 4:00 A.M. Shortly afterward, Wilberforce and his friends burst from their chambers out into the dark, snow-covered street and celebrated like schoolboys, running around, clapping each other on the back, shouting their joy. When the group gathered for a quieter celebration at Wilberforce's house, he turned to a friend who'd worked with him through the years of struggle, illness, ridicule, and defeat, and said with a twinkle in his eyes, "Well, Henry, what do we abolish next?"

William Wilberforce, the life of the party on a fast track through parliament, could never have waged that lonely struggle through the years without the authority of Scripture. Without Christ's Word sustaining him, he certainly could never have emerged from that protracted battle with a light in his eyes.

The opposition had its share of isolated biblical texts, but Wilberforce stood on the whole thrust of Scripture, its swelling through the Old Testament prophets calling for justice on behalf of the oppressed, its climax in the New Testament verity that every man is claimed by Christ—to this Wilberforce could give his wholehearted allegiance. His daily reading, his familiarity with the spirit of Scripture as well as its clear commands, gave him the energy to stand so eloquently for its principles.

Open allegiance perseveres when confronted by evil. It is strengthened by a tradition of prophetic protest. Ezekiel, for example, was repeatedly told, "Set your face against" evildoers and the wickedness on high places, because the Lord Himself said resolutely, "I will set my face against them."

Taking such a stand involves resilience, a willingness to resist wrong "to the point of shedding your blood," a willingness to wrestle against even "the powers of this dark world and against the spiritual forces of evil."

Proving What's Best

Open allegiance opposes injustice, but it also does more: It demonstrates that God's way is best. This is another essential component. God-breathed Scripture "is is useful for teaching...and training in righteousness..." The Bible enlightens as well as confronts. Those who take a stand with it should teach as well as rebuke, show as well as tell. It's not enough to complain about fallen standards. One must also present the values of the Word in place of what's wrong. Open allegiance requires a feisty faith in the ability of the eternal, the unseen, to outperform the things that are more immediately tangible, but temporary. Those whose minds are renewed by the Word are eager to "prove what the will of God is, that which is good and acceptable and perfect." They believe that the "good fight of faith" is capable of embodying eternal life to the world. They believe that it *is* possible to "do it all for the glory of God," demonstrating that His way is best. Here's where our allegiance must become the most creative, fashioning experiments where the Word can demonstrate its veracity.

Hudson Taylor, the man of the "exchanged life" who founded the China Inland Mission, learned to take the Word as an active authority early in life. He was renting a small room in a workman's cottage while taking medical studies and hoping that someday he might go to China as a missionary. In the meantime, Taylor conducted religious services in the slums that Victorian England habitually ignored. By subsisting on oatmeal, he usually managed to give away most of his meager income each month.

One Sunday evening a destitute neighbor asked him to go and pray for his dying wife. Taylor entered the man's wretched room and found the woman lying on a pallet with five small, sunken-cheeked children around her. He tried to say a few words of comfort; they fell flat. He struggled through a prayer, but felt he was mocking God. His problem was the half-crown coin lying in his pocket. That was all he had to live on for weeks to come. A basin of water-gruel awaited him for supper, and he had enough oatmeal left for breakfast, but that was it. After a few moments of struggle, Taylor was struck hard by a verse of Scripture: "Give to him that asketh thee." He concluded that "in the word of a King there is power," pulled the half-crown out of his pocket, and gave it to the desperate husband. Now he could talk with feeling about trusting God as a heavenly Father.

Taylor walked home to his lodgings humming a hymn; the Word had been expressed. After his basin of gruel, he knelt down and reminded the Lord of His promise: "He that giveth to the poor lendeth to the Lord." Taylor asked that the loan might not be a long one, or he would have nothing for lunch the next day.

In the morning a postman knocked on the cottage door while Taylor was finishing his porridge. He didn't usually receive letters on Monday, but the landlady came in with an envelope. Taylor couldn't make out the return address, and the postmark was blurred. There was no message inside, only a pair of kid gloves. When he opened the gloves, however, a half-sovereign fell to the ground.

Hudson immediately made a connection: "Praise the Lord, four hundred per cent for twelve hours' investment—that is good interest! How glad the merchants of Hull would be if they could lend their money at such a rate."

For this man, God's promises were something to stake a claim on. They must find expression in real life. This experience, and others like it, moved Taylor to a decision: He would depend on God alone to finance his mission to China. No begging, no appeal letters, no hinting about needs. If all those statements in Scripture about God's faithfulness and watch-care were true, why not demonstrate it—in the remotest corner of the world?

So Taylor went to China. He had a special burden for those who had never heard about Christ, so he didn't remain on the coast but traveled far inland, where Europeans ventured only at the risk of their lives. He sailed up remote rivers, visiting village after village as a healer and teacher. Taylor managed to survive unscathed and also to attract others to his quest.

In 1876, after ten years of labor, more than seventy people had devoted their lives to spreading the gospel in the vast hinterland of the Middle Kingdom. Financial support for them had never failed; 52,000 pounds had been received—all without making any kind of appeal for funds—and the China Inland Mission had never once been in debt.

But still more millions waited to hear the Word. At the beginning of 1887, Taylor and his fellow workers asked God for what seemed impossible: one hundred new volunteers that year, and ten thousand pounds of additional income to support them. After a great deal of prayer, but no appeals for money, the year ended with the last of "The Hundred" on their way to China and eleven thousand pounds of extra income.

Taylor wanted the entire project based on the biblical assurance of Jehovah Jireh, God provides. Everyone had to accept the experiment: Go to God directly to take care of needs, relying entirely on His benevolent will without any nudging of human wills.

Taylor was not reluctant to talk about the need for missionaries. He published a periodical called *China's Millions* to arouse complacent Christians. He acknowledged gifts received in the magazine, and the mission attracted its regular supporters. But he wanted God in direct control. He would never ask for money. While recruiting missionaries, he sometimes spoke at Christian conferences back in England. More than once someone would rise to take up a collection after one of his stirring messages. But Taylor always stopped it. He didn't want money coming in because of his eloquence, and above all he didn't want to divert funds from other church missions. If the Lord wanted a certain project to go forward, He Himself would have to direct people to supply the funds.

Time after time, Taylor and his friends tested the authoritative Word and found it dependable in meeting specific needs. Once while traveling by train from a conference back to London, Hudson met a certain Count Bobrinksy. The Russian nobleman had heard of the China Inland Mission. Taking out his pocketbook, he said, "Let me give you a trifle toward your work."

Taylor glanced at the bank note handed to him and thought there'd been some mistake. "Did you not mean to give me five pounds?" he said quickly. "Please let me return this note; it is for fifty."

The Count was a bit surprised, too, but reflecting a moment he replied, "I cannot take it back. It was five pounds I meant to give, but God must have intended you to have fifty; I cannot take it back."

When Taylor arrived at the mission headquarters on Pyrland Road, he found a prayer meeting in progress. The workers there were about to send a remittance out to China, but the money on hand was short by forty-nine pounds and eleven shillings. As usual they did not accept such a deficiency as inevitable, but had made it a matter of prayer—going to the Source and His unfailing promises. When Taylor laid the bank note he'd just received on the table, it did seem to have come directly from a heavenly Father's hand.

Hudson Taylor took a stand in China. Amid a complacent Christendom that gave lip service to God the Provider but would never think of really depending on Him, he demonstrated there was a better way. He did not harangue Victorian England about its pathetic lack of genuine faith. He didn't rebuke Christians for not putting their money where their mouths were. He simply showed that God had a better way.

There are times when we have to fight an evil like slavery head-on. The explicit Scripture passages about justice impel those who accept its authority to go into battle. But other matters require that we express our allegiance in a different way. Asking for money is not an evil. Scripture does not prescribe fund-raising methods; it encourages generosity. But it also encourages people to trust God implicitly about everything. Hudson Taylor wanted to demonstrate that. He wanted to isolate God's gracious provisions on canvas, in stark outline, brightly lit, cutting away every extraneous bit of the scenery, every prop that might suggest the composition was flawed. And he succeeded in crafting a compelling piece of artful goodness.

A Place for Others

Taking a stand on God's Word can sweep away the trivial, spotlight important truths, oppose real evil, and demonstrate that God's way is best. It can also create room for other people to stand.

The faithful, those who gave their ultimate allegiance, are described in Hebrews as a great cloud of witnesses encircling us who cheer on those coming after them, giving them more reason to persevere. Standing in faith against the tide, they had to think in terms of a better country, a heavenly one, where the Truth they sacrificed for would find fulfillment. They welcomed that promise from a distance, admitting that it lived in exile on the earth. The world was not worthy of them, but their allegiance created a legacy on earth that nurtures moral courage.

When we look around at our moral landscape, it's those making stands who hold up the scenery. Acts of faithfulness keep the faith alive. The faithful help us see that the Word is worth it all.

* * *

AS ROWS OF SUBDUED WAVES stroked the Guam shoreline, a crescent of palms nodded off to sleep in the breeze. Two men squatting on a gnarled piece of driftwood gazed out at the dusk settling over the bay.

Captain Graff's voice was calm now, even kind: "Mosley, we've got a big job to do over here. It's going to take all we've got."

"Yes, sir," answered Chief Yeoman Ramon Mosley in a voice that was even quieter.

"We're not out on some Sunday school picnic. This is war. The Navy has got to maintain complete discipline."

"Yes, sir."

"Mosley," the captain said, sounding like a longsuffering parent, "you know what I'm going to have to do, don't you?"

The chief yeoman looked down at the moist sand and replied, "Yes, Cap'n. What you've got to do, I guess you've just got to do."

Captain Graff slowly stood up, spit into the sea, and ambled back to the line of forest-green tents.

An unnerving fact had been pressing down on Mosley for some time. Anyone refusing duty in battle conditions was subject to execution. It was hard for him to imagine getting shot by his own countrymen, and yet slowly, persistently, the formal confrontations were leading to that point.

The monochrome monotony of the sea stretched out before him like an unintelligible scroll. Somewhere across its endless reach, his wife Frances wrote letters. For Mosley there would be only piquant fragments. As a sailor under arrest, confined to the base, even his incoming mail was censored.

That other world where people loved, raised corn, and had reasons for life was becoming more and more intangible. He drifted as an odd speck in a world turned upside down. Maybe they were right. Maybe he was crazy. Maybe he was the only one holding to such bizarre opinions.

And yet how could he forget those moments when the Truth took on a strong presence—he and Frances praying earnestly on their apartment building rooftop. Looking out over New Orleans, they had wondered out loud to their Lord about their growing conviction that they should keep the Sabbath truly as the Lord's Day. My father and mother began to believe that the commandment to do no work on this day, to set it apart as holy time, was God's will for Christians. For a few months the newlyweds cherished an island of meaning and peace, earnestly studying the Word as if for the first time in a world convulsing madly with total war.

The test had not come at first, not until their convictions had solidified and the couple had slipped in too deep to get out. For a while, out on shore patrol in the Gulf with the Navy, Mosley had been able to arrange for weekly time off. But finally the immovable object dropped in front of him: a direct order to work on the Sabbath.

Mosley painfully remembered the letters to Washington asking for hospital duty, the refusals, the changes of status, the verbal blasts from an assortment of officers. It all led to one ingenious solution: "Well, Mosley, we're going to see what you do on your Sabbath when the Japs get after you."

The incorrigible sailor was put on a transfer to the Solomon Islands and assigned to a Higgins landing craft unit. Surely one good landing amid machine-gun fire would cure him of his scruples.

Mosley sailed out of New Orleans on a huge transport ship. Leaning over the steel deck rail into the salty, raw gusts of the night, he knew exactly why he was being shipped out. His faith would permit no compromises. But there was no warm feeling welling up inside, no cymbals crashing. He felt only the cold wedge of conscience with which he had tried to fend off their attacks: "If you operate on what you think is right, you just can't take any other stand."

Funny, it had been only four or five months since then, yet it was hard for Mosley to remember when he hadn't been surrounded by this grim, leaden ocean, always somewhere lost in it, hearing the pounding of guns, circling nameless islands, locked in meanderings comprehensible only to an elite huddled somewhere else.

Mosley had made chief yeoman on board ship and, as chief petty officer, was placed in charge of the personnel office on Guam after the Marines established a beachhead.

Technically on a seven-day work week, he had managed to quietly arrange for time off during the Sabbath. But one day the commanding officer walked into his tent and found him studying his Bible lesson. The trouble began all over again.

Now, as the sky blackened overhead, Mosley knew he would be facing increasing pressures to give in. But he also knew that the cold wedge was still in place. Mosley stood up, spit into the sea, and strolled back to his quarters.

The next day a summons came from Captain Graff's tent. Mosley walked in and saluted. He knew what was coming—another "session." Graff, several executive officers, marshals, and the chaplain sat in full-dress uniform in a row around him. Their clustered brass gaudily displayed the authority Mosley had been drilled to obey without question.

"You have a duty to your country."

"Men are being killed all around you."

"How come you're so sure you're the only one who's right?"

Each one in turn whipped out a biting monologue, threatening, pleading, shaming this man they could not fathom.

After an hour the chief yeoman's face began betraying his weariness and confusion. He couldn't answer all their accusations. Then Captain Graff struck a final, swift blow: "Mosley, in this situation you have no choice. You cannot disobey a direct order. You WILL work seven days as scheduled."

Out of his haze the lone sailor managed to reply, "Sir, I have to do the only thing left for me to do. It is impossible for me to carry out—"

Graff blew up. "You will work, Mosley!" Medals and insignia shook on the captain's chest. "If you think you can defy this whole command, you're in for a big surprise, sailor." Graff continued with an assortment of ear-burning epithets before thundering, "DIS-MISSED."

When "deck court" finally arrived, it was almost a relief. At least the sessions would end. Mosley had at first been docketed for a court martial. But a sympathetic Christian, a full commander on a Navy ship, wrote a letter to Admiral Nimitz on his behalf. He pointed out that the right of people to worship as their conscience dictated was one of the things the Navy was defending in the Pacific. Probably as a result of that letter, Mosley faced a less punitive deck court.

Beside two flags and three stiff marshals, Captain Graff read the charges and his prepared verdict. Mosley was reduced to first class yeoman, reprimanded for insubordination, and stripped of his duties in the personnel office.

The captain then ordered him out to a rusting, decrepit barge that accommodated a few cubby-hole offices. Confined to the base, Mosley spent months in uneasy limbo, trying hard to find work that would keep him from further confrontations. But he felt grateful to have survived and not betrayed his Lord.

LEGACY

One day an ambulance pulled up near the old barges. A young man with lieutenant's bars stepped out and began asking for a guy named Mosley. Everybody knew about Mosley. The yeoman was quickly brought out. He saluted and identified himself.

The lieutenant extended his hand and said, "Glad to meet you. I'm a Sabbath-keeping Christian, too."

Mosley stood there for a moment, stunned. He felt like a man long wandering in the desert who catches the scent of water. So there was another one in the world, right there in front of him. So he wasn't all crazy. Suddenly tears burned in Mosley's eyes. He struggled for something to say to keep the mirage from disappearing. "How did you find out—I mean—"

"Well, our hospital ship landed on the other side last week, and I heard about this odd guy who was having trouble over his religion."

"I haven't been able to locate anyone who shares my beliefs since I left the States."

"Hey, well—listen, there are some more believers on the ship, too. And we're thinking of trying to start some sort of church service here."

"Sounds great."

"I think we've got some of the Guamanians interested, too. We really think this is a providential opportunity. This may be our only chance to start a church on the island."

After they retired to Mosley's tiny office, the lieutenant explained that Guam had been dominated by a powerful bishop who would permit no other religious mission to enter the island. When the Japanese took Guam, they captured the bishop and sent him to the Philippines. So if the GI's moved fast, they might be able to get something going.

"There's only one problem," the lieutenant said. "We need a place to meet."

It would always remain a complete mystery to Mosley how he managed to walk into the office of the commanding officer he had last seen at deck court. But there he was with his request, saluting a stone-faced Captain Graff. "Captain," he began, "we have some Christian sailors in a hospital company here who'd like to meet together, and we need some kind of place to worship in."

The commanding officer looked down at his desk and began writing. Mosley decided to go on. "I saw this old storage tent, sir, down by D barracks that nobody is using. I wonder if we could perhaps borrow it, Cap'n."

Suddenly Graff stood up and stared into the yeoman's eyes. "Listen, Mosley," he said, pointing his finger. "You don't have to use that thing. Let me get you a good tent."

The captain marched out of his office and led his awed subordinate over to a corrugated tin warehouse. There he ordered the supply officer to get Mosley a good tent, "just the size he wants."

Next Graff took Mosley over to the Lutheran chaplain. "This man is going to start a worship service. Fix him up with whatever he needs," Graff commanded.

Quickly Mosley's arms were filled with gold and silver bowls, cups and crucifixes. Being in no position to refuse such a weighty gesture, he thanked the chaplain and left.

Graff wasn't finished. "Now, Mosley let's see, you're going to need something to transport this stuff. Let me arrange for a truck and driver."

A truck was requisitioned and loaded. Mosley hurried off to check out at his barge. When he returned the captain had added to the church paraphernalia a portable organ for good measure. He also had ready an unrestricted base leave for his sailor. Mosley tried to thank him, but Graff just waved him off to the truck.

Rumbling along in the truck past mangled greenery and gashes in the earth, First Class Yeoman Mosley carried the embryonic elements of the first Protestant church on Guam. He noticed a warm feeling welling up inside. He heard cymbals crashing. Mosley looked down affectionately at his unwieldy load of holy ware. They were, after all, symbols of a world reclaimed, vessels for celebrating that Body that had become invisible for such a long, harrowing time.

In the future that tent would grow into a fruitful medical, educational, and evangelistic mission. The bread and wine would multiply a hundredfold in good soil. But for now Ramon Mosley was brimful just holding the seeds on the winding, dusty road.

MY FATHER DIDN'T TALK THAT MUCH about his experience during the war. I managed to coax all the details out of him only recently. But it was always there for me growing up. This man was willing to put it on the line for his convictions. His belief about the Sabbath did not become the center of his life. He held firmly to the gospel, all the more so as he grew older. But it had been a stand he felt compelled to take. Even in the midst of a world at war, God's will took precedence.

The value of my father's allegiance really sank in during my freshman year in college when I saw the James Dean film *Rebel Without a Cause*. There's a scene where Dean is facing a terrible dilemma and seeks help from his father. But this thoroughly conventional man can't rise to the occasion; he's oblivious to sharp moral edges. The Dean character, a youth caught in a no man's land between cruel peers and indifferent society, breaks down and begs his father to say something, anything. He pleads for some kind of guidance. At that point the awful emptiness of a person who finally sees that his father stands for absolutely nothing becomes apparent. This wrenching confrontation sends Dean out to his last tragic act of alienation.

It was then I realized how much it means to have a father who made a stand, and how tragic it is to try to face the world in a vacuum. My father's allegiance became an eloquent statement for me. Looking back I can see that I grew up with something to cling to, something straight and true. Right and wrong were woven clearly into the world around me. I always had a place to stand.

Great painters have their legacies. Generation after generation walks through art galleries and tries to touch their genius. Those who give their full and open allegiance to the Word create a legacy, too. Generations to come find shelter in their courage.

14

ABUSIVE BIGOTS &
ELOQUENT MARTYRS

IN THE YEAR A.D. 250, when Decius was emperor of Rome, a Christian elder named Pionius was led into Smyrna's city square through a large double gate. He was paraded between two colonnades extending more than a hundred yards and packed with a holiday crowd, then led to a temple to pay sacrifice and eat pagan meats.

Polemon, a temple official, arrived on the scene and explained, "You know, of course, about the Emperor's edict and how it bids you sacrifice to the gods."

"We know the edicts of God," Pionius answered, "in which he bids us worship him alone."

The pagans attempted to pressure Pionius into submitting to their temple rites, but instead of being intimidated he made a speech before the crowd explaining his position. Pionius quoted from certain Greek heroes who had died for philosophy. He protested the unjust treatment of Christians and warned of a judgment to come.

Later, when officials continued trying to coax him into compromising, he told them, "I wish I could persuade you to be Christians." They roared with laughter: "You can't make us willing to burn alive!"

Pionius replied, "It is far worse to be burned when you are dead."

While he was being escorted back to prison, some in the crowd who'd been impressed by his erudite speech exclaimed, "Ah, what education."

"Not that sort of education," Pionius answered back, wanting them to be impressed by something else. Referring to some recent disasters in the area, he said, "Recognize, rather, the education of those famines, deaths and other blows by which you have been tried." He hoped they might look up to the God of heaven out of their sorrows.

His listeners didn't quite get the point. "But you too went hungry with us," someone said.

Pionius replied, "But I had hope in God."

He died in that hope, crucified facing east in the city of Smyrna.

* * *

Crowds in Pergamum were eager to light the fires and consume another unyielding Christian before a darkening sky rained on them. Their victim, a man named Papylus, though hurried toward the pyre, still gazed fiercely at the Truth. "Here the fire burns briefly," he told them, "but there it burns for ever, and by it, God will judge the world. It will drown the sea, the mountains, and the woods. By it, God will judge each human soul."

* * *

When a believer named Colluthus was about to be executed, a hopeful judge misinterpreted the light in his eyes and said, "I can see it in your face; it tells me that you want to be saved. Don't you see the beauty of this pleasant weather? No pleasure will come your way if you kill yourself. But listen to me and you will be saved."

Colluthus answered, "The death which is coming to me is more pleasant than the life which you give."

THE NOBLE AND THE SCANDALOUS

Pionius, Papylus, and Colluthus were a few of the countless early Christians who took a stand by laying down their lives, bearing persuasive and open witness to a truth bigger than themselves even as they faced the flames. There was great nobility in the way many followers of Christ declared their allegiance—but among others there was much that was scandalous.

Alexander, Bishop of Alexandria, couldn't just explain why the views of Arians were unbiblical. He had to launch into loud abuse: "These knaves…are driven insane by the devil who works in them." Bishop Theodoret couldn't quite see eye to eye on some issues with Cyril, so when the latter died, the bishop wrote: "The living are delighted…May the guild of undertakers lay a huge, heavy stone on his grave, lest he should come back again and show his faithless mind again. Let him take his new doctrines to Hell, and preach to the damned all day and night." The orthodox were told of the Manichees: "Their moral code is a mass of falsehoods, their religious beliefs are shaped by the devil, and their sacrifice is immorality itself." To a man whose doctrine Jerome deemed not completely pure he wrote this: "You distill from the dunghill of your breast at once the scent of roses and the stench of rotting corpses."

Church historian Paul Johnson comments, "The mind boggles at the lists of offenses with which distinguished ecclesiastics accused each other." They seemed to have had the idea that anyone adhering to imperfect views of the Truth had of necessity to be also engaged in the worst kind of immorality, so even the most damning allegations were correct in principle.

From earliest times in the history of the church, we see two contrasting ways of declaring one's allegiance: the eloquence of martyrs who gave their lives for the Truth, and the virulent abuse of those who attacked others on its behalf. There were also some who made effective stands simply by living a certain way.

An Italian patrician born near Spoleto in about 480 decided one day to do something about the decadence and depravity of religion at Rome. Benedict left the Eternal City, where he was being educated, and found a cliffside cave in wild country to the south where he could live simply and think about God. Emperor Nero had built a palace in that area that was now overgrown. Benedict set up his silent protest there at the scene of so many profligate pleasures in the past. He wore a hair shirt and ate only bread that a friend lowered to him in a basket from above the cliff.

Benedict took a stand as an ascetic, but his statement did not center on self-torment. After he'd begun his monastic movement he heard of an admirer who had chained himself in a cave; Benedict sent the woman a message: "The true servant of God is chained not to rocks by iron, but to righteousness by Christ." Benedict sought to be useful as well as pure and founded a monastery on the heights of Monte Cassino where monks could become efficient farmers. His reform spread and proved incredibly fruitful. It was his monasteries more than anything else that transformed a Europe in disarray after the fall of Rome into a stable and productive society with a sound agricultural economy. And he had managed to awaken an indulgent church to the values of devotion and simplicity without raising his voice in anger.

Many other angry voices persisted, however, in fighting for their piece of truth. When the church grew as powerful as the state, vehement polemics became physical torture. Christians declared their allegiance to the truth by submitting those in error to the horrors of the Inquisition. Another kind of authority replaced the winsome voice of the Word.

Battling for the truth also took on a geographic dimension. Crusades to recover the Holy Land from unclean hands aroused Christian passions and mobilized fervent masses. Truth quantified into certain locations had to be possessed; the fervent knight had to raise his banner over it or die trying.

Down through the centuries a church made powerful has always found it difficult to resist the authority of the sword. But still there were always those who proclaimed a more open allegiance. The Waldensians went about Europe preaching New Testament truths in the vernacular and exposing the worldliness of many clergy by their simple lifestyle. They rejected most traditions that could not be based on the Word, so the church persecuted them. Many were slaughtered.

In the fourteenth century Oxford scholar John Wycliffe based his call for reform on the primitive church described in the New Testament. The church had grown powerful and overbearing in his day and he made a plea for innocence, purity, and simplicity. Standing against England's state religion—a lethargic bureaucracy dedicated to keeping itself fed—Wycliffe declared that there could be no religious power without virtue. Tithes should be withheld from priests who neglected their duties. In this he was taking a stand against his own self-interest as a clergyman. But he saw all around him friars growing fat and monasteries wealthy in parishes where a wheat cake the size of a man's fist fed wife and children for a day. So he insisted in one typical sermon, "A cup of cold water given with kindness and warm love is a greater gift than all the lands and kingdoms of the church." And in another he declared, "If there is a rule most necessary to virtue, it is one which demands the church forsake worldly riches for the riches of God and Christ as the apostles did."

Wycliffe believed the statements of the Bible created one universally applicable utterance and that the truth of the whole gave truth to the parts. He felt that the words of Scripture were not dead on the page, but spoken by God; therefore that divine voice should sound out in living English as well as formal Latin. As a result he began his famous translation of the Bible that would enlighten all of England.

BRIGHT WORDS AND NEEDLESS BLOODSHED

One of the most luminous stands in history was made by a Czech reformer named Jan Hus. The official church could not persuade him to abandon his position that Scripture must be the sole criterion of Christian faith, so he was condemned as a heretic. "Fearing to offend God and to fall into perjury," he would not recant before the bullying of the Council of Constance in 1415.

What is most moving about Hus's courageous allegiance is its utter lack of self-righteousness. In his final declaration to the Council he told them he could not denounce his biblical teachings, but "I would most gladly recant before all the world every falsehood and every error I ever have thought of saying or have said."

At the execution grounds Hus underwent an elaborate "ceremony of degradation." Officials disrobed him, cut off his hair, and gravely pronounced curses. Hus remarked that he was quite glad to suffer shame for the name of the Lord. When the bishops present intoned a final curse—"We commit your soul to the devil!"—Hus replied, "And I commit it to the most merciful Lord Jesus Christ."

As the wood and straw piled up to his neck were lit, Hus began singing, "Christ, Thou Son of the living God, have mercy on us." His lips were still moving silently when he died. Hus stood heroically firm, but even until the end he was always a man willing to learn, eager to be shown his mistakes. Hus wrote:

> From the earliest time of my studies I have set up for myself the rule that whenever I discern a sounder opinion in any matter whatsoever, I gladly and humbly abandon the earlier one. For I know that those things I have learned are but the least in comparison with what I do not know.

What a remarkable statement from a man who willfully faced a horrible death rather than endorse error! It was only because church teachings blatantly contradicted the Word of God that he took an irrevocable stand.

During the age of Reformation, many godly men like Martin Luther made courageous stands on the Word alone, but it was extremely difficult not to make an armed camp out of one's doctrinal position. Allegiance to gospel Truth all too frequently got tangled up with political allegiances. Blood flowed freely on both sides of the Reformation, and in the resultant clamor of vengeful voices, few heard more tolerant ones. Giordano Bruno sought to encourage a middle way of reform between the Protestants and Catholics. But in Venice he ran into the Inquisition. He was charged with having stated, "The procedure which the church uses today is not that which the Apostles used, for they converted the people with preaching and the example of good life." For asserting that people should not be tortured into the faith and that the Catholic religion he loved had need of great reform, he was burned alive as a heretic in Rome.

The Anabaptists also sought a more open allegiance to the Word. Their problem was that they insisted on reforming ahead of their time—and so met both Catholic and Protestant opposition. These peculiar believers would not accept the legitimacy of any kind of state-sponsored religion. They wanted to go beyond doctrinal correctness and have a daily walk with Christ, which meant resolutely obeying the "bright and clear words of the Son of God, whose word is truth and whose commandment is eternal life." The Anabaptists, as a rule, would not fight for their beliefs with the sword or defend themselves when persecuted. In their communities they expressed love concretely, redistributing their wealth to those most needy. Many died eloquently for their New Testament Truth.

Some reformers stood resolutely on the Word; others tried to use the sword to enforce its authority. Even Luther could be vicious; his diatribes against Jews and certain radical Protestant sects are painful to read.

Sometimes the church, wandering from the important truths emphasized in the Word, made tragic, pathetic stands. Reform was a real possibility in the Russian church early in the reign of Czar Alexis. A group of "Zealots of Faith" traveled through the land calling clergy and lay people to sincere spiritual devotion. But the movement broke up over disputes about correct forms of worship. The official church insisted that the sign of the cross be made with three fingers raised instead of two, and that the three-fold Alleluia, not the two-fold, be sung in worship. Thousands of "Old Ritualists," who believed such liturgical changes signaled an end of the world, sacrificed their lives in opposition.

Other zealous believers have made a stand on the wording of the Eucharist and its precise chemistry. Where Scripture only hints, they want to declare dogmatically. And so the clear teaching of the Bible about salvation in Christ is overshadowed by more polemics, more angry debate, more needless bloodshed.

THE WORD MADE FLESH AGAIN

In the nineteenth century, men like George Whitefield and John Wesley declared their allegiance to the living Word against a lifeless orthodoxy that stifled the Spirit. The Word needed to be made flesh again. It had hardened into dogma in the established churches, where clergymen gave dry dissertations to parishioners nodding off to sleep in agreement.

The church wanted exposition of the Word carefully regulated; Wesley believed its authoritative call should be spread everywhere. He declared his allegiance:

> God in Scripture commands me according to my power to instruct the ignorant, reform the wicked, confirm the virtuous. Man forbids me to do this in another's parish; that is, in effect, to do it at all, seeing I have now no parish of my own, nor probably ever shall. Whom then shall I hear: God or man?

Wesley took a definite stand all over England, traveling more than 250,000 miles in his evangelistic career and preaching some forty thousand sermons. He converted thousands of the spiritually starving and faced violent opposition. The gentry, who feared any kind of revival among the "lower orders of people," often incited mobs against him.

Wesley was often beaten by these crowds, but even in the midst of riots he maintained his stand. Some of the most violent trouble-makers were won over by his self-possession and earnestness. Once when a mob had beaten him until blood was flowing from open wounds, he managed to gain their attention and began a sermon. Unfortunately he soon lost his voice, and the crowd set on him again. However, he began praying at the top of his lungs, and one ruffian listening to those holy words emerging from the bloodied mouth stepped forward and said, "Sir, I will spend my life for you. Follow me, and not one soul here shall touch a hair of your head."

Wesley was a courageous man with enough drive and stamina to foment a religious revolution in England. But he relied on only one kind of authority: the power of the gospel to transform. Wesley always attempted to persuade; he reasoned from Scripture, always looking a mob in the face, never meeting violence with any force other than the Word. When an angry crowd attempted to break up his meeting at St. Ives, he went out to confront them: "I went into the midst and brought the head of the mob to the desk. I received but one blow on the side of the head, after which we reasoned the case, till he grew milder and milder and at length undertook to quiet his companions."

AGAINST THE TIDE

In 1939 a young German theologian on a lecture tour in America was urged by his friends to take up some safe work in the States and not return to the deteriorating situation in his homeland. But he couldn't. As his diary states: "The short prayer in which we thought of our German brothers almost overwhelmed me." He decided to take a stand with fellow believers about to be engulfed in the madness of Nazism, and so departed on one of the last ships to leave for Germany before the war.

Dietrich Bonhoeffer became a leader of the "Confessing Church" which resisted the philosophy of the brown-shirted fanatics of a new era. Because of his participation in a plot against Hitler, Bonhoeffer was captured, imprisoned, and finally executed shortly before World War II ended. In his *Letters and Papers from Prison* one gets a glimpse of the source of this man's courageous stand against a tide that overwhelmed most of his Christian contemporaries.

Many of his letters reflect on the meaning of Bible passages he'd been studying. He talked of "a way of seeing the God of the Bible, who wins power and space in the world by his weakness." Scripture was more than just a source of theology for Bonhoeffer; it remained his personal companion and comfort:

> The heavy air raids, especially the last one, when the windows
> of the sick-bay were blown out by the land mine, and bottles
> and medicine supplies fell down from the cupboards and
> shelves, and I lay on the floor in the darkness with little hope of
> coming through the attack safely, led me back quite simply to
> prayer and the Bible.

To a young man home on leave with his wife, Bonhoeffer wrote, "I am very glad you will be able to read the Bible together again morning and evening; it will be a great help to you, not only for these present days, but for the future." He followed his own advice: "I am reading the Bible straight through from cover to cover, and have just got as far as Job, which I am particularly fond of. I read the Psalms every day, as I have done for years; I know them and love them more than any other book."

Bonhoeffer reacted to life through the Word. One of his predecessors in the cell had scribbled over the floor an ironic note: "In 100 years it will all be over." Reflecting on the feeling that time spent in that prison was a tragic blank, he wrote:

> "My times are in thy hand" (Ps. 31:15) is the Bible's answer. But
> in the Bible there is also the question that threatens to dominate
> everything here: "How long, O Lord?" (Ps. 13).

Bonhoeffer would conclude: "If this earth was good enough for the man Jesus Christ, if such a man as Jesus lived, then, and only then, has life a meaning for us."

The Word went deep. An English officer imprisoned with Bonhoeffer during his last weeks remembered him this way:

> Bonhoeffer...was all humility and sweetness; he always seemed
> to me to diffuse an atmosphere of happiness, of joy in every
> smallest event in life, and of deep gratitude for the mere fact
> that he was alive....He was one of the very few men that I have
> ever met to whom God was real and close.

HERE AND NOW

Clarence Jordan, a Baptist pastor in Georgia, took a stand in the late 1940s on a Greek word: *koinonia*, fellowship. He believed that the fellowship early Christians practiced, pooling their possessions, sharing their lives and their spiritual commitment, bearing each other's burdens, and helping the poor—was worthy of imitation in the twenti-eth century.

Jordan saw as a constraining authority the biblical passages that demanded brotherhood, peacemaking, reconciliation, and love for one's enemies. The Sermon on the Mount was, for him, not a lovely speech to be honored in the abstract, but a command of Christ that must be put into practice here and now. Here was Sumter County, Georgia. Now was November 1942.

Jordan gathered a few like-minded believers around him and began to build Koinonia Farm on four hundred treeless, eroded acres near the town of Americus. They plowed and fertilized the land until it yielded good crops, raised corn and hogs, set up an egg marketing cooperative, and helped a number of neighboring farmers start their own poultry flocks. They planted apple, pecan, peach, walnut, pear, plum, fig, and apricot trees and dug a large vegetable garden. There was always an abundance to share with neighbors—white and black. They raised a dairy herd and established a "cow library" from which poor families could check out a cow, milk her, and return her for another. They conducted vacation Bible school and Sunday school for the kids near them, mostly black. They welcomed anyone into their farm who was willing to try *koinonia*.

The good citizens of Sumter County responded. They organized a boycott to prevent the farm from selling its produce and buying necessary supplies; lobbed explosives into their roadside market; harassed children from Koinonia in the public schools; destroyed the farm's beehives; cut down three hundred apple, peach, and pecan trees; set fire to farm buildings; and rode by in their cars night after night firing shotguns toward the houses. Then the leading citizens of Americus paid Pastor Jordan and his colleagues a visit and politely asked them to leave the area to avoid inciting further violence.

The idea that the fellowship Christ commanded might include people of color proved an unbearable outrage to most of Sumter County's white residents. For them, the convention that the races should sleep, eat, learn, and worship separately loomed large as a statute carved on Sinai, and the explicit appeals of Christ to tran-scend racial barriers trickled away unnoticed.

Southern Georgia, among many other places at the time, suffered from what we might call nominal fundamentalism. It took the worst from two worlds, the secular and religious. It cherished the most fla-grant of anti-Christian hatreds toward those on the outside and sought unquestioned authority for this in selected fragments of Scripture torn from their context.

Clarence Jordan could not ignore the weight of evidence from the

Bible. To ignore his calling would have required him to "tear out of
the New Testament all those pages which proclaim the universality
of the Christian brotherhood." He took Scripture both literally and
seriously. The whole weight of Christ's teaching had moved him to
those four hundred acres near Americus. The Master's words were
the source, not just the justification, of his vision.

His stand counts in the end. It lives as evidence of the authority
and vitality of the Word. It is art that still speaks.

AND SO WE HAVE these many and varied witnesses to the authority of the Word. It's a great tradition of people willing to lay down
their lives for it, and a frightening history of people willing to kill
others over it.

Intolerance has been a big problem for those adhering to absolute
religious truth. Today most of us pride ourselves on our tolerance,
but it's a rather cheap variety: the tolerance of people who don't
believe much of anything. We don't war over theology, but only
because we don't take it seriously. We have plenty of other "important" things to fight about.

The tolerance that matters is found in people who *do* take religious truth seriously, who believe that an authoritative Word has
eternal consequences, and yet who refuse to force others under it.
They bear witness to its power to win, and no other power.

Looking back on our tradition of eloquent martyrs and abusive
bigots, we must ask how we can express the authority of the Word in
our world. Faithfulness to it means focusing on the essential. How
can we become part of that cloud of witnesses who make room for
future generations to make a meaningful stand?

STANDING IN THE GAP

The American and European "enemy nationals" ordered to an
internment camp in Shantung Province by Japanese occupation
forces in 1943 were a varied lot who were to endure months of boredom, frustration, overcrowding and fear. Personalities clashed, tempers flared. The two groups thrown into sharpest relief were the
businessmen and the missionaries—they held each other in strictest
contempt. Petty squabbles proliferated. The businessmen couldn't
understand why the missionaries had to sing hymns at six in the
morning. The missionaries were bothered by the businessmen chat-
tering late at night about their "lurid escapades."

Only one man seemed able to span the gap between these two

groups, a man described by an internee as "without a doubt the person most in demand and most respected and loved in camp"— Eric Liddell, a missionary from Scotland. A Russian prostitute in camp would later recall that Liddell was the only man who'd ever done anything for her without wanting to be repaid in kind. When she first came into camp, alone and snubbed, he put up some shelves for her.

Another internee recalled, "He had a gentle, humorous way of soothing ruffled tempers and bringing to one's mind some bygone happiness or the prospect of some future interest round the corner 'when we got out.' "

At one irate meeting of the internees, when everybody was demanding that someone else do something about the restless youngsters in camp who were getting into trouble, Liddell came up with a solution. He organized sports, crafts, and classes for the kids, and began spending his evenings with them.

But he would not oversee games on Sunday. Liddell believed in keeping that day holy to the Lord. In fact, this former world-class sprinter, portrayed in the film *Chariots of Fire,* had sacrificed a gold medal at the 1924 Olympics in his favored event, the 100 meters, because the race was scheduled on Sunday. Though pressured by everyone from his coach to the prince of Wales, he stood firm. He would not violate principle for Olympic glory. So the team reluctantly scheduled him for the 400 meters, considered a distance race at the time. Liddell, not knowing any better, sprinted all the way around the track and won the gold.

At the Shantung compound he told the youngsters he was sorry, but he couldn't take part in sports on Sunday. Most of them protested and decided to organize their own field hockey game anyway. It ended in a brawl since there was no one to officiate.

The following Sunday, Liddell showed up on the field to act as referee—a small act that sheds a great light on his stand. He would not go for Olympic gold if he had to break the Sabbath doing it, but he would keep a handful of imprisoned youngsters from fighting.

Eric Liddell's stand is winsome and eloquent. He didn't use his position as a club, but as an expression of unchanging principles, principles he was nurtured on every morning at 6 A.M. when he tiptoed quietly past sleeping companions, settled down at a low, Chinese table, and lit a small lamp to illuminate his Bible and notebook.

THE BIG
OBSTACLES

15

BURNED OUT
ON BEING GOOD

IT WAS SET amid the ocean breezes and tall palms of the Rio Grande Valley in Texas. Nice place. Almost perfect weather, amiable teachers. But when I remember the Christian boarding school I attended, I think mostly of casualties. Cherry, that lissome lass so cheerful toward everyone, froze her lungs sniffing freon. Sally ran off with a truck driver to parts unknown. Lester the loner was discovered with a great deal of local appliance store merchandise hidden away under his bed. Crazy J.T., good at basketball, fried his brains on some nameless drug and disappeared. James, frequently picked on, a shy kid who wanted more than anything in the world to belong to a hot car, died in a head-on collision. Andrew, who talked about girls a lot but couldn't ask one out, became a projectionist in a porn theater. The list goes on.

These aren't just sad statistics for me. They're faces I laughed with, played football with, dated, feared. Frozen in the yearbook, they stare back at me now with uncanny, ghostlike smiles.

SO MANY CASUALTIES
Going through high school at a religious academy means you're on twenty-four-hour call to certain regulations. We existed in a sea of well-intentioned ethical imperatives. But few of us ever learned to swim. Rules laid out in the school guidebook hemmed us in on every side, protecting us from an evil world, but very little ever sunk in.

There were a few who flailed about in the water for a time. I remember Mother Guilliard especially and his conversion. Guilliard was, or seemed, a bit older than the rest of us and had a knack for mending things, so we began calling him Mother. Guilliard didn't mind our jovial devotion until the day someone tried to give him a rose during a Mother's Day tribute at church.

His freckled, angular features bearing a wide smile suggested impish benevolence. He came from one of the small towns in Texas, I think; at least he didn't show traces of the decadence of Dallas and Houston.

Guilliard had participated in some of Lester's midnight ventures into local stores, and when the two were caught, he experienced the catharsis of terror. Fear drove the pleasures of sin far out of sight, and he repented in earnest. Lester, more ambivalent in his guilt, was kicked out of school. Guilliard, who humbled himself before faculty, merchants, and the whole student body, won a reprieve; he was solemnly placed on probation. Soon after his narrow escape from expulsion he determined to toe the line as laid out in the good book and church manual. Mother Guilliard tried to follow all the rules and obey God. He tried for about three weeks.

But the good life was just too much for him. He was tall and very thin, and you could almost see his shoulders sag from the weight of the straight and narrow. One night he told me, "I just can't do it. I can't make it." For some reason he would not look at grace or mercy; the vast body of religious regulations dominated his field of vision. So Mother Guilliard closed his eyes.

There's a photograph in the yearbook that documents his return from the precarious height of religious resolution. He's standing in a corner of his dorm room, cheerfully eating an onion. Guilliard had shouted out some obscenities within hearing of the dean and had to make expiation with the onion. But he got the whole thing down, eyes watering, almost with relief. He'd made his public statement. He'd shut the door on attempts to be good and could now relax and live a normal life. We had good ol' Mother Guilliard back again.

Burning out didn't take long for this boy—his willpower fell in the medium-to-low range. Others with more backbone last longer, but still there are so many casualties, so many people burning out on being good.

PUTTING IN TIME

Someone I was close to grew up earnest as a stalk of wheat, a good boy without guile who wanted to serve God. Jesse handed out tracts for evangelistic meetings when he was eight. He kept himself unspotted from the world, and he mumbled to himself a lot. In fact there was a time during his adolescence when he mumbled to himself all the time. What no one knew was that he was asking for forgiveness constantly. Behind those thick glasses and the buck teeth of raw innocence, a monk labored long and hard. He'd heard someone from the pulpit quote a revered religious writer to the effect that one unconfessed sin could keep a person out of heaven, and he was doing his best, quite logically, to keep from having any unconfessed sins left in his record that might come up and damn him in the Judgment. Maybe there was something he'd overlooked. And who knew what trivial action might be regarded as impure from the holy height of heaven? So it was best to cover all the angles and confess everything, all the time.

Jesse eventually grew out of his obsessive confessing, but the burden of goodness remained with him. It was reinforced at the Christian high school he attended by teachers who modeled the same vast body of regulations that had defeated Mother Guilliard. That sensitive, earnest boy who'd struggled under a mind-boggling load finally gave up. It just wasn't worth it. Jesse collapsed on the treadmill of being good, reviving himself only after he went to college out in California and learned to lay back—at a comfortable distance from God. He remained a very likable, decent young man, but he avoided like the plague that perilous height of religious resolution.

Weak-willed people burn out. Conscientious people burn out. I see their faces still, pressed against the wall of righteousness, fading in the yearbook. For so many believers trying to be good, the endless demands of righteousness draw them down a spiritually exhausting one-way street. There are always more moral demands than they can ever catch up with.

When I try to find a reason for all the casualties, legalism leaps up as the prime suspect. It's the common bond that ties all the faces together. We all certainly struggled in a world dominated by do's and don'ts. But it's important to identify this often-fingered culprit precisely. Many Christians tend to look at legalism simply as being strict in behavior, following a lot of rules. Often we end up suspecting as a legalist anyone with higher moral standards than ourselves. If they're stricter, they're legalistic. With this kind of mind-set, the solution for legalism is to loosen up the rules a bit.

Paul wrote the book on legalism and its antidote, so it's best to approach the problem from his perspective. He zeroed in his sharpest warnings on those who were attempting to be "justified by works" or "justified by the law." The essence of legalism is attempting to earn salvation and acceptance with God by performance. We pursue good deeds or religious ritual or whatever as a method of being considered worthy.

There are strict legalists and loose legalists. The former believe they must attain a high level of performance in order to be accepted;

they're never doing enough. The latter believe they must attain a minimum level of performance in order to be accepted; they're doing just enough to get by. The person flailing himself because he didn't witness enough this week and the person congratulating himself because he's not a murderer or adulterer may seem polar opposites in religious outlook, but they're operating on the identical principle: legalism, performance as the key to acceptance. Having a few rules or having a lot of rules is not the main the problem; it's how we regard them. This is the root of legalism, and Paul hacked away at this root by wielding the gospel again and again in his epistles.

People on the way to moral burnout are working by the hour. They're not artists, but day laborers. At the boarding school I attended, all of us worked by the hour, in more ways than one. There was this generic task called hoeing weeds that occupied our hours when there were no ditches to dig or garbage bins to dump. When all else failed, the boys could always be sent out after the weeds. So we'd straggle out over the campus lawns with that looping shuffle of paid-by-the-hour peons, dragging our hoes behind us. We'd check out a few weeds, ponder their relative merits, then begin bothering one to death. There wasn't any realistic hope of getting all the weeds, for our campus included several wide fields. We were just putting in time.

Legalism, the real thing, traps people in a paid-by-the-hour contract with no assurance they'll get wages at the end. They just have to keep hoeing and hoping. There are always more weeds popping up in their lives and they can never keep up with that ubiquitous black soil in the heart. But they keep trying.

FIRST, ADMIRATION

I believe there's a healthy way out of this rut. We can preempt this slide toward moral burnout by encouraging art—creative expression —instead of just performance. How do day laborers become artists? First of all by getting some inspiration.

Mother Guilliard lacked inspiration in his trudging down the straight and narrow. He wasn't moved by admiration for a God who loved him. A human being is not big enough for both happy admiration and legalism, especially strict legalism. They can't occupy the same ground. We need to admire the God who loves and accepts us. The first step is not imitation, but admiration. Don't imitate until you've admired the One who accepts you.

That point is hinted at in the structure of the Old Testament. God could sum up His principal moral expectations in the Ten Commandments, but He laid out one hundred and fifty psalms for us. Jehovah seems to shout, "Just admire Me. That's enough. Don't do anything at first, just look at Me." This is how we begin the good life; it's the only way to begin. You've got to be properly inspired to have artful goodness. You can't just knuckle down and churn it out.

Trying to be humble is one great way to burn out. People who don't focus on admiring someone greater than themselves, but instead try to chip away at the self—a mechanical process of negation—end up with little self left with which to press ahead. But light humility is continually reinvigorated by its admiration for God. The juices keep flowing, law and spirit interacting.

As Paul emphasized, we make progress not by performance to earn credit, but by faith. It's the connection that inspires art, not just isolated labor. Artful goodness is a gift expressed. The legalist is not moved ahead by an awareness of God's great gifts. That's a telltale sign: People watching a legalist at work sense sweat more than giftedness. But people are turned on to the religious life if they have something to admire deeply. Holding up God, bearing witness to His gracious acts in our lives, gets people on the road. We are ready to reach for artful goodness not just when we've learned the rules and doctrines, but when we've come to the point of admiring God.

The Atonement is another great weapon against burnout. This strikes at the root problem of legalism. The cross takes the treadmill right out from under the feet of those trudging dutifully toward never enough. It proclaims loudly against a thundering sky over Golgotha: This perfect life of Christ, His perfect obedience to the law, stands in your place; He is your substitute, not just in bearing the penalty of sin, but also in earning the reward of righteousness.

So, as Paul urged the Galatians, stand free. Don't submit to that old yoke of slavery. You are justified by grace. Mother Guilliard couldn't take the cross seriously. He was unable to grasp such grace and labored under a yoke. His efforts were not motivated by admiration and thankfulness but by a desperate desire to imitate the law. No cross, no spirit, no art. Burnout.

The cross wasn't big enough for Jesse, either. Other things overwhelmed it: the example of his legalistic teachers and his own obsessive confessing. Jesse couldn't stop and just admire. For Jesse, Jesus did not seem visible on the cross as substitute; He remained primarily a Great Example, and that role that tended to overshadow the facts of grace.

Artists are in this way the opposite of day laborers. The latter hold up the fruits of their labor, the bundle of torn-up weeds, and ask for payment and approval at the end of the day. The former receive gracious approval first from the God they admire, and then find some way of expressing that grace.

Inspiration for the Long Haul

Healthy goodness has to flow out of the Atonement. It's not just the first chapter in the Christian life that, after conversion, leads to other chapters under the heading "sanctification." It must remain the center. Our moral life has got to keep flowing directly from it: I am accepted, I am honored, I am cherished. Then artful goodness can begin as an expression of such truths, extending to others the honor that fills us up.

It's hard to get burned out on the quality of honor. As a way to express God's act of grace, it's open-ended. We use our freedom, as Paul urged, to serve one another in love—in many different ways according to our talents. We're people who have received special abilities:

> As each one has received a special gift, employ it in serving one another, as good stewards of the manifold grace of God. Whoever speaks, let him speak, as it were, the utterances of God; whoever serves, let him do so as by the strength which God supplies; so that in all things God may be glorified.

The emphasis is on using gifts. We all have the ability to excel in some area. God's many-faceted grace bursts out in many forms. There's a creative process at work: receiving inspiration from God, giving it expression.

Those afflicted with strict legalism are always up against specific requirements, difficult acts, an interminable list, an unmasterable quantity. But honor compelled by grace is a skill to learn. We're motivated to master a quality.

With this background of an admirable God and His grace, we can then relate to the authority of the Word in a new way. Its principles are no longer barriers on the road to acceptance but challenges which the accepted can embrace. The honored want to take a stand. They see statements worth making, principles worth fleshing out in daily life.

Legalists typically see no great statements to make. Instead of embodying big principles, they're following isolated rules, not bad in themselves but not sufficient to keep moving their spirits. And when certain rules lose their meaning, the legalist has a hard time seeing beyond them. Clinging to dead symbols is a flag of the strict legalist. When the Spirit has abandoned the symbols and moved on, the legalist cannot move with Him. When believers were haggling about vestiges of the old ceremonial system, Paul declared: "Circumcision is nothing; uncircumcision is nothing. The only thing that counts is a new creation." What matters is that we keep creating from the Spirit, keep expressing. What matters is artful goodness.

Artful goodness is a healthy alternative to strict legalism. It doesn't just deal with symptoms by loosening up the rules a bit; it goes to the root. The key difference between day laborers and artists is the difference between imitation and inspired expression. Only those driven by something to express can keep going on the long haul.

The painter, for example, is continuously motivated and invigorated in his work with pigments, brushes, and canvas precisely because he's not just a painter covering surfaces. He works to express and experience something beyond the canvas. In the same way believers must work to experience and express something beyond their isolated moral acts. They may express the many-faceted beauty of God's holiness. They may experience something of what it's like to be God Himself. They express the beauty and wonder of the Atonement, extending honor. They embody the Word in new ways, making a stand on a principle that really matters. Seeing goodness as an art form of the Spirit transforms duty into a many-faceted means of glorifying God.

There's more to the good life than a pedantic following after requirements. We've got to see through them to the big picture. The painter Fuseli, an eccentric figure of early Romanticism, once wrote this aphorism: "Indiscriminate pursuit of perfection infallibly leads to mediocrity." Instead of desperately trying to get all the weeds, the chosen, the honored, are focused on expressing essential principles. They are no longer day laborers grimly aiming at that black soil but chosen artisans who "proclaim the excellencies of Him who has called you out of darkness into His marvelous light." Giving form to God's excellence—that's the kind of aim that can become a healthy passion.

I wish now I could revisit those faces in the yearbook. Some are gone forever. Others have disappeared into the world they were isolated from for so long. Some linger on the edges of religion. If only someone had held before them the possibilities of art instead of just imitation.

I BELIEVE IN YOU

Pastor Glenn Coon came from the same subculture that produced the despair of Jesse and Mother Guilliard. On the surface he appeared the spitting image of conservative religious goodness, thoroughly conventional. His dress and language and mannerisms were those of that older generation of church leaders who had battled over whether wedding rings constituted jewelry and whether playing with Rook cards was just as bad as playing with poker cards, and who generally tied down every loose end of life with a paragraph in the church manual.

Pastor Coon lived and breathed in this atmosphere, but he was not "of it." In his own life he followed rather strict standards, but they did not define him. He expressed something bigger and more animated. When this pastor spoke, people's hearts burned with the love of Jesus. Somehow he managed to turn that cliche into a very present reality.

Glenn Coon had a theme, not just isolated acts of goodness. He had something to express: Jesus believes in us, hopes for us, loves us, forgives us, and that's how we must relate to each other. Christ's gracious regard was so powerfully real to Coon that it overshadowed all other factors that influence relationships. It was something that just had to be expressed. He found a fruitful ministry among the many in his denomination on the road to burnout.

Once one of Pastor Coon's church members, a man we'll call Ralph, left his wife and children. He went to a nearby city and rented an apartment for himself. This naturally caused quite an uproar in the church. One of the elders came to Pastor Coon and exclaimed, "You know, that man must be dealt with at once." The implication was that Ralph needed to be strongly disciplined, perhaps disfellowshipped right away.

The pastor promised he would phone Ralph and make an appointment. But the elder thought that was a terrible idea. "Call him on the telephone?" he said. "Why, I should say not! If he knows you want to talk with him, you'll never get to see him. The only way to get to see that man is to come on him suddenly, like cornering a lion in his den."

Pastor Glenn thanked the elder for his concern and then, after much prayer, called Ralph. And this is how he began the conversation: "Ralph, I'm your new pastor. I have some wonderful news for you! Something you will like very much. But I have to see you alone. I'd like to meet you in my car, in my driveway, so we can be entirely alone."

This "fallen church member" who'd been declared all but unreachable quickly agreed to come. He promised, "I'll be there tonight." At the appointed time, Ralph walked up to Pastor Coon's driveway and stepped into the front seat of his car.

The minister turned to him and said enthusiastically, "I have something wonderful for you, as I said. It's nothing financial, but I've come to bring you victory over sin."

At the words "victory over sin," Ralph seemed to slump down in his seat. He stared out the window into the darkness. The man seemed to be wondering, *Is this pastor just trying to gather information to use against me?*

Pastor Coon continued talking, assuring Ralph of his genuine concern and of his experience in dealing confidentially with similar problems. He mentioned other people he'd known who had come out victorious after serious moral failures.

The minister talked for thirty minutes, forty minutes, and still there was no response. But he persisted in hope, saying he was a friend who was there to help Ralph. "I know you can be saved," he said. "I believe you will be saved."

Suddenly Ralph dropped his head and began to sob like a child. He turned to the minister and said, "Pastor, I don't believe there is any hope for me."

Pastor Coon put his arm around him and quoted 1 John 1:9: "If we confess our sins, he is faithful and just and will forgive us our sins and purify us from all unrighteousness."

Pastor Coon was fanning that tiny spark of hope. He continued presenting Scripture promises about God's acceptance, forgiveness, cleansing, and rest. And he added fervently, "Jesus is bringing you victory now. You are His child. You are turning to God."

The pastor, now weeping himself, was so moved by faith that he told Ralph about the great work for God he could do in the future. Suddenly Ralph raised his head and looked the minister in the eye. "Brother Coon," he said, "I'm going home."

Faith had produced its wonderful fruit. Ralph had seized that ray of hope. Pastor Coon was, of course, overjoyed and received the assurance that Ralph would return to his wife and children the very next day.

That meant the pastor had time to go and prepare the wife for this homecoming. Early the next morning he hurried over and told her, as enthusiastically as possible, "Jo Ann, your husband was converted last night, and he is coming home. And he is going to serve the Lord."

This woman looked back at the pastor as though she could eat nails and replied with a sneer, "Oh yeah? He needs to be converted!"

Pastor Coon's heart just about sunk through the floor. He saw his victory of hope melting away before his eyes. But the minister bravely pressed on. "Yes," he told Jo Ann, "God came in last night in a wonderful way, and the Holy Spirit melted your husband's heart."

"Hmm!" the woman shot back, "better melt it! Better melt it!"

Now it was getting harder and harder for this minister to keep showing faith. He was greatly tempted to give this woman's sneer right back to her. *Anything but a Pharisee!* he thought. *What can you do for a self-satisfied religionist?*

Pastor Coon felt like walking out the door. Then he remembered his encounter with her husband the previous night. Ralph had expressed faith, and God had acted. Couldn't this woman benefit from confidence expressed in her as well? The pastor shot a quick prayer heavenward, asking God to help him inspire Jo Ann with hope.

He found the strength to say these words: "Jo Ann, do you know what you're going to do when your husband comes home? I'm going to make a prediction. You'll rush out on the front porch and throw your arms around him. You'll give him the warmest welcome of his life. He needs it, and it will mean his salvation."

Jo Ann's reply shocked even this pastor who was trying so hard to hope. The woman's sneer disappeared, a light came on in her eyes, and she declared, "That's just what I'm going to do." Pastor Coon could scarcely believe what he'd heard, but he recovered enough to suggest they kneel down and pray together. The two joyfully gave thanks to God for what He'd done.

A few days after his conversations with Ralph and Jo Ann, Pastor Coon spotted their son in a grocery store. The minister edged over to where the boy was picking up a few items, bent down, and asked quietly, "How is everything at your home?"

The boy immediately straightened up tall and said with a beaming face, "Daddy's back home!"

IN THE CAT'S PAW

Pastor Coon's motivation as an artist made all the difference in this encounter. If he'd just been playing a pastor's game, throwing out beatitudes as a duty, it wouldn't have struck home. Coon did communicate an extravagant faith, but it sprang from a divine regard that shimmered above him, very real, palpable. It just had to be expressed. It demanded fleshing out.

After his many encounters with the casualties of legalism over the years, Glenn Coon could have easily burned out or at least burned low. He had to work against the grain most of the time. Those of his generation were still deeply committed to the ideals of regulatory reform. But through five decades of ministry, he inspired audiences with a simple, straightforward account of the matchless love of Christ. When Coon spoke about such things, it wasn't the same old story. It came alive. He was an artist at work, not a day laborer. His phrases about grace and faith and forgiveness flowed out of a lifetime of artful goodness.

Pastor Coon once received an urgent call from the business manager of a Christian high school who'd been cornered by an irate parent. Glenn jumped into his car and hurried to the school. He walked into the business manager's office to find a woman giving him the tongue-lashing of his life. She was upset over some financial mixup and went on and on about how monstrously she'd been treated. Coon listened to the tirade for a few moments, unable to get a word in, and felt his sympathy for the business manager growing by the second. So he grabbed onto something called "righteous indignation" and interrupted the woman's accusations with a word to his friend: "Do you know what I would do if I were you? I wouldn't even stay in this room with this woman."

The business manager seized on this as wonderful advice, and the two men walked out the door. They were on the second floor and proceeded down the stairway to the first floor. About halfway down, Glenn stopped. As he put it, "The Lord caught up with me." This pastor felt he had condemned the woman and acted contrary to the gospel of Jesus. This was not Christ's way of honoring. He told the business manager, "I made a mistake. I gave you poor counsel."

The man replied, "I think you gave me great advice, and I'm going to take it." He began hurrying even faster down the rest of the stairway.

But Glenn called out, "I've made a mistake, I have to return."

Glancing up, the business manager said firmly, "If you go back, you're going alone."

Glenn now regretted more than ever getting into the argument. He was going to have to settle up with the woman. "I remembered some good counsel I had received years before," the pastor wrote in describing the incident. "It was that I am to apologize to another as though I were the chief offender, whether I really am or not."

Glenn had condemned this woman, and, however much she seemed to deserve it, he had to make it right. So he started back up the stairs, the hardest stairs he'd ever had to climb in his life. When he got back up to the business manager's office, he found the woman had stomped on up to the third floor. Glenn thought for a moment, *Oh, you've done enough now. It isn't necessary to walk up another flight.*

The pastor had to pray himself up the long stairway to the third floor, one foot at a time. He finally found the woman holed up in the attic. She cast a glance his way as if to nail him to the wall.

"Sister," Glenn began, "I've come to apologize to you for what I said. I want you to forgive me."

"Well," she shot back, "how sorry are you?"

Glenn kept praying hard. "Sister, I am very sorry," he continued. "And I hope you will forgive me."

The woman wasn't through. Like a cat toying with a mouse it doesn't want to release or quite kill, she whined, "Are you sure? Are you sure?" And she continued to punish the pastor with sarcasm for some time.

Finally Glenn managed to say, "Sister, I don't know what the burden of your heart is. But I know there must be a great burden there. And I know that God can take it away. I am sorry that I have condemned you. I should have been praying for you and helping you to bear your burden. I have come up now to pray for you, and with you. And I wonder if you would let me pray with you now?"

The cat peered at its prey for a few seconds and then replied, "Well, okay, if you're sure you mean it."

The pastor prayed for his adversary, and as he prayed he felt the warmth of the Holy Spirit. "The change was in me," he wrote later, "I had changed from the spirit of condemnation to one of trying to help someone. And the Lord could do something through me."

After Glenn's heartfelt petition, the woman began praying and immediately broke down weeping. The pastor listened to the most wrenching confession he'd ever heard. The woman confessed she was to blame for everything that had happened. She described in detail how and why she was at the bottom of all the trouble. Afterward Glenn was able to lead her to make a new spiritual commitment.

Without light humility, Glenn would have never made it up those stairs. The insulted self would have been too heavy. But in admiration of God's kind of forgiveness, he was inspired to go up, all the way to the attic.

Glenn did not place himself in the cat's paws out of a sense of inadequacy, a need for approval. He didn't apologize to be accepted. He apologized to express God's greatness. He humbled himself before this obnoxious woman from a position of strength, not weakness. That gave him leverage. Those who flop down as doormats because they lack backbone have no leverage; they're simply walked over. But those who become meek as a deliberate expression of God Almighty's grace are a show of force. They may not always be successful. They may be ignored. But their statement still stands, meaningful because God is meaningful. As artists creating a work, they're satisfied with what the act expresses.

It's so hard for us to grasp that people don't learn to apologize by experiencing condemnation. They learn to seek forgiveness when someone seeks theirs. But this pastor expressed that truth with some eloquence, and he continued a successful lifelong ministry amid the arid ground of legalism, continually rejuvenated rather than burned out because he had so much to express.

═ • ═ • ═ • ═ • ═ • ═ • ═

16

BORED OUT

OF THE PICTURE

IN MY PRESENT surroundings—a comfortable Southern California suburb—I see casualties of a different kind from those at my old academy. People here rarely get burned out on religious goodness. Most have simply bored themselves out of the picture.

The call of the moral life just never caught on. Yuppies in hot pursuit of transcendental acquisition drive by with a wave at the basics: Don't hurt one another. The less upwardly mobile settle into mortgages and credit payments, and just don't have the time. Others are continually wearied by what they perceive as life's demands, and just don't have the energy.

But almost all of us here gather at least once a week under the high, vaulted ceiling of our mall and proceed in slow procession past the show windows, pausing here and there to stare appreciatively at the wealth of merchandise. Glorious as cathedral windows they are, but with no light from the outside, of course; it's all carefully controlled electricity. Saints posed in stained glass couldn't possibly compete with the designer suits, VCRs, and spy novels found there.

FANATICALLY COMFORTABLE

Everything in our world massages us. We're not so much evil as fanatically comfortable. We could spend a lifetime just sampling all the options on cable TV. We will never catch up with all the must-see movies and must-hear albums that are hyped our way. We can never really digest all the infotainment or take in all the slick adformation paraded into our living rooms. God's still, small voice doesn't even need to be ignored. It's all but inaudible.

With so much glitz and dazzle filling our senses, we find spiritual concerns quite unexciting and tend to reduce them to a minimum. Loose legalism finds good soil here in a world of horizon-to-horizon department stores. Fulfill the requirements of basic decency—surely God wouldn't make any more demands on our time. Love those close to you. Be true to your own truth. A few greeting card axioms and we're on our way. Holier commands just don't compute.

Of course, one doesn't have to be a yuppie to be complacent and apathetic. There are beer-bellied truck drivers lulled out of a walking slumber only by the Indy 500 who couldn't care less; rednecks out fishin' an' huntin' who never give a thought to goodness; and New York City drama critics who think of hard moral principles as some tasteless mistake like corny living room furniture.

Boredom with the holy isn't cultural. All kinds of people fail to be moved by the good life and, by default, opt for loose legalism. They cannot see virtue as a great pursuit; they want just enough morality to get by. Even a great many people with a thoroughly secular lifestyle still hold the idea in the back of their minds that they can keep God at bay with a few token gestures.

The fanatically comfortable don't have too many stories—no dramas like those of Guilliard and Jesse. Their lives are a smooth videotape, humming along, a tragedy in slow motion.

How can goodness become compelling for them? Let's look at a way out of loose legalism.

First, people must be confronted by a God who is almighty and overwhelming—up close. Acknowledging God from a distance isn't the solution; it's part of the problem. A remote, vague deity is rather easy to manipulate. We can reimagine Him in our own image of the moment and ventriloquize some nice, nonintrusive words of approval from on high. But that's not possible if we take a close look at Jehovah aroused, speaking face to face, passionately opposing idolatrous imitations of every kind.

Loose legalism is based on making everything relative: I'm not any worse than the next guy; I'm close to the average. This kind of horizontal perspective maintains the status quo of complacency. But all that falls apart when we get an earful from the God who doesn't just whisper suggestions but who thunders out His non-negotiable moral demands from a quaking mountain. Looking up at this very specific deity with a very concrete covenant in His hands blows the lid off the legalism of the complacent.

Jehovah's oversized qualities have to press up against us. We have to get a clear glimpse of the sovereign God, the One whose justice and mercy overshadow all our cheap imitations. Look up and begin admiring. Here is Someone utterly beyond you, utterly more than you and all you can possess. Admiring Him, being inspired by Him, gives us the leverage to move off our fat, stolid selves. This is the beginning of artful goodness and the beginning of the end for complacent legalism.

SOMETHING TO GET EXCITED ABOUT

Many believers react to the challenge of the spiritually bored by railing against materialism and complacency. It's always useful to point out that greed is a dead end. But it's better to give the apathetic something to get excited about, something to inspire them to move beyond their present horizons.

Peter liked to exalt the God "who called us by His own glory and excellence." Here we have a person beckoning. On what basis does He do that? Fear, authority, power? No, God's character—His glory and excellence—compels us to come to Him. If we truly see it up close in its heroic dimensions we'll be drawn out of the comfortable boundaries of the self. Attracted to Someone greater than us, we are enabled to loosen our tight grip on the acquisitions we've kept busily piling around ourselves as a security blanket.

After becoming a bit buoyant and vulnerable, we're ready for the real blow: the Atonement. Christ's passion on the cross, if seen in its stark and elemental light, is the weapon of choice in dealing with loose legalism.

Some of us are afraid of talking about the cross when confronted with complacent people who already think they've made deals with God on very generous terms. Maybe they've heard about mercy a little too much; something on fiery judgment seems more to the point.

But the cross, up close, provides a spectacle to awaken the most calloused. It shows us to what lengths God will go to uphold His moral character. It wasn't possible for Him to offer us arbitrary forgiveness. That would have made a mockery of His law; He wouldn't have been true to Himself. So He determined to meet the law's demands as a man and pay the penalty for breaking it. It was God's costly statement: I can be just and the justifier of cruel men who place their faith in Me.

Up close, Christ sweats blood. He writhes on the wood, slowly suffocating. Sin is this serious. Up close, He's dying for a drink. Up close, He's taking care of His mother at the bitter, blinding end. He's shaking in the thunder and lightning, but He won't budge an inch before the mockery of those He's trying to save. Up close their words bite: "He saved others but can't save himself." Yes, indeed, He will not save Himself at our expense. Up close, the spikes tear open the flesh, but the observable brutality only hints of the greater, wrenching agony which that chasm between Father and Son builds to a black, despairing climax: "Why have you forsaken me?" Up close, that cry pierces.

From a distance the cross is a nice gesture, but up close it is raw passion—and we're standing there with this man's blood on our hands. In the drama of the cross there are no bystanders, only participants. Those who walk away from this man's noble suffering can't go back to complacency; they'll always have His eloquent death to reckon with. The images of Scripture struggle to bring us up close to the spectacle and see it as if for the first time: Lamb unblemished and spotless, fated to shed His own innocent blood before the foundation of the world; Lamb burning on the altar, smoke ascending like a prayer, Father forgive them; derelict between thieves, by His stripes we are healed, sacrifice consumed.

Sometimes believers have used the cross to instill a morbid kind of motivation: You're wounding Christ anew with each sin you commit. Identification with the crucified Lord has led to imitation rather than inspiration. The devout have taken to whipping their backs or their psyches as a way to participate more fully in the Atonement.

But the end result of the Atonement is to eliminate penance, to bring guilt to its proper relief, not keep reinforcing it. Grace comes out as the point of the drama, so grace is what Calvary should move us to express. Christ honored us on the cross. We are honored by it, valued immeasurably, not reduced to whimpers.

Becoming aware of how seriously Christ honors us moves people out of a complacent regard for the goodness that this suffering Servant makes available through bloodshed. Righteousness had to be molded out of stubborn human flesh for us. How can we treat it lightly? We can't if we get close. Getting close, we tear off the layers of abstraction that mummify this familiar event, and we face the raw flesh extended to the limit to establish righteousness on the earth. Paul got close, so close that the cross took on a visceral power. Through it the world was crucified to him, and he to the world. The Atonement had enormous weight, throwing down an iron curtain between him and the seductions of the carnal nature.

Admiration makes the loose legalist buoyant, vulnerable to the hard shove of the cross, and finally the Word comes in to finish him off. Its moral authority is what he needs to get going in a specific direction. The insights of the writer of Psalm 119 are a big help here. Remember him rhapsodizing because he had found the Word sweeter than honey? He dug into that wealth of counsel and came up with gems. The complacent need to get close to the law, too.

Strict legalists are up too close to the law. They don't see the forest, a glorious whole, because of the trees and limbs and twigs and leaves in their oppressive multiplicity. Loose legalists are too far away. They don't smell the green, are not moved. The law's specific principles don't take shape in their immediate world.

But the Word asks us to stand somewhere, not drift. And we usually have to stand against the tide. The Word, if given half a chance, will stake such a claim in people's hearts. Its principles demand fulfillment. Some inherent energy drives them at us and through us. The apostle Peter reminded his flock that they had been born again "through the living and abiding word of God." That imperishable, eternal seed bears fruit. Continually spoken by God, never just a sign on the page, it awakens our best energies and demands to be made flesh.

Those bored out of the picture of righteousness need to hear the call of artful goodness. Conventional religion will not attract them. Small-time virtues won't catch on. They need something big to express, a big God who is sovereign over all, a cross that redefines all humanity, a Word with authority to pierce our innermost hearts. The complacent desperately need the inspiration of these themes up close and face to face.

'WE'RE ALREADY DEAD'

Gravel crackled under the tires as Nabe coasted up to his small, two-story home. In the quiet of the night the car door slammed. The young man climbed his porch stairs carrying under his arm three large canvases.

Inside, his wife, Yuki, waited, rocking a baby in her dimly lit kitchen. Nabe mumbled a greeting but did not look at her as he set his canvases in a hallway closet.

Yuki laid the baby in its crib and heated some tea. She fumbled with a scoop in the rice cooker and with difficulty spooned white grains into a glazed bowl. Shuffling into the living room, she knelt beside her husband and carefully set rice, seaweed, and tea on a low table. Without speaking, she moved slowly back into the kitchen.

As Yuki began rinsing dishes, Nabe asked, "How were the kids?"

"All right," she replied, her voice trembling.

After a long pause Nabe spoke, "Okay, so I was late this—"

"It's twelve-thirty," Yuki interrupted.

Nabe went on, "You've got to understand. It takes a lot of work to get anywhere in the art world."

"*I've* got to understand?" Yuki burst out. "You leave me alone with the children every night when I can hardly...." She shook her gnarled, arthritic knuckles at her husband, tears spilling down her cheeks. "Don't you see? You never give a thought to how hard it is for us. You're always off in your crazy dream world."

Nabe looked down. "When we were first married you told me you liked my abstract paintings. You even encouraged me."

"Yes, you were full of promises then—fame and independence, a nice big house. 'Just wait a few years,' you said. Well I've waited too long. All I get is the pain."

"Yuki, listen to me. A man has got to pursue something with his life. If he doesn't have a dream he might as well be dead."

"We're already dead as far as you're concerned. This house might as well be a tomb."

Nabe grimaced and shook his head. He rose quickly from the table, spilling his tea, and walked out to the balcony for some cool air.

No Way Out

As soon as Nabe passed through the massive wooden gates of Ryoan Zen temple, he felt different. It was always like that. The hassles of life seemed to dissolve as he walked by the stone garden with its quiet streams and ancient statues. The quotas and accounts at his father's steel wire factory, where Nabe worked, faded into insignificance.

He bowed low in greeting before his teacher-priest and exchanged a few polite remarks about the blooming cherry trees. Slipping into a dark robe, he entered a small room sided by classical wall paintings of the gods and sliding paper doors. Nabe crossed his legs on the *tatami* straw mats and became perfectly still.

But before he could empty his mind for *zazen* meditation, a flood of turbulent thoughts rushed in for attention. There were so many conflicts in his life that he couldn't resolve or escape. Even "Gutai," the avant-garde art group to which he belonged, had problems. It had started out so well—everyone full of ideals and enthusiasm for the artistic life. They had disdained the competition and pettiness of the "normal" business world.

Nabe's father was a typical example of the man who'd "made it," comfortably situated atop his profitable enterprise. He believed that his tidy accounts showing a positive cash flow had earned him the right to spend most nights away from his family drinking and gambling. In his small but steady prosperity he seemed safely insulated from any higher calling.

Nabe, ever since his restless high school years, had struggled for a way out of this material world which seemed deaf and blind to any spiritual qualities. He finally found an escape in art. Now "Gutai" was making a name for itself. Even foreign critics had come for a look. The group had put on a successful show in Osaka featuring some of its mechanized pieces and outlandish performance art.

But now Nabe saw the group being infected by the same dog-eat-dog mentality they had all disdained. Some of the artists were selling, some weren't. He noticed more and more jealousy and backbiting—all the things they'd sought to escape in art. There seemed no way out of the dark side of human nature.

And then there was Yuki. It was hard to watch her slowly contort into an arthritic invalid. He felt terribly guilty about leaving her and the children alone so often. But how could he give up the only significant thing in his life? Nabe's whole mind and heart were compressed into his trademark works, his metallic tableaus of dense geometry. He longed to make history with his canvases.

Why did life always get twisted into such knots? Why did someone always have to suffer?

Nabe hoped Zen would provide some answers. If only he could have that peace he had seen in the eyes of those few priests who had attained *satori*—enlightenment. Nabe shook his head and tried to concentrate again on the "perfect whiteness."

THE MAN FOR HUMANITY?

After a few minutes of mandarin oranges, rice crackers, and small talk, Perry's study group settled onto two sofas and opened their Bibles. Perry began to talk about the parable of the prodigal son. Nabe listened and watched intently as the young missionary's hands grew animated and his eyes sparked. Perry's face was always so transparently eager when he spoke on the Gospels.

That was what had attracted Nabe in the beginning. He had first met Perry at an English school where he was studying the "international language" so he could communicate with foreign artists and critics. Something about the Canadian teacher struck Nabe as soon as he walked into the classroom. It was just a subjective impression, but the look on that nineteen-year-old kid's face seemed like the serene countenance of enlightened priests who had taken decades to achieve their state. Nabe had even heard of some priests who committed suicide because they failed to reach *satori* after thirty years of *zazen*.

Nabe had not been interested in attending Bible class when other teachers invited him. After all, he was an Eastern man who needed to pursue truth in an Eastern way. But Perry fascinated him. Nabe had decided to check out his Bible class just to see what made him tick.

At first he understood nothing. The God of the Bible was a mystifying stranger. Then he began to notice parallels to Zen thought in Scripture: the "all is vanity" theme in Ecclesiastes, for example.

More recently, Nabe had come to understand something of the uniqueness of Christ. Perhaps He was the man for humanity. Really, who could resist this character portrayed in the Gospels? Jesus made an art out of life itself. His blank canvases were blind eyes, crippled limbs, and hard hearts. With a single word or touch, He created beautiful new images.

As Perry expounded on the prodigal son and the father's unconditional love, a lot began to click in Nabe's mind—Christ's sacrifice as the solution to that dark side of human nature, living by faith, being born again. It certainly seemed as if God's kind of love was what he and his family desperately needed.

SMEARED PAINT

Nabe slid open the bedroom closet door, folded up two futon mattresses, and shoved them into the shelves. He began vacuuming the smooth tatami mats. Yuki was out in a nearby park with the kids. Nabe had decided to clean up; it wasn't half bad, really. Being a good husband and father mattered more than he had realized.

Just the other day Yuki had said how surprised she was at the change in him. Nabe wasn't aware of it, but his wife said he was much more considerate. He *was* aware that she listened now when he talked with her about the things he was learning from the Bible. It had taken a while for it to sink in—for both of them.

After vacuuming, Nabe reached into the closet shelf for the futons. He felt something hard beneath them and pulled out a small red notebook. Curious, he leafed through it and recognized Yuki's handwriting. It was her diary, containing entries for the last several years. His name kept popping out from the lavender pages.

Nabe read about himself for hours in that quiet, empty bedroom. He couldn't stop. By the time the sun brushed against trees on the horizon, tears were flooding down his cheeks. He saw what it was like to live with someone like himself. It looked so different from the other side: an endless corridor of pain, thoughts of suicide. All the ugliness swept over him like paint smearing together, blotting out a composition. And for the first time, Nabe accepted it.

He remained staring out the window with the diary in his lap, remembering scenes that had only half-registered before, until his children's voices filtered up from the driveway.

UNPROMISING CANVASES

A large van pulled up and stopped between two oaks and a quiet stream. Nabe stepped out and looked around. A trail led up a hill to a grassy, level spot surrounded by pines. Perfect spot for a picnic. He climbed on top of the van and began handing down wheelchairs to several assistants. They helped about a dozen youths into the chairs and then everyone moved slowly up the trail.

An affable breeze rustled through the leaves and brushed against their faces. A couple of birds kept up a cheerful dialogue. Sunshine filled the glen with bright greens and deep shadows.

Nabe breathed deeply of the crisp air. This was the life. It was always exciting to see the faces of the handicapped light up when they were brought out into God's world. His "Helping Hand" project had created a lot more joy than he'd bargained for.

Nabe and Yuki had begun the ministry less than a year after their baptism. They had both been won principally by the boundlessness of God's love. Now they wanted to share it with those stuck in the "unsightly" corners of society.

In the pine-enclosed clearing, Yuki rolled herself over to a table and began fixing lunch. Several of the guys played a modified version of baseball. Nabe's two kids played tag, zipping happily between wheelchairs.

Nabe looked around at all the sunny faces. These people, too, were the objects of God's handiwork and the targets of His grace. Each one had broken through his or her physical restriction in some way, like the spastic kid who pitched with amazing accuracy. After each convoluted windup the ball somehow always found the strike zone. Every person there embodied the promise of re-creation, of transcending the distortions that sin brought into the world.

The truth Nabe tried so hard to find in abstract designs and strong colors now cried out in the lucent eyes around him. Here was all he had attempted to create on canvas: spiritual beauty in the superficially unattractive, a winning grace in the harsh angles of disabled limbs.

Nabe believed God would work His wonders on these unpromising, overlooked canvases. And Nabe was part of His artistry. Bursts of laughter existed now where there was lonely silence before, uninhibited play beneath a wide sky where there had been only cramped suffering.

Nabe looked over to see his wife stirring a large pot of stew, her face animated in conversation. Their eyes met. Yes, this was an art they could both understand.

DURING MY STINT in Japan I was always struck by how fragile spiritual life can be in a secular world, how easily it withers away in the arid soil of materialism. I walked by a multitude in the train stations every day who never seemed nudged at all by the call of the holy.

So I took great comfort in my friend Nabe and his escape from the blind-and-deaf confines of an environment so insulated from the Spirit. He always seemed rejuvenated in doing good. He and Yuki had discovered a God one could personally admire; He was not just a transcendent abstraction. They had come to see God's way of honoring people through the cross as the most important event in history. It still lived for them. And they were faithful and eager students of the Word who took its authority seriously.

Nabe found a way to express these things. I once asked him if he ever thought of going back into painting. He said no, it had become too commercial for him. Toward the end, every time he went to the canvas, he was thinking about how much a certain work might sell for rather than what he wanted to say. Unfortunately, that avenue of art had closed for him.

But another opened up, one no less articulate, no less compelling. Nabe's gallery of unpromising canvases splashed with bright colors stands in such telling contrast to his own upbringing, enveloped in the monochrome comforts of the material world.

17

ABSTRACTIONS

ON THE SIDELINES

* * *

Professor P: But if the woman in a prison camp, cut off from the husband and children who need her badly, can only be released if she becomes pregnant, then doesn't she have the moral right to commit adultery, say, with a prison guard?

Doctor L: Her "adulterous act" is actually a courageous expression of how much she loves her family and wants to care for them.

Reverend J: Well, what if the only way this woman can escape and be reunited with her family is to kill a prison guard? Would murder then become a courageous expression of love?

Doctor L: Would murder really guarantee her escape?

Reverend J: That's not the point.

Professor P: Well, murder can sometimes be justified; yes, I would affirm that. If some raging lunatic were about to machine-gun my family and I could prevent that by killing him, I would.

Doctor L: Some violence to prevent worse violence. But when that violence is generalized, as in war, the justification really falls apart. We start computing which populations may be sacrificed in order that other populations may survive, be free, or whatever.

Professor P: Really? Say four raging lunatics were about to machine gun twelve families and you could toss a grenade. Why would that be any less justified?

Doctor L: War is simply never that neat an equation. There's no possible way to say you're really saving more lives in the end.

Reverend J: We must treat violence as inherently evil. And I would go back and say that, with the woman in the prison camp, although her adultery may produce good in the end, we must regard it also as an evil.

Doctor L: But what does that mean? If something produces a good result, why is it bad?

Professor P: I'll give you another one. Say a sensitive young man has been sexually humiliated. He feels he's not a man any more, that no woman will ever love him, and he becomes suicidal. Now what if a caring, older woman could gently lead him through a sexual experience and affirm his manhood. Wouldn't that act "outside of marriage" be totally good in itself?

Reverend J: What he needs is love, not necessarily some sexual experience.

Professor P: But what if that act of fornication, or whatever you want to call it, would save the young man from falling apart? What if it saved him from suicide?

Reverend J: I suppose we could become hypothetical to the point of absurdity. What if I say I'll kill myself unless you cut Doctor L's index finger off. Would you be justified—

Professor P: Is sexual impotence really so hypothetical? Besides, don't we have to uncover primary principles? What's more valuable, saving a life or maintaining chastity?

Doctor L: Sometimes we have to choose between saving a life and economics. How much of our medical resources should we invest, for example, in expensive kidney machines? Dialysis is black and white, it spells the difference between life and death. Yet there are a lot of other medical needs that are going unmet, like care for the infants of the poor.

Reverend J: Don't we all just save as many lives as we can? That's still the goal no matter—

Professor P: But let's say you could save twelve infants with the same money that would save thirty older people on dialysis. What would you do?

Doctor L: You have to talk about probabilities, guesses. No one knows how many babies we can save with X amount of resources.

Professor P: But we do have to make very real choices about who gets the dough.

Reverend J: Mercy, what primary principles are we uncovering this time? The value of youth versus age?

Professor P: Yes, if you like. I hope we're not afraid to face the fact that an infant has more life ahead of him than an eighty-year-old.

Doctor L: There's no question that some heroic measures to save babies wouldn't normally be used on the elderly.

Reverend J: As a matter of effectiveness, I would hope. An eighty-year-old's shorter life expectancy shouldn't make him automatically expendable.

Professor P: But what if you could save the lives of two hundred infants right now by actually pulling the plug on....

* * *

When people hear terms like "ethics" and "morality" they often think of discussions like the one above, where elaborate moral conundrums keep experts debating heatedly on different sides of the issues. There's some problem that must be worked over, somewhat like a math equation, until the correct answer emerges. There are plenty of hard questions in our world to chew on. Medical technology creates an ever finer and more artificial line between life and death. Nuclear weapons set up a fragile balance of terror and force us to look for peace on the edge of blowing up the planet.

So we conduct studies and hold debates. Pondering how we would apply abstract principles to hypothetical situations can be useful, on occasions even necessary, but sometimes it gets in the way of practical goodness. Intellectually oriented people too often use a preoccupation with "ethical questions" as a substitute for virtuous behavior. Goodness takes place far away in some dilemma that can be resolved only through speculation. It's a specialty, an academic question that must be answered on paper. One can talk at length about obligations to humanity and creating the most good for the most people without having to deal with the guy next door. People come to believe that the really significant energies are expended on figuring out the right answers.

Cop-Out

Those with a penchant for abstractions, which is no small talent, can get abstracted out of the picture. The call to holy living is overshadowed by the call to examine it from a distance. Exceptions to the rules get all the attention, and everyday acts of decency are ignored. The message inadvertently and subtly proclaimed by our traditional ethical discussions is that all the action is on the edges of the law. The real ethical experts are hovering on the borders, and only they can come up with coherent answers from the maze of ethical dilemmas all around us.

There's a type of public cop-out in our age of specialists. I recall a TV news anchor commenting on some thorny current affair that had a few ethical implications, and ending with the statement, "This is a question which, in the end, only the ethical experts and theologians can settle." It's as if we expect these people to have some moral equivalent of high technology to draw on and come up with a super-strength answer. The unacknowledged assumption is that morality is some obtuse specialty with which we amateurs shouldn't embarrass ourselves.

The premise behind this compartmentalized approach to ethics is an old one. It has its roots in the Enlightenment, when the idea caught on that rationality, as opposed to religious superstition, could save mankind from its chronic woes. During the nineteenth century, as the Industrial Revolution kicked in and made progress the watchword of the day, people came to believe that humanity would just naturally progress away from primitive evil and toward the good, like a growing economy. Our basic problem was simply ignorance; the basic solution was education. At a time of widespread illiteracy, that was indeed a problem. Ignorance gives aid and comfort to a great number of vices. But education did not make humans significantly more moral; people could be just as nasty with a Ph.D. The products of highly efficient educational systems who could appreciate Nietzsche and Schubert in the morning could also preside over death camps in the afternoon.

Still, the notion that morality is essentially a matter of having the right knowledge lingers on. Humanist orthodoxy proclaims that the secret of ethical success is just figuring out what's right. Once we do that, these monumental problems of our time will be solved. But goodness, moral behavior, isn't just a science; it's an art. The right information doesn't produce it any more than the right color theory creates great paintings.

Again, information isn't bad. Education probably helps a lot of people morally. And debating complicated ethical questions has its place. A professor of ethics, for example, is going to concentrate on complicated cases in order to sharpen his students' thinking. Rigorous thought can certainly be an ally of the good life.

But all that is only the form, not the substance of moral life in our world. Speculation doesn't generate artful goodness. The real action lies elsewhere.

A GOOD, HARD LOOK

Moral excellence is most of all an ability acquired through discipline and practice. The discipline starts with taking time to admire God. People who have abstracted themselves over to the sidelines of the good life need badly to take a good, hard look at this Person with extraordinary moral qualities, instead of looking only at precepts. They need to admire His concrete life on earth, not just manipulate ethical variables. It's this revelation of a God-in-the-flesh who touches other lives so masterfully that best inspires people to get involved in learning the craft of goodness.

This is where a lot of people divide: inspiration versus information. The intellectually oriented typically turn up their noses at mere "inspirational literature," unable to abide soft heads turning out soft aphorisms. They don't think these niceties make much difference in the world.

It's true that a lot of what passes for inspirational literature isn't intellectually inspiring, but that doesn't mean it's the wrong ball game. It's the mental mediocrity that's at fault, not the aim to inspire. We're inspired in different ways, of course. Some like more penetrating analysis than others. But the thing to remember is that we've got to acquire a certain ability, not just information.

So we must be inspired first—by looking carefully and devotedly at God. The light humility that comes with admiration isn't a bad thing to have around, either. It's so easy for the knowledgeable to become proud and so easy for the proud to acquire blind spots— some obnoxious sin close by and cuddly is ignored while that evil on the horizon is fired upon. Proud people debating ethical issues can get trapped in self-serving dishonesty as they wrestle a bevy of lofty principles into certain shape just to maintain their chosen position. The proud often presume to pontificate about problems they have little heart knowledge about.

Humbly learning about God—that's the place to start. That's how we get beyond the omnivorous self that would much rather possess principles than practice them.

Putting God in the picture also helps us a great deal with the content of ethical dilemmas. If He's active in our world, that should change a lot of things. How can we say we're up against the wall— forced to do evil in order to accomplish good, for example—if the Almighty is around? Does He have to betray Himself and His explicit commands to help that mother in the prison camp and the humiliated young man? Surely He has other resources at His disposal.

The presence of God helps unravel a great many moral conundrums, but again, that's not His most important ethical role. First He wants to move us. How can we express the qualities of the infinite God? That's the driving question. And when we do get nudged off our lofty selves, God moves us toward the cross.

From Calculating to Expressing

Jesus nailed up there on Golgotha does something to inflated knowledge. It grabs all those abstractions and forces them to relate to a specific, bloody sacrifice. After that they're not so nimble in our hands anymore. We thought we had managed to quantify the concept "love" and mark off its reasonable boundaries until this Man turned up forgiving the men who drove spikes into His limbs. We thought we had subdivided justice properly and calibrated its domain until this Man threw pardon over the whole mocking, calloused world and allowed its sins to crush Him to death.

The Atonement throws a wrench into all our comfortable formulas. Our centuries-long effort to quantify obligations is overshadowed by one hard word: *honor.* Suddenly ethics is no longer a closed circle in which one good can be balanced against another and cancel it out. Now we're not so sure we can measure anything. We can only echo a grace far bigger than ourselves; point to it with whatever eloquence we can muster. Honor is open-ended, limitless. The equation of investment and return doesn't have to come out right. Honoring is an art form in itself; it is its own justification. The sacrifice of the innocent One pushes us beyond calculated goodness. We're moved from calculating to expressing, creating.

Now we're ready to hear the Word. A lot of times people don't hear it as much as organize it. The abstractionist typically goes in for micro evaluation and misses big principles. He needs to see something bigger than himself to express. He needs to listen. Learning to admire God helps him start listening. Being involved by the cross moves him to express the Word instead of merely evaluating it.

A big part of the Word's power is its authority to make promises. They are tucked into passages throughout the Bible, challenging us to flesh out spiritual truth. These promises are given to us that we "may participate in the divine nature." The Word is designed primarily to make us participants, not analysts. The emphasis is not on figuring out the right thing to do but on experiencing what it's like to be God, having His instincts move us, His feelings arouse us, His perspective guide us. Then we can be morally creative in the way He is.

The apostle John equated "whoever keeps his word" with a person in whom "the love of God has truly been perfected." The Word is much more than textbook information; it's a way to perfect a quality called love. A way to acquire an ability. Art, not science.

We obey the Word in order to know what love is. Love is defined by the Word, not vice versa. Usually the theoretician will reduce the law to a manageable concept like love. But that one naked word can't carry the moral weight we need. Loosened from its moorings it becomes a near empty set, and we begin to define love by our behavior. But in Scripture that value is expanded, given content, and constantly reinvigorated. In his second epistle John asked what love is and answered by saying, "that we walk according to His commandments."

Many people have problems basing their moral life on absolute commands. They correctly point out that rules can get in the way. Many of those conundrums that ethicists try to figure out are based on a rules versus people diagram, like the woman who hypothetically could go home and be with her family if she disregarded the rule about adultery. What's the bottom line, we're asked, rules or people? The correct answer, of course, is people. To paraphrase Christ, the law was created for mankind, not mankind for the law.

But here's where the discussion gets slippery. Saying that people have a priority over rules often leads to the corollary: if a rule is against my best interest, I shouldn't obey it. Honoring a rule is not worth sacrificing myself.

At that point the authoritative Word and its underlying premise of Truth must interrupt. The Bible gives us not only a specific picture of God's law, but also a specific picture of what mankind is. We learn what's valuable about human life. And part of our value is in giving allegiance to a principle greater than ourselves. In fact, that's how we become human beings. Paradoxically, a person is less than a human being if he does not transcend his own interests. It's that bull's-eye proverb of Jesus again: "He who would save his life must lose it." Every act of giving declares that something outside of me is worth sacrificing for.

If we use the scrawny term "rules" in contrast to "people," the answer is all but predetermined. But if we ask, "Is love more important than me? Does mercy weigh more than my life? Is justice worth sacrificing myself for?" Then we're moved to a different point. We recognize that heroic stands are what make human life most worthwhile. Using our existence as a canvas on which an eternal value is inscribed does have great significance.

The Word gives us those values worth standing for. We can stake out ground on what it emphasizes, on what it declares central to human life. The Word asks us to stand and declare our open allegiance, not just comment from the sidelines. Instead of always delineating the boundaries, we move inside, deep inside the Word, to artful goodness.

To Be Cut Off

In the 1860s, leprosy reached epidemic proportions among the natives of the Hawaiian islands. They had no natural immunity to this disease, nor to many others brought by white men in trading vessels. The very survival of the Hawaiian people seemed threatened. As a result, the government passed and began strictly enforcing a segregation law. All confirmed cases of leprosy had to be removed from society and kept in complete isolation. The quarantine site chosen was Kalawao on the island of Molokai. It was a stony but verdant promontory edged in between the pounding surf of a rocky coastline and a massive cliff, which no one in poor health could climb.

Many Hawaiians understandably regarded the leprosy law as inhumane. They distrusted the ability of white medical authorities to prescribe for Hawaiian bodies, and began calling the Board of Health the Board of Death. White officials complained that the Hawaiians continued to eat, drink, and sleep with leprous relatives and hide them from those who "strive to root out the evil thing."

For the Hawaiian, there was something worse than death: to be cut off from a loved one forever. They weren't as appalled by the disfiguring illness as their white contemporaries. They still wanted to touch the afflicted relative. Whatever the consequences, he must not be cut off from the group. All Hawaiians needed to reaffirm physically, by touching, their share in a common humanity.

Thus, segregation of the diseased violated the deepest fabric of Hawaiian culture. Yet that segregation seemed the only way that culture could survive. This was the dilemma that faced the island people, and the dilemma that Christian missionaries in Hawaii labored over. It was a profound moral question worthy of thorough reflection. Forty-eight ministers gathered at an annual meeting and talked about it. They considered at length all the factors involved and came up with what they considered a correct answer. The men took a stand. They decided that the greater evil was "a loathsome, incurable, deadly disease fastening itself upon the 'vitals' of the nation," and which, in a few years, could mean "the disorganization and total destruction of civilization, property values, and industry, of our churches, our contributions, our Hawaiian Board and its work of Missions."

The men also stated what sort of action should be taken: "While striving to comfort and strengthen with the love of Jesus the afflicted hearts of the lepers and their friends," we must "teach and persuade all the people to obey the law of God and segregate the lepers from among us," and "teach every leper who cleaves to his people and refuses to go away, that he is sinning against the lives of men and against the law of God."

It's easy from a distance to criticize the minister's statement as harsh and unfeeling. We know better how to control leprosy now and don't see it as the awful threat everyone did then. But in the 1860s, forty-eight sincere people came up with a credible choice of the lesser of two evils. There would be heart-rending partings at the docks in Honolulu, but that meant that a whole population would not be decimated.

What the ministers did not come up with was artful goodness. That would take someone else—a Belgian farm boy named Joseph De Veuster who had an enormous appetite for serving God. At the age of twenty he entered holy orders. Prostrated before an altar, he was covered with a black mortuary pall, sprinkled with holy water, and then raised up to poverty, chastity, and obedience with the Congregation of the Sacred Hearts. Joseph thrived in this environment of radical consecration. During his training, the words of Christ, "Go teach all nations," impressed him deeply, and he developed a yearning for missionary service.

Superiors doubted his abilities at first. They didn't think he could manage the ecclesiastical studies one had to pursue to become a priest. But Joseph surprised them, stubbornly poring over Latin texts hour after hour until he could decipher them and pass the necessary tests. He still didn't have the intellectual equipment to balance a variety of moral factors and come up with the correct sum. What he did have, however, was a passion to echo Christ, to live as He did.

Joseph, now called Father Damien, finally got his chance to go and teach: He was sent to a district on the island of Hawaii where the population was scattered over a thousand square miles of volcanic peaks and steep slopes. It took him six weeks of strenuous hiking just to get around to his parishioners. Most men would have collapsed after a few months, but Damien found a congenial challenge in this physically demanding life: carrying candles, sacraments, and portable altar on his back over rugged terrain, calling the faithful with a conch shell. He became an accomplished builder of chapels. When felling trees in the highlands or hauling up shipped-in logs from the beach, he enjoyed carrying the heaviest beams himself.

After several years of ministry, this physical Christian was confronted by the thorny issues of leprosy, segregation, and the settlement on Molokai. And he came up with an answer. It was Easter; Damien was thirty-three. He deliberately crossed from the world of the well to the world of the mortally ill, choosing to minister to and live with the people at the Kalawao settlement. It was a simple matter in a way. The lepers needed a priest, and Damien volunteered. He was sent on a temporary basis, but then he found the work of his life.

'WE LEPERS'

This man was no aging or sickly saint deciding to spend his remaining years in heroic service, but a robust, active priest described by contemporaries as a man "in the prime of life...and the perfection of youthful health and vigor." He did not come to the island blindly.

"You know my disposition," he told superiors. "I want to sacrifice myself for the poor lepers." But neither was he a morbid holy man looking for martyrdom. "I am not yet a leper," he wrote his brother, "and with the miraculous help of God...I hope I never will be."

Damien arrived on Molokai with little more than a breviary. But he quickly built himself a shack, began visiting the people in their huts, and started services in which he addressed the congregation not as "my brothers" but as "we lepers." Damien touched the people, physically as well as spiritually, and won many converts.

A doctor once assigned there had the habit of setting his medicines on his gatepost so that the afflicted could receive his help from a distance. They didn't want it. Another doctor who made rounds at the settlement hospital conducted physical examinations by raising the rags on a diseased body with his cane. A minister who had visited the island preached the good word only from the elevated and safe distance of a veranda.

These men were being quite reasonable and correct. If segregation was necessary, self-segregation must also be practiced. One had no right to take any taint of the disease back to the land of the living.

But Damien was not a visitor. He entered squalid huts, cleaned and bandaged open sores, applied salves and ointments, prescribed pills. He also labored for souls face to face: "Here I give words of sweetness and consolation; there, I mix in a little bitterness, because it is necessary to open the eyes of a sinner."

Damien ministered willingly, but he wasn't a plastic saint impervious to the physical horrors around him. He wrote to friends of the fetid odor arising constantly from toes and fingers worn away. The smell of the congregation at his church was so bad that at communion time he feared he wouldn't be able to swallow the consecrated wine. "Sometimes, confessing the sick," he wrote, "whose sores are full of worms like cadavers in the grave, I have to hold my nose." But Damien would not turn away. He stuck it out in the confessional and struggled to overcome overwhelming nausea and headaches that lasted for days.

He also started smoking a pipe to disguise the odors that clung to his clothes, and he had someone send a pair of heavy boots to protect his legs from the "peculiar itching which I usually experience every evening after my visiting." Damien stayed; he continued to touch; he continued to say "we lepers." And in time he no longer had to force himself; he lived and worked cheerfully, and he ate with a good appetite.

There was plenty of work to do. The Hawaiians there had a saying: "In this place there is no law." After all, what legal punishments could threaten those already imprisoned for life, awaiting an unpleasant death? So the weak huddled in dark houses, wrapped in filthy bed clothes, hoping that somehow they could crawl out to the boat that brought shipments of food and get their fair share. And the strong, grown accustomed to taking from others whatever they desired, "seem to want for nothing from soft slippers to hair-oil."

Children suffered the most, especially those whose parents had died or simply abandoned them. The unscrupulous sometimes used them as drudges or child prostitutes and then simply threw them out when they became too deformed by the disease.

Surrounded by such tragedies, Damien pleaded and preached and sometimes threatened. He was known to invade a dance place called the "Crazy Pen," where drunken men and women cavorted, and break up the festivities with moral outrage and a walking stick.

He also began taking orphans under his wing, building dormitories and kitchens for them near his presbytery. Slowly Damien created beauty amid this harsh, forbidding landscape of the dying. He gave music, fashioning flutes out of old coal-oil cans which the lepers managed to play with only two or three fingers. He took great pains to ensure that charity was not given in anonymous bulk but that every man, woman, and child at the settlement received a gift package addressed individually.

Each Sunday, young and old believers gathered at his church, St. Philomena's, the women in long-sleeved gowns and beribboned straw hats, the men in calico shirts and white trousers, all of them draped in flower leis. They sat quietly in the brightly painted interior, a poignant mixture of hope and decay. The candles were usually set at odd angles, the holy water font was a tin cup, and the decorations were rather tawdry. But the occasional visitor came away impressed by the beauty of the congregation's singing, the fervor of their prayers, and the earnestness with which they brought their broken, doomed bodies forward to receive the sacraments.

On these occasions Kalawao became a community. It was no longer just a place where the dying fought for food and tried to forget their misery in drunkenness. Here was Christ's body, a living part of the whole. Here human beings could grow in the Spirit.

To build it, Damien had to endure years of isolation. He frequently begged his superiors to send another priest to work with him, but that was, understandably, a difficult assignment to fill. For more than half the time he had no one, and he felt it keenly: "Being deprived of the companionship of my colleagues of our dear Congregation is more painful to bear than leprosy." But still, the man stayed on.

The Price of Touching

Father Damien outlasted three complete population turnovers at Kalawao, but after twelve years of ministry there, his "we lepers" invocation became a physical reality. He lost all feeling in his left foot, and then telltale atrophy of the skin began to appear. Damien did not fall apart at this death sentence. He simply prayed that his Lord would grant him grace to carry this cross "on our peculiar Golgotha of Kalawao." He had taken the risk with eyes wide open; this was the price of touching.

Still Damien was no ascetic seeking the dissolution of the flesh. He tried an experimental treatment using hot baths until it became apparent it wasn't working.

Damien used his strength to the end, redoubling his efforts into what a biographer called "a kind of priestly perpetual motion." A visiting clergyman was astonished to find him on top of a church putting on the roof, energetically directing masons and carpenters. The disease by now was grossly evident: puffy face, ears swollen and elongated, eyes red, voice hoarse. But Damien expressed thanks that his hands, though quite sore, were not yet crippled.

Father Damien made a priceless statement, one that never occurred to the men arguing the implications of the leper problem on property values and civilization. This man did not solve a math problem; he lived out his passion. He gave the world a luminous work of artful goodness because he was compelled to express something greater than himself. Such a work could only have been created by a man who'd acquired an ability, a disciplined skill, rising each day at 5 A.M. for "morning prayer—adoration and meditation until 6:30." Father Damien knew how to admire, how to meditate on the Word—how to make a stand. In his Personal Rule he admonished himself: "Unite your heart with God.... May passion lead you to whisper these words continually: 'I wish to be dissolved and to be with Christ.'"

A visitor at Kalawao, walking with Damien by the shore one day, stopped to cool off and waded into the water. Looking back to the beach, he was impressed by the "quiet way" Damien "sat down and read and prayed while I bathed, retiring at once into that hidden life which was so real to him." The master artist getting in touch with his sources.

SKILLFUL
REVELATION

18

The Discipline of Seeing

FATHER DAMIEN POINTS US toward the common ground, the fertile soil, of all artful goodness: the devotional life. We've seen that light humility comes from admiring God, hard honor from being moved by Christ's act of honor, and open allegiance from accepting the authority of the Word. And we've seen how people who've burned out on being good, bored themselves out of the picture, or abstracted themselves to the sidelines can escape their respective ruts with the help of these qualities. Each of these virtues and each of these strategies depend ultimately on the discipline of contemplation for their success. That's how artful goodness begins; that's how it is sustained.

How to Really See

Without a credible devotional life we have no realistic hope of doing more than imitating. Taking regular time to prayerfully see God in His Word is the key to inspired virtue. The discipline of seeing is as vital for the believer as for the painter. Both must develop it as an integral part of the skill of expression.

So how do we really see the Word devotionally? Obviously it doesn't always inspire. Its familiarity puts a lot of people to sleep, in fact. I remember as a kid bogging down in Leviticus for the fifth time as I tried to make it all the way through Scripture. A lot of people have settled on thumbing through the Bible to look for some quick fix. They don't know whether to take the job in St. Louis or the one in Chicago, and they hope that some stray verse in the Psalms will nudge them one way or the other. Or abrasive Aunt Martha is coming for two weeks, and they need some high-potency verse of exhortation in the epistles to shore up their civility.

Sometimes we do need spiritual first aid in emergencies, and God is often happy to oblige us on the run. But quick fixes don't help us see. They don't build up skill. We need something more regular and more in-depth—say an hour each morning. We need a time to look intently and admire.

Most of us could learn something in our relationship with the Word from the way artists have related to nature. Nature, the visual world, is what the painter traditionally has attempted to express. That part of creation is where he looks, with concentrated gaze, as his source of inspiration. He does not approach it casually.

In 1904, Paul Cezanne wrote this to a friend:

> I am progressing very slowly, for nature reveals herself to me in very complex forms; and the progress needed is incessant. One must see one's model correctly and experience it in the right way; and, furthermore, express oneself forcibly and with distinction.

Cezanne defined the "true path" of painting as "the concrete study of nature" as opposed to "intangible speculations." Here was a man wholly dedicated to seeing profoundly so he could express what he saw. He wasn't just grabbing a quick view of pretty trees over there or lovely flowers here. For him there was a reality out there to be experienced in the right way. He wrote, "To achieve progress nature alone counts, and the eye is trained through contact with her."

Those who hear the call of artful goodness must train their eyes in a similar way. Our "nature" is God's creative Word. One can make progress only by regular contact with it and one must be trained for something more than roving over the verses for a quick fix.

William Bougeureau, who exhibited in France's official salon for fifty years, once wrote that he respected all schools of painting "which have as their basis the sincere study of nature, the search for the true and the beautiful." The devotional study of the Word must be a similar quest, a search for the true and the beautiful, an effort to see deeply and thus admire.

Simply thumbing through Scripture is one pitfall we face on our way to a genuine devotional life. Another one, on the opposite side of the road, is the habit of approaching the Word basically as a textbook full of doctrinal information. Some people tend to comb through passages, pulling out texts and phrases and words that support a certain position. They build up data to insert into the appropriate categories and fine-tune theories to fit them together. The more scholarly pore over Hebrew and Greek nuances and analyze grammatical structure. The less scholarly grab whatever proof texts come in handy and hang on for dear life.

The Bible does, as a matter of fact, have a lot of doctrinal information, and objectively analyzing and putting together its data is important. But devotional study is something different; it goes beyond information. I happen to do a lot of analytical Bible study for various writing projects, and I do it regularly in the morning, but I've come to realize that it's possible to come away from all my neat categorizing and amassing of data with no more inspiration than from an hour of underlining a tome on biology. I need something more to make it devotional. I need to admire.

The Italian Eclectic School of painting attempted to pull together the best from various artists and create a perfect synthesis. It seemed quite reasonable to combine all possible perfections into a whole. These artists set about to capture the fire of Michelangelo, the design of the Roman School, the glowing color of Lombardy, the action and light and shade of the Venetians, the grace of Correggio, the symmetry of Raphael. However, the sum of it all didn't quite make it; the experiment failed. The men of the Eclectic School were good painters, but far behind the greatest. The perfect parts they amassed did not become a living whole.

Our primary purpose in looking at the Word is not to put theories or creeds together but to know a whole Person better. Trying to get all our doctrines to come together just right is worthwhile, but God can get lost in the shuffle. He can be fragmented into abstraction if we approach Him only through the many layers of our correct theology. The painters of the Eclectic School responded to nature only through the layers of other men's great painting styles. They lost that directness, that spontaneous expression that makes a work of art live.

Great men have produced a wealth of tools that can be helpful in Bible study. We have our commentaries and theological dictionaries and histories and introductions. But they should never become a substitute for seeing the Word. Paul Cezanne's call to painters is one we can all heed: "We must not…be satisfied with retaining the beautiful formulas of our illustrious predecessors. Let us go forth to study beautiful nature." Leonardo da Vinci advised students to avoid just imitating other painters' styles: "One must have recourse to nature herself rather than to the masters who have learned from nature." Franz Pforr, in trying with other members of a communal society called the Lukasbund to rejuvenate German art, wrote: "Look at nature. Can one surpass its precision? I doubt it."

The finely focused zeal of such artists should speak to us. We must train the eye of our hearts by looking directly at the Word. Let's consider a few ways we can do that.

TRAINING THE EYE

The epicenter of the "nature" on which we base our art is the life of Christ. He is the Word perfected, at full strength, flawless and fully expressed. So start (and end) by looking at Him as intently as possible. Notice His every gesture. Try to hear the inflection in his Words. Spotlight the economy and potency of His every action. Watch for the reactions of those around Him. Stare down His adversaries. Check out every participant in His encounters with publican, Pharisee, leper, scribe, beggar, fallen woman, disciple, multitude, lawyer, corpse, mother, governor. Try to climb into the scenes. Feel the weather; touch the faces; sense expectation, danger and suspense, imagine Christ's emotions. And always, always, relate your impressions to the whole person you are attempting to know.

Seeing as an artist means we become participants as much as possible. We don't just stand on the sidelines taking documentary photographs. Instead, we try to capture the shades of color, the textures, the mood, the barely visible harmonies and rhythms. We have to try to feel as well as comprehend.

Insights we gain from such looking will motivate us to flesh them out in life. Gustave Courbet, a realist painter, was confident of this:

> The beautiful is in nature, and it is encountered under the most diverse forms of reality. Once it is found, it belongs to art, or rather to the artist who discovers it. Once the beautiful is real and visible it contains its own artistic expression.... Beauty as given by nature is superior to all the conventions of the artist.

We can have a similar confidence in the Word; it contains its own beauties that will be revealed to us. When we begin to see intently, we begin to make discoveries. We uncover another level of meaning in some healing incident; detect a hidden point in some familiar saying; find a new application for an old command. Putting ourselves in the scenes helps bring the data home: The words and actions bounce off our present problems and challenges; we take in the counsel, hope, conviction, encouragement, reprimand, and love, as well as write it down. Above all, we discover more to admire in the matchless person of Christ.

From the epicenter we can move off into other, supporting members of the cast of Scripture. Biographical studies often yield new pictures out of familiar historical narrative. Try fashioning a whole portrait from the incidents left to us of the lives of Joshua, Solomon, or Nebuchadnezzar. What character traits do they exhibit? How did God woo, correct, and reward them? Putting the pieces of a life together is a good way to practice seeing intently. Often we see

Christ reflected in a variety of ways through these characters. Moses pleading for wayward Israel, Jonathan befriending his rival, Daniel standing firm in an alien nation—they all add their colors to the primary picture. Our admiration deepens.

Some characters have left us not so much lives as statements, a body of work that documents their religious passion compressed into its dual essentials of judgment and redemption. These are the prophets. They speak with great conviction, but sometimes their messages can blur together. We get lost in long passages against Moab and Edom or in oracles outlining a hoped-for kingdom we have never seen. Thematic studies can help us see here. Each prophet has a unique voice, and his passion has its own shape. Try to uncover what he's emphasizing, what's unique. Draw a dominant message out of his "thus saith the Lord" that can give you a clear picture on which to concentrate.

Giving form to almost all Jeremiah's messages to proud, corrupt Jerusalem was an uncompromising call to surrender, and it echoes down to us who cling so stubbornly to a threatened ego. Daniel had a habit of somehow coming up with God's sovereignty at the end of his long passages full of symbolic beasts. That's a particularly meaningful point for a man to make who's been waiting seventy years for Jehovah to restore His people. Amos the shepherd consistently cried out for justice against all the decadence a nation on the skids could throw at him. That point helps bind up his book into a compact projectile.

Coming up with themes can help us admire the whole when the details don't seem particularly inspiring. There's a point to it all. The prophets deliver fiery warnings and offer glorious hope, all in an attempt to move their people toward a certain kingdom, a certain point in time when the Christ fulfills both judgment and redemption in His crucifixion and resurrection.

There's a place in devotional study for putting pieces together, as long as the Word remains the center of focus and not our theories about organizing it. The words of landscape artist Thomas Cole are relevant here:

> The most lovely and perfect parts of nature may be brought
> together, and combined in a whole, that shall surpass in beauty
> and effect any picture painted from a single view. I believe...
> that it is of the greatest importance for a painter always to have
> his mind upon nature, as the star by which he is to steer to
> excellence in his art.

Combining parts into a whole, yes. Getting the big picture from various viewpoints, certainly. This can all be devotional as long as

we continue to steer our course directly by the star of the Word itself
and find our inspiration in it.

Themes help us get a handle on the prophets, but when it comes
to the epistles, the themes seem to spill over each other. There's such
an abundance of truths and principles in Paul's run-on sentences. He
sweeps up large chunks of theology in a few clauses thrown out in
passing. Peter and John are no lightweights, either.

Taking each verse apart is one way to add up the meaning, but
another method is more directly devotional. Try doing a verse-by-
verse paraphrase of a passage. The epistles contain many words and
phrases that have been worn down to cliches. "Cleansed by the
blood," "walking in the light," "victory in Christ," "justified, sancti-
fied"—such labels can become all but invisible in their vague familiarity. They're a kind of shorthand for a great deal of theological
truth, but when we see and hear them over and over, the original
wealth of meaning tends to shrink into a digit in our minds. We
know but don't feel. Rewriting the Word is similar to an artist's
sketching a scene; he only begins to see what's out there by trying to
capture it on canvas.

A good definition of what paraphrasing does is found in Edward
Hopper's explanation of his work: "My aim in painting has always
been the most exact transcription possible of my most intimate
impressions of nature." It helps to give voice to our innermost
impressions of the Word. Writing them out is one way of reflecting
its meaning back to God and letting it sink deeper into us.

Landscape artist Theodore Rousseau gives us a good motto: "In
art it is better to be honest than clever." Honestly and sincerely
responding to the Word is more important than our ability to wrap
credible theories around it. Rousseau also wrote: "All the particular,
special majesty of a portrait of Louis XIV by LeBrun or Rigaud will
be conquered by the humility of a tuft of grass clearly lit by a ray of
sun." In our verse-by-verse study we look for that brightly lit tuft of
grass, that piece of nature-the-Word that shines simple truth past
professional analysis and into our hearts.

So often we gaze dully over the same old lines. We take in the
familiar words dutifully, but little registers. We could use the enthusiasm of a Delacroix looking at something as pedantic as a flower. A
friend recalled finding him at work: "I came upon him in an ecstasy
of enchantment before a yellow lily, of which he had just understood
the beautiful 'architecture'—that was the felicitous word he used."
Delacroix really *saw*. We need the same intensity in order to discover
an illuminating architecture in the Word.

Paraphrasing is a means to that end. We read a sentence carefully, try to catch the significance of each word, dig for something concrete behind the abstractions, then write down what the sentence means in our own words. It's a way of expressing the faith of Scripture in a personal way. If Paul advises in Romans 12:21, "Do not be overcome by evil, but overcome evil with good," we might translate: "Don't let Satan push you around; you push Satan around—with Christ." If Peter informs us that God "has given us his very great and precious promises, so that through them you may participate in the divine nature" (2 Peter 1:4), we might respond: "Just think—these incredible promises in the Bible are a way to share in the character qualities of God Almighty!" Our sketches of Scripture will help us see more actively and can lead us back to that essential goal, deeper admiration.

FINDING SOMETHING NEW

All these methods of Bible study are simply means to help us truly look at the Word, to see more of it. And everyone, not just bookworms and theologians, has the privilege of seeing new and inspiring things in Scripture. Everyone has nature out there to enter into. In Ephesians Paul wrote that he always asked the glorious Father to "give you the Spirit of wisdom and revelation, so that you may know him better." He prayed that "the eyes of your heart may be enlightened" so we could really know, really see, spiritual realities. Every believer has this resource at his disposal.

The sculptor Auguste Rodin wrote:

> There is no recipe for improving nature. The only thing is to see. Oh doubtless a mediocre man copying nature will never produce a work of art, because he really looks without seeing, and though he may have noted each detail minutely, the result will be flat and without character.... The artist, on the contrary, sees; that is to say, his eye, grafted on his heart, reads deeply into the bosom of nature.

That's precisely what we must have; our eyes must be grafted to our hearts and enlightened. And the Spirit of wisdom and revelation makes it happen. Here's that Spirit again who interacts dynamically with law, with the Word, to produce artful goodness. The devotional life is the ground where they meet; it's where the sparks fly.

We've got to get beyond a mediocre copying of nature, noting each detail, but not really seeing. Devotional study seeks not just information, but revelation, wisdom that's deeply felt. Reviewing old truths does not inspire people. Going over the catechism of whatever doctrines we profess is not seeing. We need new insights in order to keep reflecting the "bosom of nature," the heart of the Word. Insights are the key to growth.

New converts tend to grow so quickly and feel so spiritually high in part because they're learning so many new things. A sense of discovery propels us toward change. Review sinks us into an easy chair. It's such a basic principle we overlook it. People need insight, revelation—that's what the Spirit tries to lead us to. That's essential energy for change.

Too often religious people try to create revival or reform by pounding in old lines and familiar phrases. We simply turn up the volume on the same old tune. It's poor strategy. Our listeners may be prodded into dull imitation, but artful goodness remains a long way off. People have to make genuine discoveries if any spiritual life is to be created.

Again, the artist offers us a parallel. He has to see something new in that familiar landscape, that cliche of a human face, in order to create a new painting. He's got to catch the light bathing some subject in a new way, bringing out colors he never noticed before. He needs a visual insight to express.

Devotional Bible study is about receiving insights from the Spirit to express—insights that should help us know God more profoundly.

Unfortunately, not all "insights" are created equal. Some people, uncomfortable over the familiarity of scriptural truth, try to find newness by digging up obscure texts to create some eccentric theory. The unbalanced major in flaky "insights" and draw off-the-wall conclusions. The wrong things take center stage. Details are dressed as pillars of the faith. Trying hard to get to something new, we can veer off into trivial detours.

Seeing is a discipline we must take time to develop, and looking at the Word carefully to detect what it emphasizes, what it builds up to, is an essential part of the discipline. There's no substitute for responding honestly to the Word. The great challenge is to uncover something that's both new to us and important in the Bible, something that increases our admiration for God. Some fine points are petty; some fine points inspire. What can we find that's a revelation and yet that really matters? It's the challenge that drives generations of artists on, and it should drive believers on, too.

We have to maintain a balance between our "intimate impressions" and faithfulness to the Word, avoiding both dull review and novel misinterpretations. Artists have faced a similar need for balance. Thomas Cole, a painter absorbed in romantic landscapes, advised: "If the imagination is shackled, and nothing is described but what we see, seldom will anything truly great be produced in either Painting or Poetry." Spirit-led imagination helps the Word come alive off the page. But Cole also wrote this about another painter's failure:

He has painted from himself, instead of recurring to those
scenes in nature which, formerly, he imitated with such great
success. It follows that the less he studies from nature, the further he departs from it, and loses the beautiful impress, of
which you speak with such justice and feeling.

We still have to keep close to our source of inspiration; we still have
to keep looking carefully.

The insights we gain don't have to be mind-boggling truths no
one ever thought of before. We will rarely make those kinds of discoveries. They simply must be new to us, a familiar phrase seen in a
new light, a glimpse of some "beautiful architecture" in a passage.
Rediscovering verities, running into old commands as if for the first
time, appreciating anew the whole person behind it all—these are
the things that can inspire us each day. The insights that matter move
us beyond groggy mental assent to seeing with the eyes of our heart.

COMPLETING THE CIRCLE

After we get an insight from the Word, there's another step we can
take to complete the circle of devotion: praise. Expressing praise to
God clarifies and intensifies our admiration.

Normally we equate prayer with a single aspect of it: petition.
Prayer is asking for things—a hurried request for watchcare before
we rush out the door. But a quick nod heavenward, like thumbing
the Bible for a quick fix, does not create a devotional life. If we want
to become artists and not just day laborers, prayer must become
more devotion than transaction. Petition is vitally important, but
praise is what best helps develop the essential discipline of seeing.
It's a way of looking intently at God.

Our natural tendency in prayer is to touch every base except God
Himself. We tug at His blessings; intercede for others; express thanks
for the trees, our job, new furniture, sunny days. We do everything
but focus on the Person of God. It takes no effort to ask for what we
need, but few of us fall on our knees and spontaneously launch into
a doxology. Participating in praise is a vital part of healthy spiritual
growth, however, not an accessory for religious specialists. So here
are a few suggestions on how to get started.

To get the wheels working, select one of the Psalms and sketch it
out with a paraphrase. The Psalms contain a rich variety of anthems
to God. Find one that gives you a striking picture, and echo its
expressions of admiration in your own words to God. Make it your
own prayer reflecting your present situation. The ardor and awe of
the Psalms are contagious, and looking through them toward God
will stimulate us toward creative praise of our own.

Make a praise collection. As you look carefully at the Word, you'll run across passages describing the character and glory of God that strike you as insights. Begin to write down those favorite descriptions. Make your own collection of praise that portrays the qualities of God in living color.

Assembling these glimpses expands your picture of the Almighty. The richness of His character grows more vivid in your mind. You discover that the God whose voice shakes the earth and whose presence causes mountains to melt like wax is also the God who gently promises not to break a bruised reed or snuff out a dimly burning wick. You see that the God who stills the tumult of the peoples is also the one who causes the dawn and sunset to shout for joy.

Focus on one character trait. As you become experienced in praise, you'll want to look closely in prayer at specific aspects of God's character and attributes. This helps sharpen your concentration and deepen your perception. Select something like *power, holiness,* or *mercy,* and think of all the biblical descriptions you can recall that illuminate that one quality. Think of God's acts in Scripture that embody it, and raise your own psalm celebrating all the ways He is powerful, holy, or merciful. This personalized psalming becomes even more effective when you remember acts of God you've witnessed that exemplify the trait on which you're concentrating.

Developing the discipline of praise enables us to see God more sharply, to fix the gaze of our hearts and minds on Him. To keep on looking, we need to keep seeing new things. Catching some new glimpse of Truth in Scripture is precisely the thing that can move us to praise with feeling.

It's important to exploit the moment. Study and prayer are a creative dynamic. Study by itself can trickle off into cold facts. Prayer by itself drones off into tired phrases. We need both acting together, the essentials of the devotional life, law and spirit, which become more than the sum of two parts.

Vincent van Gogh, writing his brother Theo about inspiration, spoke gratefully about times when "the sincerity of one's feeling for nature" becomes so strong that "one works without knowing one works...the strokes come with a sequence and a coherence like words in a speech or a letter." This is art at its best and the devotional life at its best. The Spirit wants to create in us a strong response to the Word, a response that moves us to work without knowing we work, expressing a coherent picture of the God we admire.

Our time of study and praise keeps us from merely laboring at goodness. Instead of going out to the chores, we start by looking at the God who cherishes us, who has honored us in Christ. That needs to be reaffirmed each day. We create because we're valued, not in order to *be* valued.

THE DEVOTIONAL LIFE is not an addition, an icing on the cake. It's the substance. All that lies behind the eloquent virtues—admiring the Sovereign God, being moved by the Cross, standing on the Word —is only theory without the devotional life. The discipline of seeing is never exhausted. Some drop the Word after becoming familiar with it as if it were a car manual: These are the working parts; okay, now I can drive. No, artful goodness must have inspiration from beginning to end. Or as sculptor Marsden Hartley put it: "The eye is the painter's first and last vehicle."

It's our calling to maintain a sense of wonder in the Word, just as painters managed to wonder at nature all their lives. Here's Delacroix at the zoo and natural history museum:

> Elephants, rhinoceros, hippopotamus, strange animals....I had a feeling of happiness....What a prodigious variety of species, of forms, and of destinations! At every moment, what seems to us deformity, side by side with what seems to us grace. Here are the herds of Neptune, the seals, the walruses, the whales.... How necessary it is to give oneself a shaking up...to try to read in the book of creation, which has nothing in common with our cities and with the works of men! Certainly, seeing such things renders one better and calmer. When I came out of the museum, even the trees got their share of my admiration."

Yes, we need a shaking up, to see everything as if for the first time, with all the excitement of Adam naming the animals.

─── 19 ───

MAKING THE
PICTURE WHOLE

NOW THAT WE'VE LOOKED at the essential prerequisite of artful goodness, let's look a bit closer at the quality itself.

It will help to define art in general. We have to be careful, of course, in trying to say what art is and isn't. Artists, by the very nature of their craft, constantly redraw boundaries and challenge definitions. Art can never be completely summed up. But I would like to propose a functional definition simply to put a finger on what about art has affected people most deeply down through the centuries. I've come to see this as *skillful revelation*.

When we look at most works of art we're impressed by skill. The sculptor chiseling a graceful form out of stubborn stone, the painter making daubs of color cohere into glowing flesh tones, the poet setting perfect words into a musical flow—these people move us with their skill. We're attracted by it; we stop and take a closer look. When we don't find skill, we generally keep walking.

The second element that makes art important to us is revelation. Almost all works of art reveal something to us. We see, feel, hear, and think something which the artist sees, feels, hears, and thinks. We never knew the human body could be so heroic until Michelangelo spread his figures above the Sistine Chapel. We'd never seen the stirring drama in a wheat field until van Gogh showed it to us. Composers like Beethoven and Tchaikovsky make clear emotions that most of us could only vaguely point to before. We sense a thrill of recognition when a writer makes vivid for us experiences and feelings which we'd only half-registered or which we'd always tucked away in secret.

Works of art are revelations. Traditionally they reveal beauty—

and awe the beholder. More contemporary works often reveal the ugliness and anguish in life—and can be equally moving.

Art is skillful revelation. It's not just revelation—a sharing of information. The skill with which the revelation comes has a lot to do with its impact. And it's not just mute skill—showing off some technique. The revelation intended is what gives the skill a point. The two must bind together. And the more deeply felt the revelation, the greater the work of art. This is what the dynamic of law and Spirit lead to. We absorb the law; we respond to the Spirit—and that creative tension produces skillful revelation.

DEVELOPING SKILL

Artful goodness is first of all a skill we develop. It's not something we simply memorize and do, or buckle down and do. It's a skill that comes from the discipline of a devotional life. It can't be decreed or copied into existence.

But neither is the skill of artful goodness something that just happens. There's this naive view that art is the effortless oozings of inspiration, but no painter struggling with a landscape would accept that. We don't let go and let it flow. We develop a discipline. We act on the insight we receive.

Blessed are the doers of the law, not those who just stare idly. There's an enormous secret of success hidden in this plain command *to do*. We develop skill by acting; there's no replacement for that. Nothing can take the place of participation. Artful goodness will remain a hazy glow on the horizon to those who read about it and then fall asleep in the easy chair. We've got to respond.

And when we do respond to what our devotional life suggests, wonderful things happen. The first step leads to others; the first, clumsy effort grows into surer motions. God is just waiting for that one move off dead inertia to get us into the spirit-law dynamic. But only doers open the first door. You have to do something in order to do better.

So stare at nature-the-Word, and then put paint on canvas; find a way to express it. The results may not be spectacular, but you're on your way. Skill grows on you. The art critic can do without it; those speculating on the price of the latest Picasso to go on the market can do without it; but not the artist. The artist must do.

Then there's the other side of the coin. Skill is not grunt work, laboring under a strain. Something's wrong if our goodness comes drenched in sweat. Developing skill means that our efforts will eventually appear effortless. They'll be inspired; they'll flow, but only because there's been practice behind them.

Giving expression to truths that inspire us leads to a less-labored goodness, more spontaneity. James Whistler wrote, "A picture is finished when all trace of the means used to bring about the end has disappeared. To say of a picture, as is often said in its praise, that it shows great and earnest labour, is to say that it is incomplete and unfit for view." It's the same with virtue; calculated goodness is a contradiction in terms. That's why we're advised to wash our faces and smile when we fast, to pray in the closet, and to let the left hand hang loose while the right hand is giving. Genuine virtues don't call attention to themselves; they're best seen as expressions of some great truth.

There is joy and satisfaction in developing a skill. Too many people regard every moral challenge as some pop quiz leading up to the final. We're going along on our merry way, and all of a sudden, bam, there's a difficult moral choice before us. Apprehension, anxiety —we either pass or flunk. After taking the quiz, we experience either relief that we squeaked by with the right answer, or grief because there's another black mark against us. Then we go on our way, hoping we'll be ready for the next pop quiz.

It makes such a difference if, instead, we regard moral challenges as a means of developing skill. As artists, we may be clumsy, and we may not have our technique down yet, but we're developing an invaluable skill. Every ethical experience, good or bad, is a means toward that end. Moral failings are to be regretted, yes. We need to repent, yes. But our dominant mind-set has got to be: I'm going to be an artist; I'm not a grunt. I'm learning. I still hear that high calling. The possibility of mastering a certain quality beckons me.

A PASSION TO EXPRESS

Now we come to the second part of our definition: revelation. Artful goodness is more than isolated acts to fulfill an obligation, a quantity of deeds to fulfill a quota. It expresses something beyond behavior, revealing spiritual truth to the beholder.

That is precisely what drives an artist through a lifetime of creative effort: a passion to express, to reveal. It's not just mechanically slapping down paint on a surface. It's not just finding the correct words in the dictionary. The artist longs to express something through his work—an idea, a feeling, a perspective. Artful goodness is driven by the desire to express glorious facts (like the majesty of God; Christ's act of honor on the cross; the authority of the Word).

More and more of our secularized world is specialized and fragmented. We perform isolated functions, manipulate a certain type of data, pick up pieces much more often than the whole. But artful goodness demands a whole. Just trying to be good in a vacuum won't do; you end up burned out or bored out. You need theology as well as ethics, inspiration as well as action. Just trying to isolate the truth won't do, either. You end up with theory piled on theory, and art gets lost in a game of abstractions. Inspiration shrivels when divorced from action.

Revelation requires wholeness: devotion and action joined together, law and spirit interacting dynamically, the single act speaking of a greater whole.

We also need our whole lives to express a consistent picture, like an artist's entire body of work summing up his dominant themes. All our actions are strokes applied to the canvas; all are part of the whole. Hypocrisy creeps in when we lose that sense of our whole lives revealing truth. We start wanting to express the right thing when convenient, only when the right people are watching. We go down a list to knock off certain isolated items of duty in order to earn points with critics. We want to keep our own private collection of bad art intact, in the closet, and show off only certain pieces of calculated goodness. Genuine revelation falls apart.

A true artist of the Spirit wants his whole life to be a statement, to mean something. He's compelled. He's expressing what he's learned at the feet of the Master.

Jean Pierre Camus intended to be Francis de Sale's biographer, and he drilled a hole in the wall of the man's bedroom in the episcopal residence in order to discover the secret of his holiness. He wanted to see if the man's personal life agreed with his eloquent devotional writings. Camus discovered that each day de Sales crept out of bed early and quietly so as not to wake his servant. He prayed, wrote letters, read his office, slept, and prayed again. At the peephole Camus observed the same beautiful manners, unruffled compassion, courtesy, and humility on display that many others had observed in the pulpit or at the dinner table. Francis de Sales' art was a whole statement. He showed himself to be a true artist of the Spirit, not someone putting on an act, but one who consistently revealed the truths he admired.

This habit of expressing the whole should also help us see beauty as well as truth, or to see that beauty is a part of God's whole truth. Limited as we are by our sluggish human nature, we usually grasp only one or the other. Those who worship the beautiful can't stand the sour-faced proclaimers of truth. And those who reverence truth look down on people devoting their lives to mere beauty.

The religiously oriented tend to fall into the latter category, preferring to hoe weeds rather than cultivate roses. Conservative Christian goodness has had a blind spot in this area. Francis Xavier wrote extensively about his missionary travels through India, Ceylon, and Japan. But there's no hint in all his journals that he observed anything of the natural beauty of those exotic lands. A certain leader of the Jesuits always became angry with any of his followers who dared to pick even a solitary flower. An appreciation of beauty seemed to him simple self-indulgence. The Puritans, in reacting against the fashionable excesses of their Cavalier contemporaries, took plainness in dress as a virtue, which isn't all that bad an idea. But it unfortunately led many to conspire against physical beauty in general.

The beautiful is a part of God's truth, however, not some distraction. Revealing the whole means revealing beauty, too, making our statements winsome as well as truthful, making our actions attractive as well as proper.

Beauty, of course, has tremendous variety. There is no one proper way for flowers to be. They blossom in a wild assortment of color and shape. Creation bursts with ingenious adaptation, original form, special skills. In fleshing out the richness of the Word, we ought to take a cue from the richness of nature. Principles are eternal, but styles are infinite. There's plenty of room for a variety of expression.

Most people prefer to make their conversations with the Lord quiet and private. Charles Finney thrived on a different kind of prayer. His critics used to say, "It is impossible for him to pray in secret, for he can be heard a half-mile off." Bellowing out one's petitions may seem insincere and offensive, but one man who heard Finney praying off in the woods at a great distance become so convicted by the man's earnestness that he "sought God's face for redemptive grace."

This matter of what's sincere religion and what isn't trips up a lot of people. Some find it impossible to believe that the young lady sighing sweetly about "my lovely, precious Jesus" can be for real. Others look at a man's expressionless defense of the faith and conclude he hasn't got much religion. Some balk at oratorical heights, while others question the plainspoken.

Christian people get wrapped up in great battles over style, such as whether we should raise our hands in worship. The person who sits quietly can't imagine how someone can worship God while making a big commotion. And the person who raises his hands and shouts can't imagine how anyone can worship God motionless in a pew. When we condemn other styles, we're really assuming that so-and-so can't be for real because *we* couldn't naturally express our faith that way. But of course different personalities react in different ways to the same truth.

Down through Christian history, there's almost always been pressure to confine goodness to one dimension, one style. At one time, extemporaneous prayer in public worship was scandalous; you had to go by the book. The saints used to believe that singing anything except psalms in church was an insult to God. Let's face it, conventional religion draws an awful lot of stupid battle lines.

How much better to reveal the richness of the Word to the world. Our challenge is to really see the original source of inspiration, nature-the-Word, and express it in new ways. That's how we progress. Skillful revelation. Too often we try to make all kinds of rules about styles instead of focusing on the essentials. We should be helping people create new wine instead of fiddling with the wineskins. There's plenty of room within the law for all kinds of expression. Artful goodness should have many children—enough to fill up the world.

THE LAW ENLARGED

Jesus specialized in expanding on the Word, enlarging the law. He urged His contemporaries to move beyond the confining traditions of their time and He inspired new ways of expressing old truths. There's a great gap between conventional religious goodness and the teachings of this artful Master.

When socializing, conventional goodness refrains from throwing wild parties, avoids drinking or carousing, and issues no invitations to the impure. Jesus suggested something different: "When you give a banquet, invite the poor, the crippled, the lame, the blind, and you will be blessed."

Conventional goodness submits to indignities without retaliating. Jesus wants us to express something more. How about disarming the oppressive Roman soldier who forces you to carry his burden one mile by carrying it two?

Conventional goodness fasts and prays and puts on a somber spiritual face. Jesus told us to fast and pray and put on a red dress.

He asked us to give expression to extraordinary facts, like God's lavish forgiveness. If your million-dollar debt has been wiped out, how can you possibly hold a grudge against the guy who didn't give you back the right change?

Does God watch over us? Then give it expression. In the midst of a world hunkering down over its pursuit of financial security, be a sparrow flitting about contentedly. Be a lily opened to the sun.

SHINED SHOES

The New Testament is always pushing us beyond imitative deeds to skillful revelation. There is so much in the Word waiting to be expressed; there are so many needs out there waiting for the touch of artful goodness.

When someone loses a loved one, conventional goodness prescribes that we phone our sympathy or send a condolence card. Artful goodness finds a way to flesh out comfort.

The terrible news about a car accident that killed several members of Madge Harrah's family came just as she, her husband, and children were preparing to move to another state. The house was in chaos. Madge had to fight through her grief to get ready—find the right clothes for the kids in all the boxes, get tickets to fly home so she could be with her mother, and check on details about the funeral. As she was walking around the house in a daze, aimlessly picking things up and putting them down, the doorbell rang. It was a neighbor. What on earth could he want?

"I've come to clean your shoes," he said simply.

Madge didn't understand. As she stared, the neighbor explained, "When my father died, it took me hours to get the children's shoes cleaned and shined for the funeral. So that's what I've come to do for you."

The neighbor settled himself on the kitchen floor and scraped and washed and shined all the shoes in the house. Watching him concentrate quietly on his task helped Madge pull her thoughts together and begin her own preparations. Later, when she returned from the laundry room, the neighbor was gone. But lined neatly against the wall stood all the shoes, spotless and gleaming.

HOUSE OF THE URCHIN

When confronted by a growing crime rate, conventional goodness locks the doors, bars the windows and hopes for stiffer penalties. Artful goodness checks out the streets.

In the city of Naples, Italy bands of young orphans and outcasts called the *scugnizzi* lived on the streets, begging, pilfering, and sometimes assisting older criminals. They were tough, wily, and apparently unreachable. But twenty-five-year-old Father Mario Borrelli wanted to try, so he became one of them each night after his regular duties. Dressed in the usual ragged, filthy, *scugnizzi* get-up, he started begging at the Naples railroad terminal. The other young toughs were impressed by his style: just the right mixture of humor and pathetic humility. When a gang leader swaggered up and demanded half his take, Mario beat him up.

The incognito priest slept on basement gratings covered with old newspapers, just like the others. Soon he was getting to know his new companions well as they talked around fires, heating their scraps of food in old tin cans. And Mario discovered that all of them, even the most bitter and hardened, had a longing for home, affection, and security.

One winter evening Mario informed the gang that he'd found a place for them to stay, the little, bombed-out church of St. Gennaro, which had been abandoned. Slowly he transformed the structure into a home and started providing the boys with nourishing meals.

One night Mario appeared in clerical robes. After his friends stopped laughing, he explained that he was, in fact, a priest. By this time the bonds he'd established were strong enough to make them stay; Mario had won their respect. And so the House of the Urchin was established, where young throwaways could find a home, hope, and the street-wise spiritual guidance of Mario Borrelli.

'PRAY FOR ME'

When unjustly accused, conventional goodness is filled with righteous indignation. Artful goodness tries to express something more enlightening.

One member of Howard Welklin's congregation continually aimed barbs at him. The pastor had never experienced anything like it before in his decades of ministry—not just criticism, but venomous attacks. Finally Welklin received a letter from the man in which all the accusations were massed together in one vehement assault. The pastor had a good answer for each of the points his parishioner brought up. His criticisms were totally unjustified, and Welklin wanted very much to give it right back to the guy.

But after some serious thought and prayer he decided on a different approach. The pastor wrote a reply back containing only four words: "Please pray for me."

Shortly afterward, the man's attitude changed radically. His animosity withered away, and he became one of the more supportive members of the congregation.

WINNERS AT BILLIARDS

Conventional goodness avoids questionable amusements. Artful goodness tries to turn them upside down.

A doctor of theology at a Paris college once invited Ignatius of Loyola to play billiards. Ignatius agreed provided there was a stake in the game. He pointed out that he owned little beyond his own person, and proposed, "If I lose I will be your servant for a month to obey your orders. If I win you shall do just one thing for me, and it shall be something to your advantage."

The professor willingly agreed and then lost the game of billiards.

Loyola laid out his terms: the man must read a devotional guide on *Spiritual Exercises,* and practice them for one month. As a result, the rather irreligious professor saw a marked change in his life.

WHEN WE LOOK at the possibilities of this kind of art of the Spirit we are drawn back to one artist who packed more skill and revelation into His life than any other. His short career produced a wealth of canvases we still pore over, and still rediscover as masterpieces. Vincent van Gogh said of Christ, "He lived serenely, as a greater artist than all other artists, despising marble and clay as well as color, working in living flesh." One gets a sense of how good He really was by looking at all He placed in just one canvas.

POWER TEMPERED BY GRACE

Jesus walked through the covered colonnades surrounding a spring-fed pool called Bethesda and looked out over the human wreckage hovering about it. Pale bodies racked by fatal diseases panted on filthy mats, their faces turned toward the motionless surface of the pool. The blind crouched on the stone porches, their heads cocked, ready to spring toward the first sound of water lapping on stone. The maimed sprawled in a variety of positions, trying to keep their good limbs ready for propulsion. And the most pathetic, those completely paralyzed, lay near the water, staring up at the cold columns, hoping against hope.

These afflicted people were waiting for the miracle. They believed, or tried to believe, that an angel came down from heaven periodically to stir the waters of Bethesda, and that the first one into the pool after each disturbance would be healed of his disease. So they waited each day as the sun rose overhead and fell in its wearying cycle. Some veterans of Bethesda crawled close to the water when they smelled sheep. They imagined a breeze strong enough to bring them the pungent odors of the Sheep Gate market a few blocks away might be strong enough to help that angel disturb the pool. Others had trained themselves to detect a faint rumbling underground that was usually followed by heated water bubbling to the surface.

Jerusalem was in the midst of a great holy feast, and Jesus had come to participate as a good Jew in the elaborate rituals of the temple. On this high Sabbath day, He'd gone out from the pomp and pageantry for some fresh air and been drawn to His more natural environment—the dark corners where the poor and afflicted huddled.

Jesus glanced around at those gray faces dying of suspense, meshed into a crowd where only one could win, and He longed to cause a real disturbance by healing them all. But He knew that such a mighty work during this feast day in a Jerusalem bulging with pilgrims would bring things to a climax too quickly. His ministry would be cut short. Overenthusiastic crowds had already prevented Him from ministering in certain areas.

Jesus' eye fastened on one particularly hopeless case, one of the paralytics staring up at the columns, and He walked over and started a conversation. Jesus found out the man had been an invalid for thirty-eight years, enduring a lifetime of physical limbo. Its only interruption in recent months had been a mad rush every few days in which the less disabled trampled over him on their way to the bubbling pool.

Jesus reached down into this bottomless, black well of despair and asked a simple question: "Do you want to get well?"

It seemed at first like a silly question. Of course he wanted to get well. Why else would he expose himself to cold and heat every day amid those stinking bodies? But this was Jesus' way of dropping a little hope into the well. It was the first morsel a starving man gets that prepares him for the feast later.

And it was more. Here Jesus presented Himself as servant. He was not the great miracle worker parading through who condescended to pass His wand over some lucky wretch. He was a servant asking if He could be of help. Jesus' power, always tempered by grace, was never overbearing.

The paralytic could think only of the pool. If just once he could be the first one in! He'd managed to persuade acquaintances to carry him to Bethesda, but no one wanted to hang around all day waiting for the water to move. "I have no one to help me," he said. Maybe, just maybe, this kind stranger would give him a push at the right time.

Jesus seized this ray of hope and bent it from superstition to Himself. He looked into the man's eyes and uttered a perfectly ridiculous command: "Get up! Pick up your mat and walk." He might as well have ordered the stone columns to dance in a circle around the afflicted.

But something started to happen to the paralytic's muted nerve endings and shriveled limbs. Looking up at this unassuming stranger who spoke with such authority, the invalid struggled onto his feet. Responding to the command of Christ, he found that the impossible became possible. Thirty-eight years of immobility faded away like a head cold.

Any other healer would have been content to just make a paralyzed man walk. That's a pretty good day's work—a deed glorious enough, in fact, for a lifetime. But Jesus had still more to say through this sign.

Tucked away in His simple statement that produced the miracle was a bomb that would detonate beneath the crusty pillars holding up the legalistic religion of His day. Jesus had commanded that the man *pick up his mat* and walk. And so the former invalid, bursting with gratitude and praise, walked off into the stream of pilgrims going to the temple with his mat rolled up under his arm. He probably hopped, skipped, and jumped his way through the crowd.

If ever there was a time to worship God on the Sabbath, this was it. So he joined those celebrating with his own loud praises. In his heart-thumping joy, the man didn't realize he was proclaiming himself a Sabbath breaker before the multitude of pilgrims around him. Jewish tradition clearly forbade any person to carry a mat on the Sabbath. That constituted "bearing a burden."

Word of this transgression reached the priests, and they promptly came to reprimand him. The former invalid explained that the one who healed him had told him to carry his mat. And here the religious leaders showed their true colors. An individual stood before them bubbling over with joy because thirty-eight years of humiliation and misery had just somersaulted inexplicably into perfect health. The man had been born again into a new body. But this marvelous deliverance paled into insignificance before the fact that the delivered carried a mat under his arm.

They weren't interested in his story. They wanted to know who had dared to give such a command and thereby cause this defilement of the Sabbath.

Jesus' picture-bomb detonated before the multitude of pilgrims. The values of these guardians of the law were exposed. There was no room in their holy day for divine rescues, no room for the afflicted to be saved. Their Sabbath had become a fortress within which to defend tradition against all comers. This human being so dramatically touched by grace was invisible; they noticed only his inadvertent bump against the rules.

Jesus had one last brush stroke to make before His canvas was complete. He located the former paralytic in the temple and explained that deliverance should lead to reformation. In this case, the man's destructive lifestyle had contributed to his illness, and Jesus wanted to make sure he didn't fall into the same downward spiral again.

That afternoon, in a few moments by the pool of Bethesda, Jesus deftly sketched out a masterpiece. The centerpiece was just a few quick strokes of command: "Get up! Pick up your mat and walk." Bright, basic colors against the grim walls. But how that act echoed.

The Master had drawn a lesson in faith surrounded by superstition. There were no paraphernalia attached to His healing, no grand gestures, no supernatural props to help legitimize the scene. Christ's act was so minimal that one almost misses where the miracle occurs. , But He laid out a personal transaction before a crowd clinging desperately to a pool they invested with magical powers. He made a statement: Person to person, person to God, is what counts—not person to object.

His act of healing is carefully composed as a model for salvation. We are utterly helpless in sin. Christ comes and introduces Himself. We have to want to be saved. He commands us to be whole. As we respond to Him in faith, we *are* made whole.

Finally, Jesus vividly contrasted His kingdom of grace with the dried-up religious establishment around Him.

Christ's acts express so much. They have a precision and eloquence that make people stand back and stare and study. They see skill and revelation.

—————— 20 ——————

BALANCING

THE COLORS

WITH JESUS we see artful goodness in brilliant color. The canvases on display in the four gospel galleries dazzle us with the skill and revelation of the artist. Here is something that goes far beyond the defensive reactions of conventional virtue and also blows apart that lowered horizon of moral expectations.

Jesus gives us whole revelations, full-color portrayals of divine truth. To express a similar wholeness, you and I need to have those three primary colors in balance.

Let's look at some of the ways light humility, hard honor, and open allegiance, work together to create a many-hued whole. All three tell us why goodness is so basic to human life. They show us how to become human beings—not just saints, but healthy human beings.

FILLED OUT IN FULL COLOR

Light humility makes a good background color for hard honor. It takes a solid sense of security to be able to regard with grace those who are unlovely or even threatening. In fact, there is no graciousness without security. Goodness twists into all kinds of awkward shapes without it. We try hard to be kindly in order to be accepted, and end up stepping on toes with our forced niceties. Words of encouragement inserted like commercials into a conversation fall flat and bring on uneasy silences. When our attempts to "honor" others are shoved out of an insecure personality, they always make the "others" feel put upon.

Only the secure can honor fluently. All artful goodness depends on a person who expresses naturally something he feels deeply. Our stands of allegiance also need to be colored by the security of those humbly admiring God. The insecure tend to take fierce stands against evil as a way of carving out a place for their fragile selves. They desperately need the space, and the more sharply they can define it, the better. The righteous statements of the insecure are usually more a defensive covering for all those internal holes than they are skillful revelation.

The light humility of the secure enables them to make more credible statements before the world. They already have a space; they don't need to carve one out of the moral failings of others. When the securely humble are moved to speak loudly in warning, they do so testifying about their own weakness. They bear witness to danger instead of just pointing a knowing finger elsewhere. As a result, their voices strike all the more deeply.

Our allegiance also needs the hue of hard honor—that quality as deeply colored as the dark blood running down Christ's broken flesh on the cross. When we stand against evil, we usually have to wield categories, abstractions, principles. Slavery is wrong. Revival is necessary. Freedom should be protected. Adultery must be dealt with. In our zeal to champion certain truths, people sometimes get lost. We trample on humanity in particular while trying to lift up humanity in general. Hard honor helps us keep a better perspective. In all our stands we must come back to Christ's all-encompassing stand on Golgotha, where He declared every human being redeemable.

In our fight against evil we must always ask ourselves, Am I still honoring? While grappling with injustice and oppression we can be overwhelmed by the dark, unwittingly absorb its spirit, and forget our central goal of pursuing the redeemable. AIDS may not be redeemable, but homosexuals are. Millions of aborted fetuses may not be salvageable, but unwed teenager mothers are. Drug abuse, pornography, and materialism may be gaining ground everywhere, but every human being trapped in them is still worth saving.

Without a regular infusion of hard honor, our allegiance comes to be seen as a war against; we seal off enemy encampments under the banner of a certain sin and begin whacking away at human victims with our weapon-principles.

At the same time, our taking a stand on and under God's Word also has a color of its own, a color that humility and honor need. Those two qualities can turn pale if left to themselves for too long. The humble and those giving honor can drift into a kind of passive goodness that smiles benignly at whatever's going on. It's necessary to keep in touch with the hard edges of the Word. At times we need to stand up to real evil and better it; we need to show that evil can be overcome. Compelled to stand definitely on specific ground gives our humility and honor a cutting edge; they aren't just ways for the weak to survive, but expressions of a sovereign God staked out in a world of lowered moral horizons.

All three of these primary qualities war against selfishness; they attack the omnivorous self. Pride has to clear out and take all the furniture for humility to really settle in. Honor, the verb, steals all our titles, coats of arms, and positions and turns them into gifts. We bestow all the merit we've been hoarding up for ourselves. And taking a stand pushes us under an authoritative Word. We must submit and be spoken to. The self can no longer just speak its mind.

After these three virtues enter in earnest, it seems we have nothing left. But as Jesus promised, in losing our lives we get them back again—in good health. The carnal self assaulted gives way to genuine personhood. We find a profound security that enables us to grow. We discover a priceless and imperishable honor in honoring others. And we get a piece of that elusive commodity called meaning and purpose by giving up ourselves, risking it all in open allegiance.

Light humility, hard honor, open allegiance. These three primary colors combine and fill us out in full color. We become balanced human beings growing into the image of God.

SEXUAL ETHICS

It's within the balance of those three virtues that we can best deal with the knotty ethical questions that confront us from time to time. Those values provide us with a good foundation, a means to get us moving in a healthy direction. My assumption is that motivation is the essential problem in our world of lowered moral expectations, not a lack of information. The three primary qualities do not provide formulas for arriving at the proper specific decision about a moral dilemma. They don't create airtight arguments. What they do is create a track leading us to some point within the law, moving us away from the mediocre gray and toward artful goodness.

Let's take a look at what happens to sexual ethics when we brush on our three primary pigments. Recently a Catholic priest who taught at a university began questioning his church's traditional teaching on adultery and premarital sex. He wrote about certain "committed relationships" outside of marriage that might involve sex legitimately, and he stated that in some cases even adultery could be defended. This man had not arrived at such a position lightly. The turning point came for him when he was attempting to counsel a parishioner whose wife suffered from a debilitating, chronic illness. It had progressed to the point where she could no longer have intercourse. The distraught husband looked into his priest's eyes and asked, "What am I supposed to do the rest of my life?"

That proved to be a difficult question indeed. The priest couldn't bring himself to tell this man that his sexual life had come to an end. It didn't seem humane. Surely, he thought, here was one exception to the rule. The husband had a right to normal sexual fulfillment, and in his case that meant going outside of marriage.

How would we respond to such a difficult situation? To get our bearings we need first to become aware of our starting point in dealing with the problem. What do we bring with us? To what do we cling? Light humility prevents us from being riveted to the self and its needs as our starting point. Bowing before God is how we begin as genuine human beings, acknowledging His love for us and His claims on us.

Sexual fulfillment is a legitimate, God-given need, but it is not a nonnegotiable one. If we start from the premise that we must have a good sex life whatever the consequences, we're headed for trouble. What we must do is live toward God, whatever the consequences.

After establishing that perspective we have to ask how we can live honorably in the present situation. How can we express the unconditional acceptance we've received because of God's act of atonement? In the case of this husband, he has to ask himself how he can honor the one he chose as his wife. Will he look at her only as an incapacitated body or as his cherished companion in spite of her sexual handicap? How can he express honor? The essence of honor is that we regard people as chosen and redeemable, apart from their particular attributes. In the case of marriage, spouses have the opportunity to regard each other as husband and wife, period. That debilitated wife needs to feel like the chosen one, period.

And then we come to taking a stand. How can we be open to the authority of Scripture in this situation? There is no scarcity of verses lined up explicitly and unyieldingly against adultery. One of the preeminent values the Word highlights is faithfulness. It's pictured as more important than personal gratification. Scripture also admires self-sacrifice and assures us we have much to gain from denying ourselves in order to benefit other people. It presents celibacy not as an unmitigated disaster, but as an opportunity to devote our energies to God's service in a more concentrated manner.

In this light, what statement needs to be made in our time? How can we best show our allegiance to Truth today? Do we need to rise against the swelling tide of those sacrificing their sexuality too readily? Is celibacy over-glamorized in our world? Do we need to loosen up the rules because our contemporaries are into so much self-denial? Obviously the tide has been going the other way for some time. Sexual gratification is the pursuit that bowls over friends, relatives, spouses, and children born and unborn. Almost everything these days can be sacrificed on its altar.

That priest who'd begun to modify scriptural teaching explained quite rightly that people increasingly ignore the injunctions of the church. He pointed out that the sexual practices of most Catholics bear little relation to traditional Catholic teaching. This is a real problem I'm sure, but the man's solution was to match the rules a little more closely with behavior. That's like saying the problem is so bad we had better contribute to it. It's not taking a stand; it doesn't really take evil seriously.

Declaring our open allegiance to the Word cannot simply relate to the norm. The norm in Assyria was to skin captives alive. The norm in Victorian England was children worked to death in sweat shops. For one hundred and fifty years in America it was slavery. During the 1970s in Cambodia it was genocide. Our norm is represented by an L.A. radio psychologist listening to a twenty-six-year-old caller complain that her husband went to topless bars. The good doctor informed this woman that men naturally derive pleasure from visual excitement, and, on the basis of that revelation, she advised that a sensible wife should not interfere. After the woman hung up, the psychologist informed her listeners that this caller's attitudes were insecure and childlike.

The question of how the husband could honor his wife and the fact that sexual fidelity is a part of strong marriages apparently never entered the counselor's mind as she sold her moral values to the public in the guise of pontificating on what constitutes maturity.

Every age has its blind spots, pockets of moral illness that future generations look back on with outrage. High on the list of ours must be this utter lack of honoring in sexual relationships, our habit of using and discarding other human beings solely for their ability to give us physical pleasure.

DONORS AND GRACE

Let's look at something even closer to home for good, church-going folk. Take fundraising, for example. What would happen to it if it were doused in some light humility, hard honor, and open allegiance?

There is nothing inherently immoral in asking people for money, of course. Some of the more forceful passages in Paul's epistles are requests for money, although they were appeals not for his own ministry but for the suffering churches in Jerusalem. Our discussions generally center on what kind of fundraising is ethical. We conclude that our appeals must not be deceptive and that funds received must be used for the project promoted.

All this is certainly useful, but it's even more useful to look at the statement being made by our fundraising. What are we expressing? Light humility should make us uncomfortable about harping on our accomplishments all the time, making our particular institution the center of good in the universe. I cannot imagine any fundraiser worth his paycheck who doesn't exaggerate the importance of the ministry or charity he's promoting. And in always exalting our particular group, we sometimes find it difficult to admire God apart from what He accomplishes through us.

Hard honor values people differently from the way we look at them through a data base of giving patterns. All our paragraphs smiling broadly and our purple lines of "spiritual encouragement" generally have only one object: to get the person in a giving mood. We speak of "converting" those who respond into regular donors. The gospel demands that human beings be identified as the ends of God's grace, never a means to a financial end.

So how do we take a stand in our big-budget, smooth image, high-pressure environment where getting God's people to give has been reduced to a science? What more important allegiance do we need to express?

One answer is provided by Hudson Taylor and his China Inland Mission. He disappeared in remotest nineteenth-century China on what he believed to be an obvious and pressing case of God's business, trusting Him to take care of the ministry's financial needs. Of course everybody "trusts God to take care of our needs." But for Taylor that meant not asking people for money. He wanted God Himself to do all the nudging.

He avoided altogether the hype that almost all of us now take as our commission for the glory of God (we're working for Him, aren't we?). Most of all, Taylor did not treat his particular ministry as an absolute. He was willing to fail if He could not succeed by God's direct intervention. We're in the habit of thinking our endeavor must survive at all costs; it's doing good, isn't it? We're not willing to open ourselves and our work to the possibility that God might just want to work in some other way.

Taylor declared that an objective, sovereign God is really up there, and he put his ministry where his mouth was. He built up his mission quietly, treating fellow Christians as people capable of being moved by God to give. He did not presume to lighten the workload of the Holy Spirit by inserting a slick PR operation in His place.

Taylor's experiment is probably not the only form humility,

honor, and allegiance can take in the field of fundraising. But we can't ignore this part of our heritage of artful goodness. We have to ask more than whether our last appeal letter lied outright. The important question is, What are we expressing? Are we building on a statement like Taylor's, extending it in any way?

ROOM TO EXCEL

Artful goodness declares that all the creative room is within the law, not at its edges. That's where there's room to excel. God presents His law as a light shed on the world. The prism shows us that all the colors of the rainbow are in that ray of white light, that whiteness is not some pale, blank space; it's the source of a world of hues. Black is simply the absence of all color.

Sex outside of marriage is a moral dead end. It fuels countless plots (which are, of course, stimulating and lucrative), but it shows little skill or revelation. Sexual honoring is where the action is. It's the broad canvas on which we can make beautiful and true statements. The subtle ways a husband makes his wife feel she is cherished, for example, are the skillful revelations that count, not the same old mechanical lines sexual predators throw at each other.

Murdering our neighbor, despising him—that's a dark alley without exit. All that spiteful maneuvering over each other, the petty rivalries, the pointed gossip, the strategic put-downs—it's a wasteland. The Word points us away from it: Turn around; all the room for art is in the other direction. Finding that window of redeemability, fanning into flame a spark of spiritual life, helping those encased in despair to spring a leak of hope—that's where the action is.

Hovering around the gray we miss out on the eloquent virtues that are worth expressing. Careening around the edges of the law we lose our chance in life to make an eternal statement. What can we best express? That's what matters in the end. All our ethical decisions would be illuminated if we approached them with an eye for art.

In 1941, six-year-old Elain Esposito underwent surgery for appendicitis and didn't wake up. No one at the hospital was really sure what went wrong. After a few weeks her parents ran out of money, but their "fair Elain" still lay in a coma. So Mrs. Esposito took her home to Holiday, Florida, and learned to be a nurse. Mr. Esposito worked three jobs to pay expenses.

Each day the mother would bathe and powder her sleeping child, turn her, feed her through a tube in her throat, and clip a fresh ribbon in her hair—each day for thirty-seven years. Mr. Esposito died in 1978. His wife's only prayer was that she might live longer than the daughter she regarded tenderly as her sleeping beauty. Elain stopped breathing at the age of forty-three, with her mother still keeping her bedside vigil.

Stories like this usually become prime material for ethical discussions. How far should we go in keeping the comatose alive? How about those with irreparable brain damage? How much of our lives are we obligated to invest in those who make no apparent human response? How far can virtue go without hope of being rewarded?

These are certainly useful questions to consider, but they miss the basic picture. Mrs. Esposito wasn't trying to come up with a correct answer for her serious problem. She was trying to express something precious. Her love couldn't be turned off when her daughter's consciousness went underground. It had to keep going.

It would help us greatly, in our world of lowered moral expectations, if we could simply admire this woman's action as we do works of art. She made a statement worth hearing, worth savoring: This is how precious life is; this is how irreducible a human bond can be. We could ponder that wordless, eloquent act as profitably as any master's painting. It's more than right or wrong, black or white. It's a full-color statement that deserves a place in a gallery, not just in some ethical equation.

Most people looking at Mrs. Esposito see only a life colossally wasted. She got so few returns on her oversized moral investment. But very few looking at an artist living in poverty most of his life in order to produce some masterpiece would call such a life wasted. To be able to express something felt to the depths is worth all the sacrifice. That's exactly what Elain's mother did. Her act didn't have to be rewarded; it didn't have to be efficient or fit into a neat, rational plan. Hers was an extreme devotion. But it possesses its own integrity as an act of art.

JOYFUL NURTURE

Other, less obviously heroic acts deserve the same enlightened consideration. Many of my most pleasant memories of childhood involve simply talking with my mother. Like most people recalling favorite memories of Mom, I can fondly think of apple pie, comfort during illness, story time, and so on. But, for me, conversation stands out. There's nothing earth-shaking in that, but what I distill from this distance is that Mom took genuine pleasure in my company.

During my earliest years we'd cuddle up in bed and talk. Saturday mornings were a favorite time. Later she'd take me out to restaurants and we'd talk. I remember trying to decipher the menus and learning what to make of three forks and two spoons, but most of all it's Mom's joy and my own in our outings that remains in the mind.

I grew up knowing that this very important human being valued me as a companion, not just a responsibility. She wanted to be with me. And that's quite a gift to carry into the world. It's hard for things to knock you down when you have that kind of self-worth imbedded into you.

Mother's love is about the biggest cliché one can imagine. It's obvious, expected, assumed, ignored. We're more fascinated by terrible exceptions to the rule—some Hollywood mother twisting her child into pathetic shape. The subject of good parenting doesn't fit into sizzling novels.

But I see my mother's acts from the perspective of what they've created. I am a whole human being in large part because of her regard, her hard honor. No matter what mischief I got into or what a pest I was being (and my parents were not in the least indulgent), I always knew I was cherished—not just as a kid who could smile nicely when dressed up, with face washed and hair combed for a family picture before going to church; not just because I could be good on occasion; but because she regarded me as a human being worth listening to.

For centuries we've reverently admired the mysterious lifelikeness of Leonardo da Vinci's masterpiece *Mona Lisa*. Critics declare the artist all but embodied the human soul; a real personality lies there in those self-assured eyes and that knowing smile. We celebrate this master because by his skill he has revealed to us a human being.

My mother's craft is no less noble, no less skillful. She created a whole person, spontaneously, just expressing her care. It's certainly no cliché to me. Acts like hers seem especially eloquent in a world where children are increasingly warehoused away from the attention of their parents. We try to inject a measure of regard in a few minutes of quality time. But great paintings can't be forced that way. They take time. There are irreplaceable moments for just this color, just that brush stroke.

My mother, as a matter of fact, worked as a teacher most of her married life. But I never remember her being stingy about time. There always seemed plenty for me. She made me feel wanted as an individual, someone she nurtured not just dutifully, but as an expression of her joyful love.

We certainly owe a debt to masters like Leonardo for their moving revelations. But how can you ever repay what a mother's consistent and generous regard has revealed to you? Acts like hers deserve the same careful esteem we give to one who turns blank canvas into Mona Lisa's smile.

—— 21 ——

VIRTUES AS

LUMINOUS AS ART

SHE FIRST DREW THE GAZE of the Paris art world in 1866 as "The Lady of the Green Dress" in a portrait by her lover, Claude Monet. Novelist and art critic Émile Zola wrote, "Look at the dress. It is both supple and solid, it trails softly, it lives, it says out loud what this woman is. No doll's dress there, one of those chiffon muslins which one wears in dreams; no, this is real silk in the act of being used."

Camille Doncieux did like beautiful clothes. She came from a well-to-do family and was fun-loving and pleasant. Some even saw her as a frivolous child unworthy of the attentions of the budding genius Claude Monet. But there was far more to this eighteen-year-old swept off her feet by a visionary painter than could be expressed in the shimmer of green silk. The tragedy is that almost no one seems to have noticed.

'SWEET, GOOD CAMILLE'

Camille cast her lot with Claude while he was a struggling, impoverished painter. And he remained exactly that during the fifteen years they were together. Claude's parents refused to support his endeavors. They didn't mind him being a painter as long as he was a successful one. But the road to success in nineteenth-century Paris lay through the all-powerful Academy of Fine Arts where painting was taught in the approved style: correct, finished, lifeless. Claude Monet couldn't bring himself to take that road. What was the point of merely copying the same old scenes in a certain style? Monet had to paint what his own eye saw, directly from nature. He longed to capture the liveliness of things—the interaction of light, color, and shape in one momentary impression.

Monet's parents were sure this was a dead end financially. They also insisted he cut off his relationship with Camille as a condition for their support. Such a liaison was not for respectable people. Camille's decision to live with Claude without benefit of a wedding can be faulted, but not her devotion. She gave herself completely to this man and his art.

It was Claude who would not marry the girl. She served wonderfully as a model. He was deeply attracted to her, and he wouldn't let her go, but neither would he commit himself.

Camille set up house in a tiny Paris flat and made do with the little money Claude could beg from artist friends. They were often cold and hungry. They lacked comforts of any kind, but she never complained. It was her cheery faith in the worth of his canvases that helped Claude keep going. Yes, someday the world would see and recognition would come.

Camille became pregnant. Monet wrote desperate letters, begging, shaming, arguing, demanding help from friends. A few francs trickled in; not enough. He walked the streets of Paris with canvases under his arm trying to get a pittance from art dealers for his work. No one was interested. And always, always, he kept painting, hoping that somehow the breakthrough would come before they were thrown out in the street.

Camille grew more and more pale. Monet couldn't bear to see her suffering, smiling gamely, but neither could he bear to give up his painting. Finally he hit on a scheme: He gathered up what money he could and entrusted Camille to the care of a doctor friend. He proposed to leave Paris and take up residence with an aunt, telling his family that he'd broken off with his mistress. Monet hoped they would now be willing to send money.

The ruse didn't quite work. In the end Camille simply had to bear her child without Claude, ill and lonely, without midwife or nurse. But she delivered a sturdy boy whom they named Jean.

As usual it was Camille's courage and gaiety in the face of hard times that made their desperate straits bearable. The three existed in a bare room without a fire. When the cupboard became empty or Monet's paint supply failed, he would walk the streets again, trying to sell his work.

There were a few lulls in the struggle. In the spring of 1868, Monet received eight hundred francs for a painting. That kept them fed for a while. When the money ran low they moved to Normandy, where life was cheaper. There Monet began one of his more productive periods. "I want to go on always like this," he wrote his friend Bazille, "working in a quiet and secluded countryside." Some might assume that Camille and little Jean represented a dulling domesticity that Monet needed to flee in order to be creative. Not so: "In the evening I come back to a good fire and a loving little family in my cosy cottage. I wish you could see your godson now, how charming he is. It is fascinating to watch this little being growing up."

Monet could be an affectionate companion, but hard times sometimes reduced him "to little more than a truculent neurotic, slightly haunted and of incredible endurance, but living out of touch with reality." Hard times came often. It was Camille, the woman who could live out of herself, who exhibited grace under pressure. She endured the humiliation of angry creditors knocking at the door. She watched her boy go hungry and turn blue-fingered from the cold. But there were no angry outbursts, no accusations or demands for Claude. Whenever Monet's friends mentioned his mistress, it was always "sweet, good Camille," the one who never complained. She was also the one who could face down village merchants reluctant to extend credit and the whispers of neighbors who sat in judgment.

Finally, Monet married the woman. But desperation figured more prominently in the decision than commitment. He hoped her parents would deliver a dowry of twelve thousand francs that could keep the three of them clothed and fed. As it turned out they received only a fifty-franc-per-month stipend.

But they were extremely happy and set off to Trouville after the ceremony. Camille might have seen herself in an awkward light: mother of a three-year-old son sets off on a honeymoon. But this remarkable young woman was never encumbered with position or status. Happily packing and preparing for her new husband and child, entertaining friends who dropped by, making her wide-eyed little sister, Genevieve, feel part of the group—she was too busy being gracious to feel embarrassed.

Monet by this time had become a leader in the new art movement called Impressionism, but he still couldn't sell his work. When the Impressionists exhibited their work the crowds came only to jeer. Critics had a field day. "Even wall paper…is more finished than *that*," one wrote. A newspaper cartoon pictured a policeman warning pregnant women to stay away from the exhibit.

There were more hardships, more desperate letters to friends, more disappointments, and always more canvases to paint. "I am the prisoner of my eye," Monet once said. His one unchanging goal remained to represent truthfully his own vision of life and nature.

But the strain of barely surviving began taking its toll on Camille. She steadily weakened. Her acts of comfort and kindness now took on a heroic dimension. In her frailty she somehow could always draw on an inexhaustible well of devotion. Monet was drawn to her more than ever, but he still couldn't stop painting. He felt guilty, but his obsession drove him. He hoped against hope for a breakthrough. Surely someone would recognize his work soon; his paintings would sell; they could settle into more comfortable surroundings, and all would be well.

The breakthrough didn't come. And Camille was pregnant again. Monet fretted, pleaded with friends, pawned the last bits of Camille's jewelry, and hoped she'd get better. The one thing he did not do was find some way to earn a living in order to adequately care for his wife and son. A job in an office or at the docks might delay his emergence as a great painter. That he could not bear. He could have devoted time to caricatures or some other kind of popular painting that would earn money, but he didn't see that as an option. Monet believed passionately in his art; he would not compromise it. He had to make the world see his vision.

What he didn't see so clearly was the woman who was such an integral part of his art: tall and stately Camille in the fields, in their gardens, on the beach, posed with their son, Jean. She appeared often on his canvases, but one wonders whether he ever really took the measure of this human being who showed such determined grace and good humor under the most withering of circumstances.

In Camille's sweet selflessness was a profound art that acquaintances caught admiring glimpses of but which no one made any sacrifice to preserve. Monet's integrity as an artist, his unwillingness to conform to lesser tastes, was considered heroic. And he was indeed a great painter, a great eye. But his wife also created a body of work over the years that eloquently expressed a quiet heroism—and deserved a better audience.

Monet saw only the narrow spectrum of his own particular art. As one biographer put it: "He had, like so many artists, the sense that the less creative can best justify their existence by assisting the original artist." But who was really "less creative"? Camille was happy to play the role of the person giving her life for the "original artist." And yet, though too self-effacing to realize it, she had become an artist of the spirit in her own right.

She carried her humility so lightly. In 1876, Monet painted her as "La Japonaise," dressed in a brilliantly colored kimono. She lifts a fan up beside her face, tilts her head back, and looks at us as if caught in a dance. Her bright eyes and querying smile flirt with the viewer. This is the same cheery girl who fell for a dashing young painter. There are no traces of the woman worn down by years of privation.

If Camille had been some stern-faced matron sacrificing herself because duty to one's husband demanded it, her suffering could be more easily passed over. But this woman loved life. It's the gaiety of her selflessness that makes it so compelling, her ability to appreciate and believe against the odds in the art of another when no one could appreciate her own.

In 1879, though pale and weak, with dark patches spreading in the hollows of her eyes, Camille gave birth to a fine, healthy boy, Michel. But she never recovered her strength. The next year she died of tuberculosis. Camille was thirty-two.

Monet begged enough money to bury her in the little walled cemetery that crowns a hill at Vetheuil. No one is really sure where she lies. Her stone was never inscribed.

A few years later the breakthrough finally arrived. The public had begun warming to Impressionism, and Monet's paintings started selling. His reputation grew. He was finally making it as an artist, but he grieved that Camille was not there to share his success.

Now Monet could sell his older paintings at impressive prices, but he struggled for some time with new work. He wrote, "I have scraped off all my latest canvases. I suffer anguish." Later, in another location, he said, "I've destroyed six [canvases] since coming here. I've done only one that pleases me. I'm tired of it all."

Monet had only to paint what he pleased and it would sell for almost any price he demanded. But he found himself increasingly restless and bitter. "I work hard," he wrote, "and make myself ill with wretchedness: I'm horribly worried by everything I do."

He didn't realize what an irreplaceable part of his inspiration Camille had been. One biographer concluded, "With Camille's death, his wonderful eye lost its most powerful creative force.... All the warmth, the humanity, the feeling in his pictures came from her."

Monet would actually go on to paint some of his most famous works—his series of haystacks and water lilies, for example. But a case can be made that he was now indeed merely a prisoner of his eye, and that now it remained a disembodied organ.

'A GREAT PIECE OF NEWS'

Theo van Gogh had always tried to sustain his fragile brother emotionally and financially, but now he felt himself terribly helpless in the face of this last illness. Theo wrote: "He had, while I was with him, moments in which he acted normally, but then after a short while he slipped off into wanderings on philosophy and theology. It was deeply saddening to witness all this, for from time to time he became conscious of his illness and in those moments he tried to cry —yet no tears came. Poor fighter and poor, poor sufferer."

From the mental hospital at Saint-Remy, Dr. Felix Rey had written to inform Theo that Vincent's condition was grave. He had attempted to bathe in a coal scuttle, threatened a nurse, and occupied another patient's bed, refusing to get up.

Van Gogh was terrified of the attacks that disabled him. But during the calm periods between his storms, after he'd wandered down the gloomy corridors punctuated by bolted cell doors, stared out the barred windows at the scenery, or taken walks on the hospital grounds, he was able with thick, animated brush strokes to immortalize what he saw—circular stone fountain, writhing cypress, crows flying out of an undulating wheat field.

Vincent fought desperately against his manic attacks, knowing they might destroy forever his ability to paint. But he had grown increasingly isolated. The townspeople of Arles, where he'd been painting, regarded him with hostile suspicion. He'd been a dismal failure with women and now sought comfort only among prostitutes. His physician at the mental hospital offered little hope. The Catholic sisters seemed cool. And always his disease threatened.

In the midst of this enveloping dark, one bright yellow beam of honor shone through from a most unlikely source.

Back in Paris, Theo had married a Dutch girl named Johanna. This woman now had to deal with a brother-in-law whom she knew would drain their meager finances indefinitely. Vincent had been making financial and emotional demands on his brother for years. There were no signs his position would ever improve and plenty of signs that he had become a dangerous lunatic. A few weeks previously he had attempted to stab the artist Gaugin who was staying with him. Then, tormented over his act, he'd cut off his earlobe and given it to a prostitute.

Johanna's response to all this is remarkable. She wrote him: "I am now going to tell you a great piece of news, on which we have concentrated a good deal of our attention lately—it is that next winter...we hope to have a baby, a pretty little boy—whom we are going to call Vincent, if you will kindly consent to be his godfather. Of course I know we must not count on it too much, and that it may well be a little girl, but Theo and I cannot help imagining that the baby will be a boy."

Johanna had good reason to wish Vincent a quick disappearance. Her husband worried about him constantly, and this artist who'd sold exactly two paintings in his lifetime offered no evidence of being remembered by posterity except for his eccentricities. But Johanna and Theo honored anyway, linking the identity of their firstborn child with Vincent's. In those paintings that covered the walls of their home (no one else would have them), they saw a value, something redeemable, something to honor. In *The Potato Eaters*, hanging in their sitting room, Vincent— like no one before him—had honored the impoverished, the people he had ministered to so compassionately during his stint as an evangelist.

And so, hemmed in by his private terrors in the asylum, Vincent received this gift from a woman he had never met. He wrote back to them both: "Jo's [Johanna's] letter told me a very great piece of news this morning. I congratulate you on it and I am very glad to hear it." He suggested it might be more appropriate to name the baby after its grandfather considering "the circumstances."

After the birth of the child, a boy whom the parents christened Vincent, his uncle expressed his joy by painting what he wrote was "big branches of almond-trees in blossom against a blue sky." A few weeks later he took an overnight train to Paris and there Johanna saw him for the first time. "I had expected a sick man," she recalled, "but here was a sturdy, broad-shouldered man with a healthy color, a smile on his face and a very resolute appearance." For his part, Vincent found his sister-in-law "intelligent, warmhearted and unaffected."

Johanna describes the moment all three had been waiting for: "Theo drew him into the room where our little boy's cradle was.... Silently the two brothers looked at the quietly sleeping baby—both had tears in their eyes. Then Vincent turned smilingly to me and said, pointing to the simple crocheted cover on the cradle, 'Don't cover him with too much lace, little sister.'"

Vincent spent three days with the family, "cheerful and lively," basking in this island of loving calm and in the new life of his namesake. Tragically, after his return to southern France, Vincent was enveloped by the old demons again. Theo and Johanna's act of honor wasn't enough to save him from eventual suicide, but the gift did sink in for a while. In one of his last letters, he wrote, "I am so glad to have seen Jo and the little one."

Hard honor. Johanna's naming her child Vincent, projecting health and wholeness toward a tormented, difficult man, is an act of artful goodness every bit as luminous as the painter's bright yellow sunflowers fetching their millions at Christie's.

THERE ARE SOME THINGS worth expressing in this world, some things that echo eternally. There are eloquent virtues worth their weight in Rembrandt's colors or the lines of Ingres. And the quality of our lives is determined by how much we invest in them, how much we express.

Goodness doesn't have to be conventional or colorless, nor does it have to be confined to the sidelines, trying to avoid evil. It can become a glorious pursuit.

Whatever you do, Scripture tells us, do it all to the glory of God. Make your acts speak of Him; flesh out His qualities. We can do more than just imitate from a distance. We can become participants in the divine nature. That's an art worth our lifetimes.

We can be "transformed into his likeness with ever-increasing glory" as we see Him intently, with unveiled faces, in the devotional life. This isn't a picture of a day laborer picking away at the weeds, but of an artist finding more and more wonders to express. We are people compelled by Christ, laid hold of by our spiritual muse, who "press toward the goal of the prize of the upward call of God."

The artist of the Spirit is secure enough and inspired enough to aim high, hoping to experience "the whole measure of the fullness of Christ." And why not dream? Why not excel? Our God "can do more than we ask or think through the power at work within us." Plugged into the source of creation, we echo His skill and revelation, producing acts of art that God Himself can treasure. Paul wanted us to realize "what are the riches of the glory of His inheritance in the saints." God glories in our eloquent virtues. Creativity comes full circle, from master to pupil and back again.

Artful goodness is our calling as children of God. There's no higher one, no other pursuit more valuable. It's this kind of art that we can look back on and sum up a life with. Acts of art make the most difference in our world.

REIGN OF TERROR

Early in the morning of the second of May, 1808, the citizens of Madrid rose up in revolt against the hated French forces who had occupied and oppressed their nation. Men and women took to the streets with whatever weapons they could muster and attacked Napoleon's troops. The Spaniards fought bravely but were soon overwhelmed by disciplined soldiers who counterattacked with cavalry and artillery.

In the afternoon, an uneasy silence hung over the city, broken only by the sound of reprisals. Groups of citizens were rounded up and executed by firing squads. At first only those carrying weapons were to be shot, but soon the killing became more and more indiscriminate. It lasted until early morning of the following day.

This revolt was only the first in a series of disastrous conflicts that erupted again and again on Spanish soil. The horror of the Napoleonic wars had broken over a nation that had enjoyed a century of relative peace and prosperity under the Bourbon dynasty. One man documented all this with an almost obsessive persistence: Francisco Goya, looked upon now as the greatest artistic genius of his age. One of Goya's most famous paintings, *The Third of May*, recalls the execution of the "Madrilenos" — people of Madrid. A faceless line of soldiers prepares to fire into a terrified group of citizens. The solid row of uniformed executioners bent implacably over their rifles contrasts with the wild gestures of those about to die. One lurches forward to pray, one covers face with hands, one stares in disbelieving shock, and a kneeling, white-shirted man, the center of the composition, spreads his arms wide and stares aghast, his stance screaming a mixture of supplication and protest.

The Third of May was Goya's way of taking a stand. He spoke powerfully about tyranny and suffering, and his image still moves us today. During and after the savage French occupation and the war between France and Spain, he created a series of prints called *Los Desastres de la Guerra* (The Disasters of War) that expressed what he had seen and felt. The prints are unique in their graphic depiction of cruelty and in their curiously direct titles. Goya seemed to want to shake us by the neck with these scenes. Soldiers kick and yank at a man choking to death on a rope; the title reads *Why?* A scene of mutilated bodies strung up on a tree is called *Great Courage Against the Dead!* Goya titled *What More Can One Do?* a print of a spread-eagled body being hacked up by soldiers. *Barbarians!* was his epithet for two soldiers firing on a man tied around a tree. A couple covering their faces as they look on a mound of sprawling corpses was called *Bury and Be Quiet*. Men, women and children mowed down by rifle fire is *One Cannot Look*.

But Goya made us look and shows us war at its most brutal, utterly bereft of the heroic. There are only human beings butchering each other; the weaker and less well-armed are overwhelmed by a vast, organized terror. That terror continued on for Goya and his countrymen in the years after Napoleon fell and the Spanish Bourbons returned to power. They proved they could be as savagely repressive as the French. Goya had ever more disasters to document.

He also had even more despair to deal with. His harshly eloquent stand against the cruelty and inhumanity around him didn't seem to make much difference. He withdrew more and more into his own world and began executing a series of what are called "Black Paintings" on the walls of his small farmhouse near Madrid. They were very private statements, intended to be viewed by himself in solitude.

Goya pictured *Saturn Devouring One of His Sons*, in which a wild-eyed, shadowy man claws into a tiny figure and bites off its arm.

Skeletal animal-humans cavort in *The Food of the Witches*. Women sit in a worshipful circle around a large-horned goat-god in *The Witches' Sabbath*. A couple in *The Evening Meal* who tenderly spoon-feed their infant are drawn with outlandishly grotesque features.

All this intensely personal work was dominated by scenes that can best be described as nightmares. Goya had made a forceful statement about the inhumanity of war, but he was also tormented by a private savagery. The same demonic forces he saw out there butchering his fellow citizens lurked in his own mind. He had stood against evil, but when he looked inside he could find no real alternative, no greater image. Its unending reign of terror overwhelmed his spirit.

ABOVE AND BEYOND

On May 5th, 1945, the advance of the 77th Division of American troops down Okinawa was still held up by stubborn resistance on the Maeda Escarpment. This promontory, running almost the entire breadth of the island, rose steeply from the central valley and peaked in a sheer rock cliff, from thirty to fifty feet high. The Japanese had fortified the escarpment with pillboxes and a maze of tunnels and managed to turn back several all-out assaults.

Now orders came down from 10th Army headquarters that the ridge was to be taken at all costs. The 1st Battalion, spearheaded by Company B, was assigned to attack a pillbox anchoring the Japanese line. Company B's Captain Frank Vernon tried to prepare his men for what he knew would be the fight of their lives. Some were new recruits sent in to replace the heavy casualties Company B had sustained on the island.

There was one man Vernon especially wanted along on this mission. He walked over to a soldier who sat nursing a leg he'd injured in a fall over the cliff and told him about the orders. "Doss," Vernon said, "I know you don't have to go on this mission. But the men would like to have you with them, and so would I."

It hadn't always been like that. Back in boot camp with the 77th, the other recruits ridiculed Desmond Doss as "Holy Jesus." When he quietly read the Bible and prayed at his bunk each evening, they threw boots or yelled obscenities. Doss just didn't fit in. The skinny kid with glasses was too much of a straight arrow.

When drafted, Doss had registered I-A-O and assumed he'd be assigned to a medical unit. Instead he found himself in an infantry unit and was ordered to take a rifle. Doss could not. On the wall of his family's living room in Lynchburg, Virginia, hung a framed scroll illustrating the Ten Commandments that he'd studied in awe ever since the time he could drag a chair over and climb up for a look. The sixth commandment, "Thou shalt not kill," pictured a murderous Cain standing with a dagger over his prostrated, bleeding brother.

Doss wanted to obey God's commands, even with a world at war. He'd been taught, and still believed, that they were eternally valid. But he also wanted to serve his country. He believed in the values of a democracy that was pitted against Nazi tyranny. When a shipyard official where he worked suggested he could get a deferment as someone "essential to industry," Doss declined. He would accept the call to service. But he would also try to express his greater loyalty to God, so he signed up as a noncombatant.

As a result, Doss had to face a succession of superior officers who demanded he carry a weapon. They shouted and pleaded; he respectfully refused. Finally a friendly chaplain straightened out the confusion, and Doss began training as a medic.

In the desert of Arizona, where they were being whipped into shape on long marches in the withering heat, Doss joined the men of Company B. They, too, didn't think much at first of the soft-spoken "objector" with his ever-present Bible. But he soon won their respect for his toughness in the field and skill in caring for their injuries.

Their respect grew during combat on the island of Guam when he insisted on going out on dangerous night patrols with the "dogfaces" instead of sticking to the battalion aid station. He knew even the bravest of soldiers has a horror of being wounded and left behind to the mercy of the enemy.

Their admiration turned to something approaching awe on the Philippine island of Leyte during fierce jungle fighting when Doss scurried about caring for the wounded under fire, seemingly impervious to Japanese bullets. For his continual bravery during the campaign, superiors recommended him for the Bronze Star.

So it was with good reason that Captain Vernon wanted Desmond Doss along on the mission to take the Maeda Escarpment, though he hated to ask. Doss didn't hesitate. "I'll go, Captain," he told Vernon. But then he asked permission to finish studying his Bible devotional lesson. The captain started to object. The entire American advance in Okinawa was hung up at this one spot. Then he looked down at Doss's face and saw eyes sunk deep into dark sockets from exhaustion. The man hadn't even had time to change his cotton uniform, now stiff with the dried blood of the men he'd rescued during previous assaults.

Vernon nodded. "We'll wait for you," he said, and walked off.

Doss's sunken eyes had seen a great deal during the previous months: men with chests torn open by shell fragments, men disemboweled and pleading to be shot. He'd crawled among blood-drenched, dismembered bodies, feeling neck arteries for signs of life. He'd watched helplessly as his best friend bled to death beside him. Doss was surrounded by the disasters of war. All the horrors that Francisco Goya documented so fervently and despairingly pressed against him and took their toll.

A few days earlier Doss had found himself squatting beside a can of gasoline he'd lit, staring at the flame in a daze, with tears running down his cheeks. GIs usually lit such a fire to warm up their rations, but Doss wasn't hungry. He knew he had to snap out of it, stop thinking about all his dead buddies. He'd grown edgy and irritable. His hands shook. His voice sometimes broke.

At such times he tried to focus on his trust in the Lord. He had to keep the madness at bay with the good Word; he could still be loyal to it, no matter what. God still had something to say, even in the midst of a terror that seemed to envelope the whole world. God could preserve life. Yes, life was worth preserving.

For Doss, that meant *all* life. Once he tried to treat two dying Japanese soldiers, but a couple of GIs made him back off at rifle point. On Guam he managed to rescue a few seriously wounded native Chamorros. A buddy asked him, "Haven't you got enough to do, taking care of our own men? Why try to resurrect these natives?

"Because it's not up to me to judge whether one of God's children should live or die," Doss answered. "I believe that I should do everything in my power to help all men hold on to life."

"Suppose they aren't fit to live?"

Doss explained, "Well, the way I look at it is that anybody who isn't fit to live surely isn't fit to die."

Try your best to preserve life—this was what he was clinging to desperately. He had to keep in touch with the Word, with that better image, that enabled him to make a meaningful stand in the midst of *Bury and Be Quiet, Barbarians!* and *What More Can One Do?*

So Doss, quite unaware that he was holding up the war, finished his Bible reading, bowed his head for a few moments of prayer, then stood up, testing his leg. He was relieved to find that it supported him.

The men of Company B, covered by sweeping fire from the rear, moved up and over the escarpment and managed to throw a few explosives down the main pillbox hole. A mighty rumble shook the entire hill; they'd set off an ammunition dump underground. They'd also set off the Japanese counterattack. Okinawa's defenders poured out of holes everywhere, screaming, firing rifles, tossing grenades. Captain Vernon ordered the men to dig in, but they were soon overwhelmed by sheer numbers. Retreat turned into panic as soldiers rushed madly back toward the cliff. Many were cut down by enemy fire.

Only one man remained on top doing his job: Desmond Doss, tending to the fallen amid a terrifying concentration of artillery, mortar, and machine-gun fire. Alone on the escarpment, he began pulling casualties from where they'd been cut down to the edge of the cliff and then scurrying back for more. Then he rigged a litter with rope, slipping the legs of one of the most seriously wounded men through the two loops of a bowline, passing the rope around the man's chest and tying another bowline there. He looped the long end of the rope around a shattered tree stump and slowly lowered his comrade down the cliff to safety. In this way Doss managed to move the wounded, one after the other, from the escarpment. The slope where he worked was partly shielded from enemy fire, but he had to stand up during part of the lowering process and his head and shoulders were often exposed. No one could figure out why the heavy gunfire never struck him.

Doss remained on the escarpment until he'd lowered every wounded man to the soldiers waiting below. He was preserving life with a vengeance. Seventy-five men that day would owe theirs to him. Later, for his "outstanding gallantry far above and beyond the call of duty," Desmond Doss was awarded the Congressional Medal of Honor by President Truman.

A few days after his stand on the escarpment, Doss was wounded by a sniper and had to be evacuated in an ambulance. As he was driven away, the medic suddenly gasped, "My Bible, I've lost my Bible!"

"It's okay, " the driver said. "They'll get you one on the ship."

But Doss wanted *his* Bible, the one that had carried him through the long terror, and he made the driver promise he'd pass the word to friends at the battalion aid station, asking them to look for it. Word did get back to Company B, and all the men fanned out over the battlefield, pausing in their war to poke around shell holes and under debris, keeping an eye out for booby traps and snipers, retracing Doss's last steps, until they found the small, leather-bound book that their comrade—the skinny, bespectacled "preacher" they had come to respect and love—regarded so earnestly as the Word of God.

Desmond Doss stands among those whose acts are eloquent as art. He wasn't trying to establish a rationally perfect pacifist position. Ethicists could argue at length about the consistency of Doss's stand in the Pacific. Wasn't he just as much a part of the war as those carrying rifles? But this man was making a statement, the finest he could under the circumstances, that life is worth preserving. He was willing to keep saying that under the most dangerous conditions imaginable. Doss gives us a canvas to look at, one every bit as powerful as Goya's *Third of May*.

YES, SOME PEOPLE do make of "simple goodness" a glorious enterprise, men and women whose virtue is anything but banal. And not just the obvious heroes like Desmond Doss. Johanna van Gogh's more quiet act of honor speaks to us as well, and illuminates us as the best works of art do. Charles de Foucauld's selfless devotion in the desert speaks. Spurgeon's sensitive grace with his orphans, Eric Liddell's winsome care for unruly teenagers in an internment camp, Hudson Taylor's faith ventures in innermost China—they all make the world bigger for us, embodying truths we so easily ignore. These people had a longing to express something.

Those in the great cloud of witnesses manifest a vocation as compelling as that of any artist's quest. They urge us to follow in the race. They ask us to pursue the holy with the ardor of a painter like Albert Ryder, who wrote of his craft, "The artist needs but a roof, a crust of bread, and his easel, and all the rest God gives him in abundance. He must live to paint and not paint to live."

We dare not make a lesser commitment. Artful goodness must be the passion of our innermost selves. And unless it's artful goodness, it will turn into unhealthy obsession. What a tragedy it is to be a human being and remain outside this experience! To have missed a taste of the eloquent virtues—what an unbearable burden!

But to join in their pursuit, to struggle after this skill, to make these revelations—surely that, of all things in this life, is most to be coveted.

SOURCES

(Most Scripture quotations in this book are from *The Holy Bible: New International Version,* copyright 1973, 1978, 1984 by the International Bible Society, and published by Zondervan Bible Publishers. Other versions used include the *New American Standard Bible,* the *Revised Standard Version,* the *New English Bible,* and *The New Testament in Modern English,* translated by J. B. Phillips.)

CHAPTER 1: A MORAL NO MAN'S LAND

(PAGE)	(REFERENCE)	(SOURCE)
15ff.	Stephen Dedalus	*A Portrait of the Artist as a Young Man,* James Joyce, (1916)

CHAPTER 2: INTO ACTS OF ART

28	consuming pursuit	Php. 3:14, 1 Tim. 6:11, 2 Tim. 2:22, 2 Cor. 3:18, Gal. 6:15
29	precepts trustworthy	Ps. 111:7-8
	laws eternal	Ps. 119:160
	law of liberty	Jas. 1:25, 2:12
	law is good, spiritual	Rom. 12:2, 1 Tim. 1:8, Rom 7:12-14
30	follow all the words	Dt. 29:29
31	open my eyes	Ps. 119:18
31-38	artist quotations	*Artists on Art,* edited by Robert Goldwater & Marco Treves (New York: Random House, 1972)
33	abundant fruit	Gal. 5:22-23
	potent brew	1 Cor. 12:13, Eph. 5:18-19
	speak to one another	Col. 3:16
	did you receive	Gal. 3:2
34	dwell in you richly	Col. 3:16
	searches all things	1 Cor. 2:10
35	Abba Father	Rom. 8:15
	law fully met	Rom. 8:14
	joy complete	1 Jn. 1:4
	living stones	1 Pet. 2:5
36ff.	Richard Wurmbrand	*In God's Underground* by Richard Wurmbrand (New York: Bantam Books, 1977)

CHAPTER 3: THE INVISIBLE VIRTUE

42	Thomas Mann	*2500 Anecdotes for All Occasions,* edited by Edmund Fuller (New York: Doubleday, 1961), p. 70.
43	William Congreve	*The Oxford Book of Literary Anecdotes,* edited by James Sutherland (New York: Pocket Books, 1976), p. 73.
46ff.	Charles de Foucauld	*Desert Calling* by Anne Fremantle (London: Hollis & Carter, 1950)

CHAPTER 4: ADMIRING THE ONE WHO CHERISHES

54	Lin Yutang	*Conversions,* edited by Hugh T. Kerr & John M. Mulder (Grand Rapids: Eerdmans, 1983)
61	Saul prophecies	1 Sam. 10:9-10
	the Lord rescued	1 Sam. 11:13

CHAPTER 5: WATER SPLASHED IN A BASIN

CHAPTER 6: DESERT DWELLERS & LIVELY SAINTS

128   *die together, live together*   2 Cor. 7:3, NASB

129-30   *Elizabeth & Frank Morris*   *Readers Digest*, May 1986, pp. 136-140; from *Guideposts*, January 1986

130-31   *Kathy & Steve Saint*   *By Their Blood*, by James Hefley & Marti Hefley (Milford, Mich.: Mott Media, 1979), pp. 570-576

CHAPTER 10: SPLENDID ROBES & SPECIAL SERVANTS

133   *care for poor*   *A History of Christianity*, by Paul Johnson (as cited above), pp. 74-75

134-5   *Patrick*   *The Life and Writings of the Historical Saint Patrick*, by R. P. C. Hanson (New York: Seabury Press, 1983)

135-6   *Francis of Assisi*   *Classics: Bonaventure* (as cited above), p. 195

137-8   *Mother Teresa*   *Bright Legacy*, edited by Ann Spangler (Ann Arbor, Mich.: Servant Books, 1983)

CHAPTER 11: AFRAID OF A PLACE TO STAND

144ff.   *Martin Luther*   *Here I Stand*, by Roland H. Bainton (New York: New American Library, 1950)

CHAPTER 12: INTO THE CLUTCHES OF THE WORD

151   *love one another*   Jn. 13:34

151-2   *Arthur Katz*   *Ben Israel*, by Arthur Katz (Plainfield, N. J.: Logos International, 1970), pp. 86-88

152   *God-breathed*   2 Tim. 3:16

    living and active   Heb. 4:12

    blessing—warning   Rev. 1:3, 22:19

152-3   *sound doctrine*   2 Tim. 4:3-4

153   *impelled by Holy Spirit*   2 Pet. 1:21, NEB

    angels long to   1 Pet. 1:12

154   *no room for word*   Jn. 8:37, 8:45

    hard as flint   Zech. 7:12

    dividing soul and spirit   Heb. 4:12

155   *grass withers*   Isa. 40:8

156   *no human wisdom*   1 Cor. 1:17

157   *not imprisoned*   2 Tim. 2:9

160-61   *Micaiah*   1 Ki. 22

161-2   *Josiah*   2 Chr. 34-35

162   *Word a delight*   Jer. 15:16

    way of life and death   Jer. 21:8-9

CHAPTER 13: A WITHERED HAND IN THE SYNAGOGUE

167   *for the truth*   2 Cor. 13:8, NASB

    stand fast, stand firm   2 Pet. 5:12, 2 Thes. 2:15, 1 Cor. 15:13, Php. 4:1, 1 Thes. 3:8

168   *handling accurately*   2 Tim. 2:15

    judges thoughts   Heb. 4:12

    Sabbath for man   Mk. 2:27

    synagogue healing   Mk. 3

169   *trained to distinguish*   Heb. 5:14

    pure devotion   2 Cor. 11:3

INDEX